Bilingual

VISUAL

dictionary

Bilingual

VISUAL

dictionary

DK

DK

DK LONDON
Senior Editors Angeles Gavira, Angela Wilkes
Senior Art Editor Ina Stradins
Jacket Editor Claire Gell
Jacket Design Development Manager Sophia MTT
Preproduction Producer Andy Hilliard
Producer Alex Bell
Picture Researcher Anna Grapes
Project Manager Christine Stroyan
Art Director Karen Self
Publisher Liz Wheeler
Publishing Director Jonathan Metcalf

DK INDIA
Editor Arpita Dasgupta
Assistant Editor Priyanjali Narain
Art Editor Yashashvi Choudhary
DTP Designers Jaypal Chauhan Singh, Anita Yadav
Jacket Designer Tanya Mehrotra
Jackets Editorial Coordinator Priyanka Sharma
Preproduction Manager Balwant Singh
Production Manager Pankaj Sharma

Designed for DK by WaltonCreative.com
Art Editor Colin Walton, assisted by Tracy Musson
Designers Peter Radcliffe, Earl Neish, Ann Cannings
Picture Research Marissa Keating

Language content for DK by g-and-w PUBLISHING
Managed by Jane Wightwick, assisted by Ana Bremón
Translation and editing by Christine Arthur
Additional input by Dr Arturo Pretel, Martin Prill,
Frédéric Monteil, Meinrad Prill, Mari Bremón,
Oscar Bremón, Anunchi Bremón, Leila Gaafar

First published in Great Britain in 2005
This revised edition published in 2018 by
Dorling Kindersley Limited,
80 Strand, London WC2R 0RL

目录
mùlù
contents

42

健康
jiànkāng
health

146

外出就餐
wàichūjiùcān
eating out

252

休闲
xiūxián
leisure

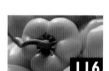

人 rén • people

外表 wàibiǎo • appearance

健康 jiànkāng • health

家居 jiājū • home

服务 fúwù • services

购物 gòuwù • shopping

食物 shíwù • food

外出就餐 wàichū jiùcān • eating out

学习 xuéxí • study

工作 gōngzuò • work

交通运输 jiāotōng yùnshū • transport

体育运动 tǐyùyùndòng • sports

休闲 xiūxián • leisure

环境 huánjìng • environment

日常便览 rìcháng biànlǎn • reference

词典介绍

图片的应用经研究有助于对信息的理解和记忆。本着这个原则，这本有着丰富图片注释的英中双语词典包含了范围很广的词汇。

这本词典按照情景划分章节，从饮食到健身，从家居到工作，从太空到动物世界，包括了日常生活的所有细节。从这本词典中你也可以找到额外的常用词汇和词组以便口语练习和词汇量的扩大。

这本词典实用，生动，易用。对所有对语言有兴趣的人来说是一个重要的参考工具。

注意事项

本词典中的中文汉字同中华人民共和国官方汉字一样为简体汉字。

本词典为普通话注音 注音标记为拼音。拼音是中国人和中文学生最熟悉的一种音标。四声的变化也在拼音的结构中显示。

所有词典项都是以同样的顺序展示 –文字，拼音，英文。例如：

午餐	安全带
wǔcān	ānquándài
lunch	**seat belt**

动词在英文词尾以 (v) 作为标记。例如：

收获 shōuhuò | harvest (v)

所有词汇在书后也有总目录可以查阅。在总目录里你可以通过查询英文 或者查询拼音找到相应的页数。这样可以很顺利地找到和拼音或英文相对应的中文文字翻译。

使用说明

不论你学习语言的目的是工作，兴趣，为旅行做准备还是仅仅在已学语言的基础上扩大词汇量，这本词典都是你语言学习的重要工具。你可以多方面地去运用它。

在学习一种新的语言的时候，注意同源词汇（即在不同语言中相似的词汇）和衍生词汇（即只在某种语言中有相似根源的词汇）。你可以发现语言和语言之间的联系。例如说，英文从中文中引用了一些关于食品的词汇，而同时也输出了一些关于科技和流行文化的词汇。

实用技巧

• 当你设身处地在家，工作场所或者学校的时候，试着看看相对应自己所在环境的章节。这样一来你可以合上书，环视四周看看自己可以识别多少事物。

• 为自己做一些词汇卡片，一面英文一面为中文和汉语拼音。时常携带这些卡片并且测试自己的记忆。记住每次测试之前要打乱卡片的顺序。

• 挑战自己尝试用某一页上的所有词汇写一个小故事，一封信或者一段对话。这样不但可以帮助你牢记这些词汇，而且可以帮助你记住它们的拼音。如果你想尝试写一篇长一点的文章，那么以至少含有2-3个词的句子为起点。

• 如果你有很强的视觉记忆，试着将书上的内容画出来或者在纸上诠释出来，然后合上书，在已有的图形下面填充词汇。

• 一但你变得更加自信，从中文目录中任意找一些词汇，检查自己是否在翻阅到相关页之前能知道其词意。

免费音频应用程序

此音频应用程序包括书中的全部单词和语句，中文和英文语音是由母语播音员录制的，吐字清晰，使得语音和重要词汇的学习更加准确和明了。

音频应用程序使用说明

• 在应用程序站（app store）搜索"Bilingual Visual Dictionary"，免费下载此程序到手机或平板电脑设备中。

• 打开程序，然后扫描书后的国际标准书号（ISBN）去解锁，解锁后视觉辞典（Visual Dictionary）就会显示在图书馆中。

• 下载与书本相配套的语音资料

• 输入页码，然后上下翻动去查看此页上的词和句。

• 通过点击词或句去播放语音。

• 左右滑动去浏览前页和下页内容。

• 添加词和句到"特别喜爱的文档中"（Favourites）。

about the dictionary

The use of pictures is proven to aid understanding and the retention of information. Working on this principle, this highly-illustrated English–Chinese bilingual dictionary presents a large range of useful current vocabulary.

The dictionary is divided thematically and covers most aspects of the everyday world in detail, from the restaurant to the gym, the home to the workplace, outer space to the animal kingdom. You will also find additional words and phrases for conversational use and for extending your vocabulary.

This is an essential reference tool for anyone interested in languages – practical, stimulating, and easy-to-use.

A few things to note

The Chinese in the dictionary is presented in simplified Chinese characters, as used in the People's Republic of China.

The pronunciation included for the Chinese is given in the Mandarin dialect and is shown in Pinyin, the standard romanization familiar to most native speakers and learners of Chinese. Accents showing the Chinese tones are included on the Pinyin.

The entries are always presented in the same order – Chinese, Pinyin, English – for example:

午餐	安全带
wǔcān	ānquándài
lunch	**seat belt**

Verbs are indicated by a **(v)** after the English, for example:

收获 shōuhuò | **harvest (v)**

Each language also has its own index at the back of the book. Here you can look up a word in either English or Pinyin and be referred to the page number(s) where it appears. To reference the Chinese characters for a particular word, look it up in the Pinyin or English index and then go to the page indicated.

how to use this book

Whether you are learning a new language for business, pleasure, or in preparation for a holiday abroad, or are hoping to extend your vocabulary in an already familiar language, this dictionary is a valuable learning tool which you can use in a number of different ways.

When learning a new language, look out for cognates (words that are alike in different languages) and derivations (words that share a common root in a particular language). You can also see where the languages have influenced each other. For example, English has imported some terms for food from Chinese but, in turn, has exported some terms used in technology and popular culture.

Practical learning activities

• As you move about your home, workplace, or college, try looking at the pages which cover that setting. You could then close the book, look around you and see how many of the objects and features you can name.

• Make flashcards for yourself with English on one side and Chinese/Pinyin on the other side. Carry the cards with you and test yourself frequently, making sure you shuffle them between each test.

• Challenge yourself to write a story, letter, or dialogue using as many of the terms on a particular page as possible. This will help you retain the vocabulary and remember the spelling. If you want to build up to writing a longer text, start with sentences incorporating 2–3 words.

• If you have a very visual memory, try drawing or tracing items from the book onto a piece of paper, then close the book and fill in the words below the picture.

• Once you are more confident, pick out words in the foreign language index and see if you know what they mean before turning to the relevant page to check if you were right.

free audio app

The audio app contains all the words and phrases in the book, spoken by native speakers in both Mandarin Chinese and English, making it easier to learn important vocabulary and improve your pronunciation.

FREE AUDIO APP

how to use the audio app

• Search for "Bilingual Visual Dictionary" and download the free app on your smartphone or tablet from your chosen app store.

• Open the app and scan the barcode (or enter the ISBN) to unlock your Visual Dictionary in the Library.

• Download the audio files for your book.

• Enter a page number, then scroll up and down through the list to find a word or phrase.

• Tap a word to hear it.

• Swipe left or right to view the previous or next page.

• Add words to your Favourites.

人 rén
people

人体 réntǐ • body

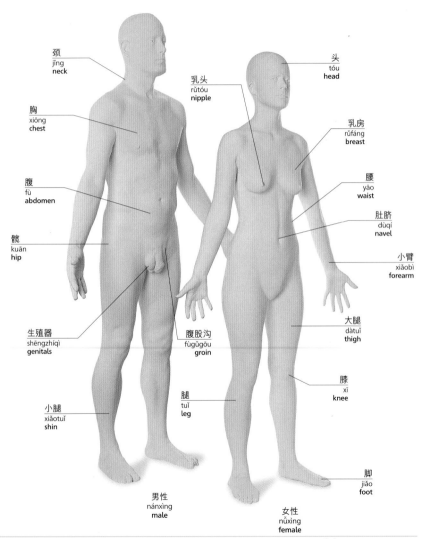

颈
jǐng
neck

乳头
rǔtóu
nipple

头
tóu
head

胸
xiōng
chest

乳房
rǔfáng
breast

腹
fù
abdomen

腰
yāo
waist

髋
kuān
hip

肚脐
dùqí
navel

小臂
xiǎobì
forearm

生殖器
shēngzhíqì
genitals

腹股沟
fùgǔgōu
groin

大腿
dàtuǐ
thigh

膝
xī
knee

小腿
xiǎotuǐ
shin

腿
tuǐ
leg

脚
jiǎo
foot

男性
nánxìng
male

女性
nǚxìng
female

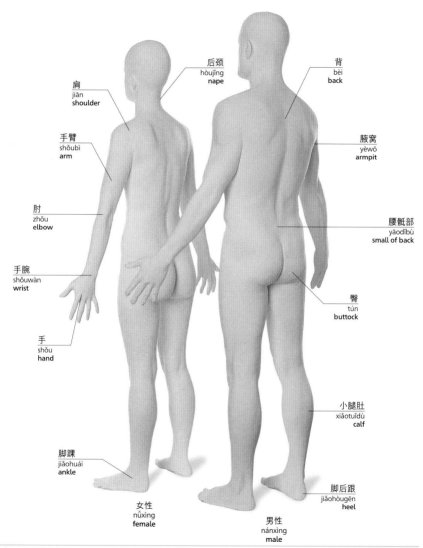

肩
jiān
shoulder

手臂
shǒubì
arm

肘
zhǒu
elbow

手腕
shǒuwàn
wrist

手
shǒu
hand

脚踝
jiǎohuái
ankle

后颈
hòujǐng
nape

背
bèi
back

腋窝
yèwō
armpit

腰骶部
yāodǐbù
small of back

臀
tún
buttock

小腿肚
xiǎotuǐdù
calf

脚后跟
jiǎohòugēn
heel

女性
nǚxìng
female

男性
nánxìng
male

面部 miànbù • face

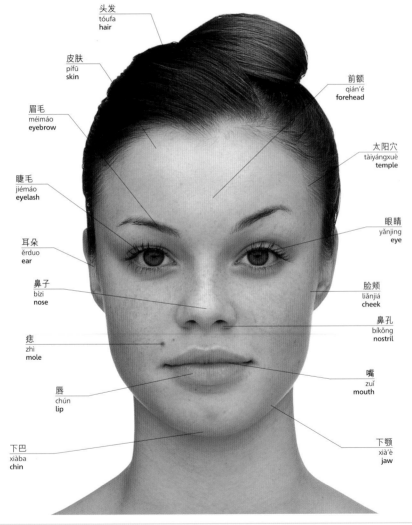

头发
tóufa
hair

皮肤
pífū
skin

眉毛
méimáo
eyebrow

睫毛
jiémáo
eyelash

耳朵
ěrduo
ear

鼻子
bízi
nose

痣
zhì
mole

唇
chún
lip

下巴
xiàba
chin

前额
qián'é
forehead

太阳穴
tàiyángxué
temple

眼睛
yǎnjing
eye

脸颊
liǎnjiá
cheek

鼻孔
bíkǒng
nostril

嘴
zuǐ
mouth

下颚
xià'è
jaw

皱纹
zhòuwén
wrinkle

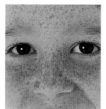
雀斑
quèbān
freckle

毛孔
máokǒng
pore

酒窝
jiǔwō
dimple

手 shǒu • hand

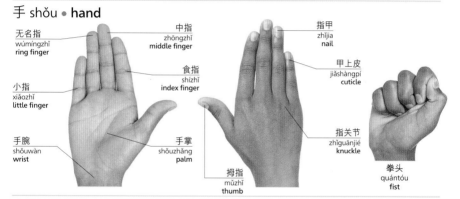

无名指
wúmíngzhǐ
ring finger

中指
zhōngzhǐ
middle finger

食指
shízhǐ
index finger

小指
xiǎozhǐ
little finger

手腕
shǒuwàn
wrist

手掌
shǒuzhǎng
palm

拇指
mǔzhǐ
thumb

指甲
zhǐjia
nail

甲上皮
jiǎshàngpí
cuticle

指关节
zhǐguānjié
knuckle

拳头
quántóu
fist

脚 jiǎo • foot

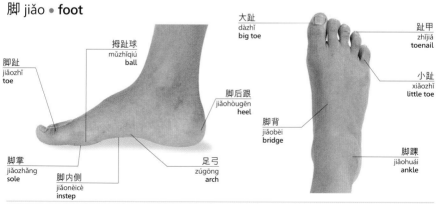

拇趾球
mǔzhǐqiú
ball

脚趾
jiǎozhǐ
toe

脚后跟
jiǎohòugēn
heel

脚掌
jiǎozhǎng
sole

脚内侧
jiǎonèicè
instep

足弓
zúgōng
arch

大趾
dàzhǐ
big toe

趾甲
zhǐjiǎ
toenail

小趾
xiǎozhǐ
little toe

脚背
jiǎobèi
bridge

脚踝
jiǎohuái
ankle

肌肉 jīròu • **muscles**

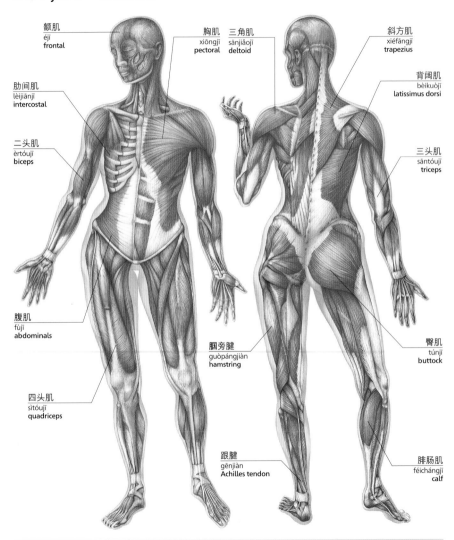

额肌
éjī
frontal

胸肌
xiōngjī
pectoral

三角肌
sānjiǎojī
deltoid

斜方肌
xiéfāngjī
trapezius

肋间肌
lèijiānjī
intercostal

背阔肌
bèikuòjī
latissimus dorsi

二头肌
èrtóujī
biceps

三头肌
sāntóujī
triceps

腹肌
fùjī
abdominals

腘旁腱
guòpángjiàn
hamstring

臀肌
túnjī
buttock

四头肌
sìtóujī
quadriceps

跟腱
gēnjiàn
Achilles tendon

腓肠肌
féichángjī
calf

骨骼 gǔgé • **skeleton**

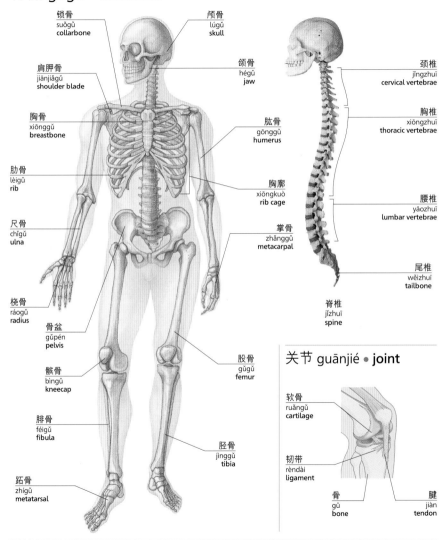

锁骨
suǒgǔ
collarbone

颅骨
lúgǔ
skull

肩胛骨
jiānjiǎgǔ
shoulder blade

颌骨
hégǔ
jaw

胸骨
xiōnggǔ
breastbone

肱骨
gōnggǔ
humerus

肋骨
lèigǔ
rib

胸廓
xiōngkuò
rib cage

尺骨
chǐgǔ
ulna

掌骨
zhǎnggǔ
metacarpal

桡骨
ráogǔ
radius

骨盆
gǔpén
pelvis

髌骨
bìngǔ
kneecap

股骨
gǔgǔ
femur

腓骨
féigǔ
fibula

跖骨
zhígǔ
metatarsal

胫骨
jìnggǔ
tibia

颈椎
jǐngzhuī
cervical vertebrae

胸椎
xiōngzhuī
thoracic vertebrae

腰椎
yāozhuī
lumbar vertebrae

尾椎
wěizhuī
tailbone

脊椎
jǐzhuī
spine

关节 guānjié • **joint**

软骨
ruǎngǔ
cartilage

韧带
rèndài
ligament

骨
gǔ
bone

腱
jiàn
tendon

内脏 nèizàng • internal organs

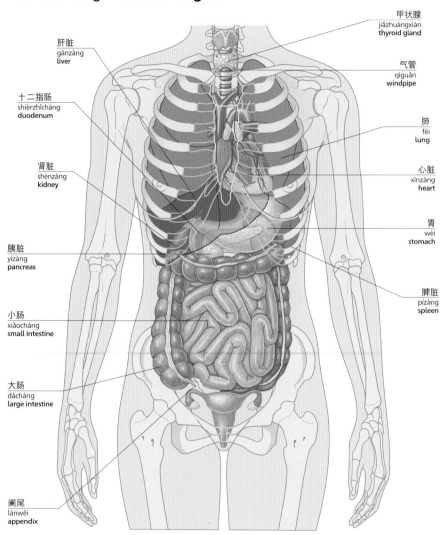

甲状腺
jiǎzhuàngxiàn
thyroid gland

肝脏
gānzàng
liver

气管
qìguǎn
windpipe

十二指肠
shí'èrzhǐcháng
duodenum

肺
fèi
lung

肾脏
shènzàng
kidney

心脏
xīnzàng
heart

胰脏
yízàng
pancreas

胃
wèi
stomach

脾脏
pízàng
spleen

小肠
xiǎocháng
small intestine

大肠
dàcháng
large intestine

阑尾
lánwěi
appendix

头部 tóubù • head

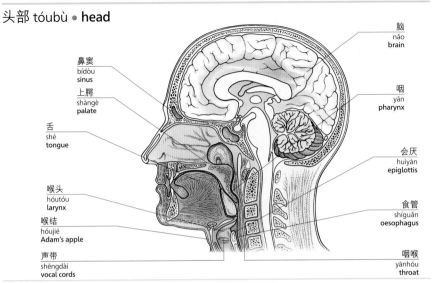

鼻窦
bídòu
sinus

上腭
shàngè
palate

舌
shé
tongue

喉头
hóutóu
larynx

喉结
hóujié
Adam's apple

声带
shēngdài
vocal cords

脑
nǎo
brain

咽
yān
pharynx

会厌
huìyàn
epiglottis

食管
shíguǎn
oesophagus

咽喉
yānhóu
throat

人体系统 réntǐxìtǒng • body systems

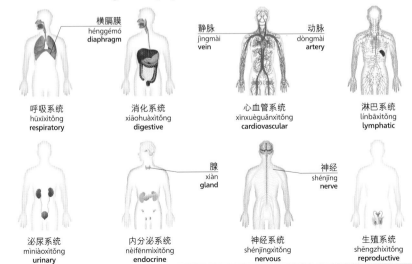

横膈膜
hénggémó
diaphragm

呼吸系统
hūxīxìtǒng
respiratory

消化系统
xiāohuàxìtǒng
digestive

静脉
jìngmài
vein

动脉
dòngmài
artery

心血管系统
xīnxuèguǎnxìtǒng
cardiovascular

淋巴系统
línbāxìtǒng
lymphatic

泌尿系统
mìniàoxìtǒng
urinary

内分泌系统
nèifēnmìxìtǒng
endocrine

腺
xiàn
gland

神经
shénjīng
nerve

神经系统
shénjīngxìtǒng
nervous

生殖系统
shēngzhíxìtǒng
reproductive

生殖器官 shēngzhíqìguān • reproductive organs

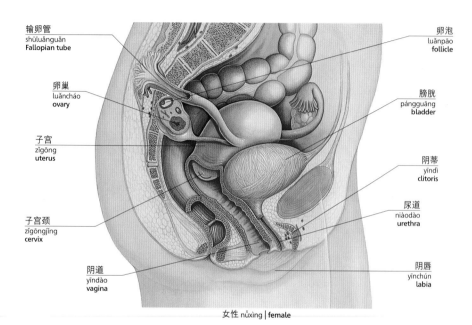

输卵管
shūluǎnguǎn
Fallopian tube

卵巢
luǎncháo
ovary

子宫
zǐgōng
uterus

子宫颈
zǐgōngjǐng
cervix

阴道
yīndào
vagina

卵泡
luǎnpāo
follicle

膀胱
pángguāng
bladder

阴蒂
yīndì
clitoris

尿道
niàodào
urethra

阴唇
yīnchún
labia

女性 nǚxìng | **female**

生殖 shēngzhí • reproduction

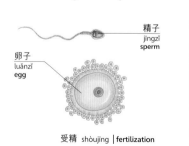

精子
jīngzǐ
sperm

卵子
luǎnzǐ
egg

受精 shòujīng | **fertilization**

词汇 cíhuì • vocabulary

荷尔蒙
hé'ěrméng
hormone

排卵
páiluǎn
ovulation

不育
bùyù
infertile

阳痿
yángwěi
impotent

怀孕
huáiyùn
conceive

性交
xìngjiāo
intercourse

有生殖能力的
yǒushēngzhínénglìde
fertile

月经
yuèjīng
menstruation

性病
xìngbìng
sexually transmitted disease

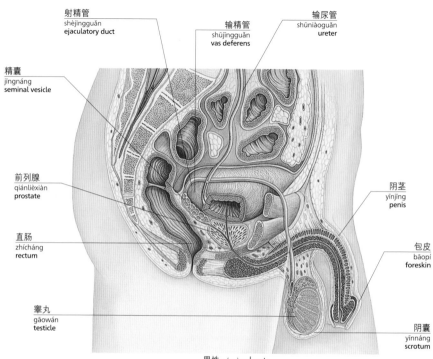

射精管
shèjīngguǎn
ejaculatory duct

输精管
shūjīngguǎn
vas deferens

输尿管
shūniàoguǎn
ureter

精囊
jīngnáng
seminal vesicle

前列腺
qiánlièxiàn
prostate

直肠
zhícháng
rectum

睾丸
gāowán
testicle

阴茎
yīnjīng
penis

包皮
bāopí
foreskin

阴囊
yīnnáng
scrotum

男性 nánxìng | male

避孕 bìyùn • contraception

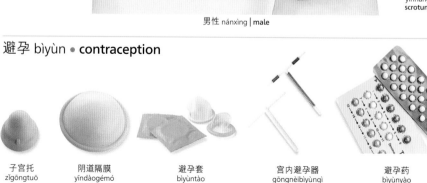

子宫托
zǐgōngtuō
cap

阴道隔膜
yīndàogémó
diaphragm

避孕套
bìyùntào
condom

宫内避孕器
gōngnèibìyùnqì
IUD

避孕药
bìyùnyào
pill

家庭 jiātíng • **family**

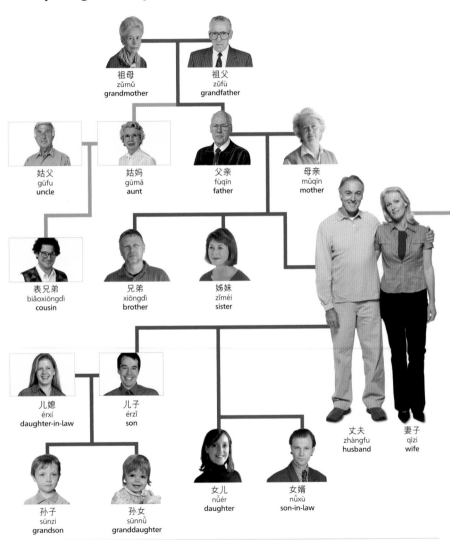

祖母
zǔmǔ
grandmother

祖父
zǔfù
grandfather

姑父
gūfu
uncle

姑妈
gūmā
aunt

父亲
fùqīn
father

母亲
mǔqīn
mother

表兄弟
biǎoxiōngdì
cousin

兄弟
xiōngdì
brother

姊妹
zǐmèi
sister

儿媳
érxí
daughter-in-law

儿子
érzi
son

丈夫
zhàngfu
husband

妻子
qīzi
wife

孙子
sūnzi
grandson

孙女
sūnnǚ
granddaughter

女儿
nǚér
daughter

女婿
nǚxù
son-in-law

词汇 cíhuì • vocabulary

亲戚 qīnqi relatives	**父母** fùmǔ parents	**孙子女/外孙子女** sūnzǐnǚ/wàisūnzǐnǚ grandchildren	**继母** jìmǔ stepmother	**继子** jìzǐ stepson	**配偶** pèiǒu partner
世代 shìdài generation	**孩子** háizi children	**祖父母/外祖父母** zǔfùmǔ/wàizǔfùmǔ grandparents	**继父** jìfù stepfather	**继女** jìnǚ stepdaughter	**双胞胎** shuāngbāotāi twins

岳母
yuèmǔ
mother-in-law

岳父
yuèfù
father-in-law

成长阶段 chéngzhǎngjiēduàn • stages

妻妹(姐)夫
qīmèi(jiě)fū
brother-in-law

妻妹(姐)
qīmèi(jiě)
sister-in-law

婴儿
yīng'ér
baby

儿童
értóng
child

男孩
nánhái
boy

女孩
nǚhái
girl

太太
tàitài
Mrs

外甥女
wàishēngnǚ
niece

外甥
wàishēng
nephew

青少年
qīngshàonián
teenager

成年人
chéngniánrén
adult

称谓 chēngwèi • titles

先生
xiānshēng
Mr

小姐
xiǎojiě
Miss/Ms

男人
nánrén
man

女人
nǚrén
woman

人际关系 rénjìguānxì • relationships

助理
zhùlǐ
assistant

经理
jīnglǐ
manager

生意伙伴
shēngyìhuǒbàn
business
partner

雇主
gùzhǔ
employer

雇员
gùyuán
employee

同事
tóngshì
colleague

办公室 bàngōngshì | office

邻居
línjū
neighbour

朋友
péngyou
friend

熟人
shúrén
acquaintance

笔友
bǐyou
penfriend

男朋友
nánpéngyou
boyfriend

女朋友
nǚpéngyou
girlfriend

未婚夫
wèihūnfū
fiancé

未婚妻
wèihūnqī
fiancée

情侣 qínglǚ | couple

未婚夫妻 wèihūnfūqī | engaged couple

情感 qínggǎn • emotions

微笑
wēixiào
smile

快乐
kuàilè
happy

悲伤
bēishāng
sad

兴奋
xīngfèn
excited

无聊
wúliáo
bored

皱眉
zhòuméi
frown

惊讶
jīngyà
surprised

惊恐
jīngkǒng
scared

愤怒
fènnù
angry

困惑
kùnhuò
confused

忧虑
yōulǜ
worried

紧张
jǐnzhāng
nervous

自豪
zìháo
proud

自信
zìxìn
confident

尴尬
gāngà
embarrassed

羞涩
xiūsè
shy

词汇 cíhuì • vocabulary

烦躁 fánzào upset	笑 xiào laugh (v)	叹息 tànxī sigh (v)	叫喊 jiàohǎn shout (v)
震惊 zhènjīng shocked	哭 kū cry (v)	晕倒 yūndǎo faint (v)	打哈欠 dǎhāqian yawn (v)

人生大事 rénshēngdàshì • life events

出生
chūshēng
be born (v)

入学
rùxué
start school (v)

交友
jiāoyǒu
make friends (v)

毕业
bìyè
graduate (v)

就业
jiùyè
get a job (v)

恋爱
liàn'ài
fall in love (v)

结婚
jiéhūn
get married (v)

生子
shēngzǐ
have a baby (v)

婚礼 hūnlǐ | wedding

离婚
líhūn
divorce

葬礼
zànglǐ
funeral

词汇 cíhuì • vocabulary

洗礼
xǐlǐ
christening

纪念日
jì'niànrì
anniversary

移民
yímín
emigrate (v)

退休
tuìxiū
retire (v)

死亡
sǐwáng
die (v)

立遗嘱
lìyízhǔ
make a will (v)

出生证明
chūshēng zhèngmíng
birth certificate

婚宴
hūnyàn
wedding reception

蜜月
mìyuè
honeymoon

犹太男孩成人(13岁)仪式
yóutài nánhái chéngrén
(shísānsuì)yíshì
bar mitzvah

节庆 jiéqìng · celebrations

节日 jiérì · festivals

生日聚会
shēngrìjùhuì
birthday party

贺卡
hèkǎ
card

生日
shēngrì
birthday

礼物
lǐwù
present

圣诞节
shèngdànjié
Christmas

逾越节
yúyuèjié
Passover

新年
xīnnián
New Year

狂欢节 / 嘉年华会
kuánghuānjié / jiā'niánhuáhuì
carnival

游行
yóuxíng
procession

斋月
zhāiyuè
Ramadan

缎带
duàndài
ribbon

感恩节
gǎn'ēnjié
Thanksgiving

复活节
fùhuójié
Easter

万圣节
wànshèngjié
Halloween

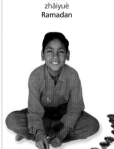

排灯节
páidēngjié
Diwali

外表 wàibiǎo
appearance

童装 tóngzhuāng · children's clothing

婴儿 yīng'ér · baby

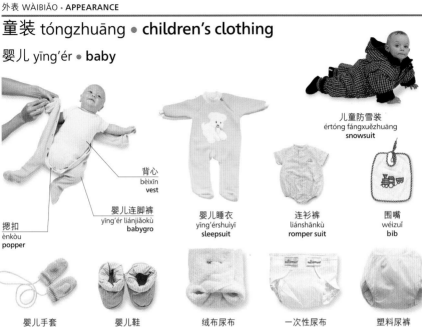

儿童防雪装
értóng fángxuězhuāng
snowsuit

背心
bèixīn
vest

婴儿连脚裤
yīng'ér liánjiǎokù
babygro

婴儿睡衣
yīng'érshuìyī
sleepsuit

连衫裤
liánshānkù
romper suit

围嘴
wéizuǐ
bib

摁扣
ènkòu
popper

婴儿手套
yīng'érshǒutào
mittens

婴儿鞋
yīng'érxié
booties

绒布尿布
róngbù niàobù
terry nappy

一次性尿布
yícìxìng niàobù
disposable nappy

塑料尿裤
sùliào niàokù
plastic pants

幼儿 yòuér · toddler

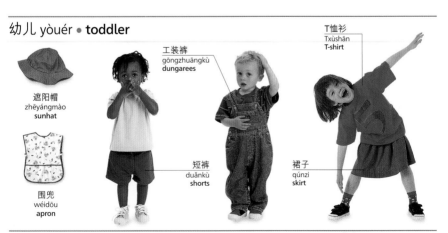

T恤衫
Txùshān
T-shirt

工装裤
gōngzhuāngkù
dungarees

遮阳帽
zhēyángmào
sunhat

围兜
wéidōu
apron

短裤
duǎnkù
shorts

裙子
qúnzi
skirt

儿童 értóng · child

连衣裙
liányīqún
dress

风帽
fēngmào
hood

牛仔裤
niúzǎikù
jeans

凉鞋
liángxié
sandals

背包
bēibāo
backpack

棒形纽扣
bàngxíng
niǔkòu
toggle

围巾
wéijīn
scarf

滑雪衫
huáxuěshān
anorak

长筒橡胶靴
chángtǒng
xiàngjiāoxuē
wellington boots

夏天
xiàtiān
summer

雨衣
yǔyī
raincoat

秋天
qiūtiān
autumn

粗呢外套
cūní wàitào
duffel coat

冬天
dōngtiān
winter

室内便袍
shìnèi biànpáo
dressing gown

标识
biāoshí
logo

运动鞋
yùndòngxié
trainers

儿童睡衣
értóng shuìyī
nightie

拖鞋
tuōxié
slippers

睡衣
shuìyī
nightwear

足球球衣
zúqiú qiúyī
football strip

运动服
yùndòngfú
tracksuit

儿童保暖裤
értóngbǎonuǎnkù
leggings

词汇 cíhuì · vocabulary

天然纤维
tiānrán xiānwéi
natural fibre

合成的
héchéngde
synthetic

这可以机洗吗?
zhèkěyǐ jīxǐ ma?
Is it machine washable?

这适合两岁的孩子穿吗?
zhè shìhé liǎngsuìde háizi chuān ma?
Will this fit a two-year-old?

男装 nánzhuāng · men's clothing

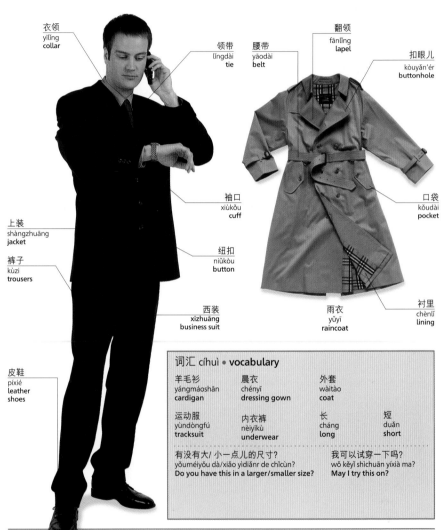

衣领
yīlǐng
collar

领带
lǐngdài
tie

腰带
yāodài
belt

翻领
fānlǐng
lapel

扣眼儿
kòuyǎn'ér
buttonhole

袖口
xiùkǒu
cuff

口袋
kǒudài
pocket

上装
shàngzhuāng
jacket

裤子
kùzi
trousers

纽扣
niǔkòu
button

衬里
chènlǐ
lining

西装
xīzhuāng
business suit

雨衣
yǔyī
raincoat

皮鞋
píxié
leather shoes

词汇 cíhuì · vocabulary

羊毛衫 yángmáoshān cardigan	晨衣 chényī dressing gown	外套 wàitào coat
运动服 yùndòngfú tracksuit	内衣裤 nèiyīkù underwear	长 cháng long	短 duǎn short

有没有大/小一点儿的尺寸?
yǒuméiyǒu dà/xiǎo yìdiǎnr de chǐcùn?
Do you have this in a larger/smaller size?

我可以试穿一下吗?
wǒ kěyǐ shìchuān yíxià ma?
May I try this on?

v型领
Vxínglǐng
V-neck

圆领
yuánlǐng
**round
neck**

休闲上衣
xiūxián shàngyī
blazer

粗呢夹克
cūníjiákè
sports jacket

马甲
mǎjiǎ
waistcoat

T恤衫
Txùshān
T-shirt

滑雪衫
huáxuěshān
anorak

运动衫
yùndòngshān
sweatshirt

衬衫
chènshān
shirt

牛仔裤
niúzǎikù
jeans

套头毛衣
tàotóumáoyī
sweater

睡衣
shuìyī
pyjamas

背心
bèixīn
vest

休闲服
xiūxiánfú
casual wear

短裤
duǎnkù
shorts

三角内裤
sānjiǎonèikù
briefs

短衬裤
duǎnchènkù
boxer shorts

袜子
wàzi
socks

女装 nǚzhuāng • **women's clothing**

上装
shàngzhuāng
jacket

缝合线
fénghéxiàn
seam

无肩带
wújiāndài
strapless

无袖
wúxiù
sleeveless

袖子
xiùzi
sleeve

及脚踝长
jíjiǎohuái cháng
ankle length

晚礼服
wǎnlǐfú
evening dress

连衣裙
liányīqún
dress

裙子
qúnzi
skirt

女士衬衫
nǚshì chènshān
blouse

裙边
qúnbiān
hem

及膝长
jíxī cháng
knee length

裤子
kùzi
trousers

连裤袜
liánkùwà
tights

鞋
xié
shoes

正装
zhèngzhuāng
formal

便装
biànzhuāng
casual

女用内衣 nǚyòng nèiyī • lingerie

便袍
biànpáo
dressing gown

衬裙
chènqún
slip

肩带
jiāndài
strap

紧身内衣
jǐnshēn nèiyī
camisole

女式短上衣
nǚshì duǎnshàngyī
basque

吊袜带
diàowàdài
suspenders

长筒袜
chángtǒngwà
stocking

连裤袜
liánkùwà
tights

胸罩
xiōngzhào
bra

女用内裤
nǚyòng nèikù
knickers

女睡衣
nǚshuìyī
nightdress

婚礼 hūnlǐ • wedding

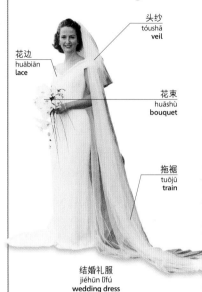

花边
huābiān
lace

头纱
tóushā
veil

花束
huāshù
bouquet

拖裾
tuōjū
train

结婚礼服
jiéhūn lǐfú
wedding dress

词汇 cíhuì • vocabulary

束腹 shùfù **corset**	**剪裁考究** jiǎncái kǎojiu **tailored**
松紧袜带 sōngjǐn wàdài **garter**	**露背装** lòubèizhuāng **halter neck**
垫肩 diànjiān **shoulder pad**	**内有金属丝的(胸罩)** nèiyǒu jīnshǔsīde (xiōngzhào) **underwired**
腰带 yāodài **waistband**	**运动胸罩** yùndòng xiōngzhào **sports bra**

配饰 pèishì · accessories

帽子	礼帽	围巾	腰带
màozi	lǐmào	wéijīn	yāodài
cap	**hat**	**scarf**	**belt**

腰带扣
yāodàikòu
buckle

柄
bǐng
handle

尖
jiān
tip

手帕	领结	领带别针	手套	伞
shǒupà	lǐngjié	lǐngdàibiézhēn	shǒutào	sǎn
handkerchief	**bow tie**	**tie-pin**	**gloves**	**umbrella**

首饰 shǒushì · jewellery

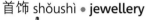

项链坠	胸针	袖扣
xiàngliànzhuì	xiōngzhēn	xiùkòu
pendant	**brooch**	**cuff links**

珍珠项链
zhēnzhū xiàngliàn
string of pearls

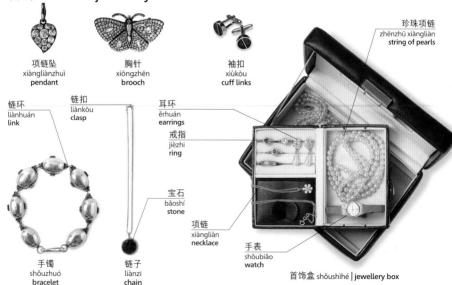

链环
liànhuán
link

链扣
liànkòu
clasp

耳环
ěrhuán
earrings

戒指
jièzhi
ring

宝石
bǎoshí
stone

项链
xiàngliàn
necklace

手表
shǒubiǎo
watch

手镯
shǒuzhuó
bracelet

链子
liànzi
chain

首饰盒 shǒushìhé | **jewellery box**

中文 zhōngwén · english

包 bāo • bags

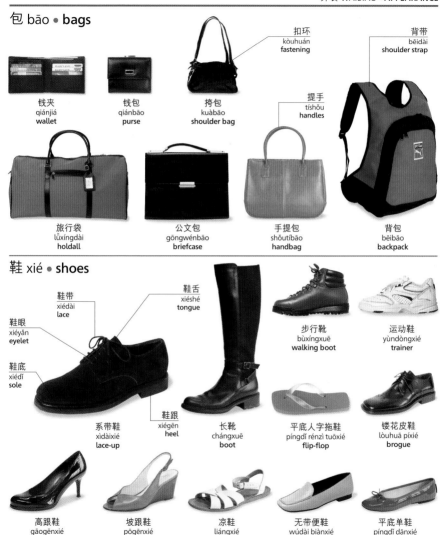

扣环
kòuhuán
fastening

背带
bēidài
shoulder strap

钱夹
qiánjiá
wallet

钱包
qiánbāo
purse

挎包
kuàbāo
shoulder bag

提手
tíshǒu
handles

旅行袋
lǚxíngdài
holdall

公文包
gōngwénbāo
briefcase

手提包
shǒutíbāo
handbag

背包
bēibāo
backpack

鞋 xié • shoes

鞋带
xiédài
lace

鞋舌
xiéshé
tongue

鞋眼
xiéyǎn
eyelet

鞋底
xiédǐ
sole

步行靴
bùxíngxuē
walking boot

运动鞋
yùndòngxié
trainer

系带鞋
xìdàixié
lace-up

鞋跟
xiégēn
heel

长靴
chángxuē
boot

平底人字拖鞋
píngdǐ rénzì tuōxié
flip-flop

镂花皮鞋
lòuhuā píxié
brogue

高跟鞋
gāogēnxié
high-heeled shoe

坡跟鞋
pōgēnxié
wedge

凉鞋
liángxié
sandal

无带便鞋
wúdài biànxié
slip-on

平底单鞋
píngdǐ dānxié
pump

头发 tóufà • hair

发梳
fàshū
comb

梳头
shūtóu
comb (v)

发刷
fàshuā
brush

刷头发 shuātóufà | brush (v)

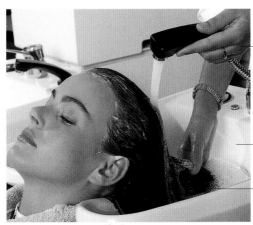

美发师
měifàshī
hairdresser

洗头盆
xǐtóupén
sink

顾客
gùkè
client

洗 xǐ | wash (v)

罩衫
zhàoshān
robe

冲洗
chōngxǐ
rinse (v)

剪
jiǎn
cut (v)

吹干
chuīgān
blow dry (v)

定型
dìngxíng
set (v)

美发用品 měifà yòngpǐn • accessories

吹风机
chuīfēngjī
hairdryer

洗发水
xǐfàshuǐ
shampoo

护发素
hùfàsù
conditioner

发胶
fàjiāo
gel

定型水
dìngxíngshuǐ
hairspray

卷发钳
juǎnfàqián
curling tongs

剪刀
jiǎndāo
scissors

发箍
fàgū
hairband

直发器
zhífàqì
hair straighteners

发卡
fàqiǎ
hairpin

发型 fàxíng · styles

马尾辫
mǎwěibiàn
ponytail

麻花辫
máhuābiàn
plait

法式盘头
fǎshì pántóu
French pleat

发髻
fàjì
bun

小辫
xiǎobiàn
pigtails

女式短发
nǚshì duǎnfà
bob

短发
duǎnfà
crop

卷发
juǎnfà
curly

烫发
tàngfà
perm

直发
zhífà
straight

发根
fàgēn
roots

挑染
tiāorǎn
highlights

秃顶
tūdǐng
bald

假发
jiǎfà
wig

发色 fàsè · colours

金色
jīnsè
blonde

深褐色
shēnhèsè
brunette

红褐色
hónghèsè
auburn

红棕色
hóngzōngsè
ginger

黑色
hēisè
black

灰色
huīsè
grey

白色
báisè
white

染色的
rǎnsède
dyed

词汇 cíhuì · vocabulary

修剪
xiūjiǎn
trim (v)

拉直
lāzhí
straighten (v)

理发师
lǐfàshī
barber

头皮屑
tóupíxiè
dandruff

发梢分叉
fàshāo fēnchà
split ends

面包
miàn bāo
beard

油性(发质)
yóuxìng (fàzhì)
greasy

干性(发质)
gānxìng (fàzhì)
dry

中性(发质)
zhōngxìng (fàzhì)
normal

头皮
tóupí
scalp

发带
fàdài
hairtie

小胡子
xiǎo hú zi
moustache

美容 měiróng · **beauty**

染发剂
rǎnfàjì
hair dye

眼影
yǎnyǐng
eye shadow

睫毛膏
jiémáogāo
mascara

眼线液
yǎnxiànyè
eyeliner

腮红
sāihóng
blusher

粉底
fěndǐ
foundation

口红
kǒuhóng
lipstick

化妆 huàzhuāng · **make-up**

眉笔
méibǐ
eyebrow pencil

眉刷
méishuā
eyebrow brush

眉夹
méijiá
tweezers

唇彩
chúncǎi
lip gloss

唇刷
chúnshuā
lip brush

唇线笔
chúnxiànbǐ
lip liner

化妆刷
huàzhuāngshuā
brush

遮瑕膏
zhēxiágāo
concealer

化妆镜
huàzhuāngjìng
mirror

粉饼
fěnbǐng
face powder

粉扑
fěnpū
powder puff

粉盒 fěnhé | compact

美容护理 měirónghùlǐ ·
beauty treatments

面膜
miànmó
face pack

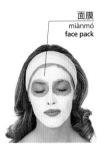

紫外线浴床
zǐwàixiàn yùchuáng
sunbed

面部护理
miànbùhùlǐ
facial

去死皮
qù sǐpí
exfoliate (v)

热蜡脱毛
rèlàtuōmáo
wax

趾甲护理
zhǐjiǎ hùlǐ
pedicure

指甲护理 zhǐjia hùlǐ · manicure

洗甲水
xǐjiǎshuǐ
nail varnish remover

指甲锉
zhǐjiacuò
nail file

指甲油
zhǐjiayóu
nail varnish

指甲剪
zhǐjiajiǎn
nail scissors

指甲刀
zhǐjiadāo
nail clippers

化妆用品 huàzhuāng yòngpǐn ·
toiletries

洁面水
jiémiànshuǐ
cleanser

爽肤水
shuǎngfūshuǐ
toner

保湿霜
bǎoshīshuāng
moisturizer

黑肤霜
hēifūshuāng
self-tanning cream

香水
xiāngshuǐ
perfume

淡香水
dànxiāngshuǐ
eau de toilette

词汇 cíhuì · vocabulary

肤色 fūsè **complexion**	油性(皮肤) yóuxìng(pífū) **oily**	棕褐色皮肤 zōnghèsè pífū **tan**
皮肤白皙 pífū báixī **fair**	敏感性的 mǐngǎnxingde **sensitive**	纹身 wénshēn **tattoo**
肤色较深 fūsè jiàoshēn **dark**	低致敏的 dīzhìmǐnde **hypoallergenic**	抗皱 kàngzhòu **antiwrinkle**
干性(皮肤) gānxìng(pífū) **dry**	色调 sèdiào **shade**	棉球 miánqiú **cotton balls**

健康 jiànkāng
health

疾病 jíbìng · illness

发烧 fāshāo | fever

气雾剂
qìwùjì
inhaler

头痛
tóutòng
headache

流鼻血
liúbíxiě
nosebleed

咳嗽
késou
cough

喷嚏
pēntì
sneeze

感冒
gǎnmào
cold

流感
liúgǎn
flu

哮喘
xiàochuǎn
asthma

痉挛
jìngluán
cramps

恶心
ěxin
nausea

水痘
shuǐdòu
chickenpox

皮疹
pízhěn
rash

词汇 cíhuì · vocabulary

中风 zhòngfēng stroke	糖尿病 tángniàobìng diabetes	湿疹 shīzhěn eczema	寒战 hánzhàn chill	呕吐 ǒutù vomit (v)	腹泻 fùxiè diarrhoea
血压 xuèyā blood pressure	过敏 guòmǐn allergy	传染 chuánrǎn infection	胃痛 wèitòng stomach ache	癫痫 diānxián epilepsy	麻疹 mázhěn measles
心肌梗塞 xīnjī gěngsè heart attack	枯草热 kūcǎorè hay fever	病毒 bìngdú virus	昏厥 hūnjué faint (v)	偏头痛 piāntóutòng migraine	腮腺炎 sāixiànyán mumps

医生 yīshēng · **doctor**
诊断 zhěnduàn · **consultation**

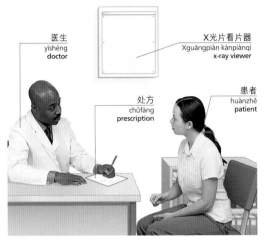

医生
yīshēng
doctor

X光片看片器
Xguāngpiàn kànpiànqì
x-ray viewer

处方
chǔfāng
prescription

患者
huànzhě
patient

护士
hùshi
nurse

体重计
tǐzhòngjì
scales

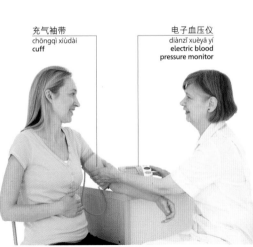

充气袖带
chōngqì xiùdài
cuff

电子血压仪
diànzǐ xuèyā yí
electric blood pressure monitor

词汇 cíhuì · **vocabulary**

预约 yùyuē **appointment**	接种 jiēzhòng **inoculation**
诊疗室 zhěnliáoshì **surgery**	体温计 tǐwēnjì **thermometer**
候诊室 hòuzhěnshì **waiting room**	体检 tǐjiǎn **medical examination**

我需要看医生。
wǒ xūyào kànyīshēng.
I need to see a doctor.

这儿疼。
zhè'er téng.
It hurts here.

创伤 chuāngshāng · **injury**

医用吊带
yīyòng
diàodài
sling

颈托
jǐngtuō
neck brace

扭伤 niǔshāng | **sprain**

骨折
gǔzhé
fracture

头颈部损伤
tóujǐngbù sǔnshāng
whiplash

割伤
gēshāng
cut

擦伤
cāshāng
graze

淤伤
yūshāng
bruise

刺伤
cìshāng
splinter

晒伤
shàishāng
sunburn

烧伤
shāoshāng
burn

咬伤
yǎoshāng
bite

蜇伤
zhēshāng
sting

词汇 cíhuì · **vocabulary**

事故
shìgù
accident

大出血
dàchūxuè
haemorrhage

中毒
zhòngdú
poisoning

他/她没事吧？
tā/tā méishì ba?
Will he/she be all right?

紧急情况
jǐnjí qíngkuàng
emergency

水泡
shuǐpào
blister

电击
diànjī
electric shock

哪里疼？
nǎli téng?
Where does it hurt?

伤口
shāngkǒu
wound

脑震荡
nǎozhèndàng
concussion

头部损伤
tóubù sǔnshāng
head injury

请叫救护车。
qǐngjiào jiùhùchē.
Please call an ambulance.

急救 jíjiù · first aid

药膏
yàogāo
ointment

创可贴
chuàngkětiē
plaster

安全别针
ānquán biézhēn
safety pin

绷带
bēngdài
bandage

止痛药
zhǐtòngyào
painkillers

消毒湿巾
xiāodú shījīn
antiseptic wipe

镊子
nièzǐ
tweezers

剪刀
jiǎndāo
scissors

消毒剂
xiāodújì
antiseptic

急救箱 jíjiùxiāng | first-aid box

纱布
shābù
gauze

包扎
bāozā
dressing

医用夹板 yīyòngjiābǎn | splint

橡皮膏
xiàngpígāo
adhesive tape

复苏术
fùsūshù
resuscitation

词汇 cíhuì · vocabulary

休克
xiūkè
shock

脉搏
màibó
pulse

窒息
zhìxī
choke (v)

您能帮帮我吗?
nín néng bāngbāng wǒ ma?
Can you help?

不省人事
bùxǐng rénshì
unconscious

呼吸
hūxī
breathing

无菌
wújūn
sterile

你会急救吗?
nǐ huì jíjiù ma?
Do you know first aid?

医院 yīyuàn · hospital

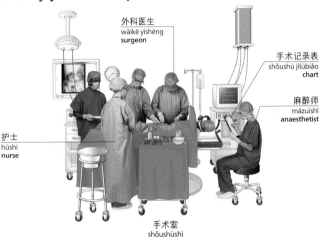

外科医生
wàikē yīshēng
surgeon

手术记录表
shǒushù jìlùbiǎo
chart

麻醉师
mázuìshī
anaesthetist

护士
hùshi
nurse

手术室
shǒushùshì
operating theatre

验血
yànxuè
blood test

注射
zhùshè
injection

X光
Xguāng
x-ray

移动病床
yídòng bìngchuáng
trolley

呼叫按钮
hūjiào ànniǔ
call button

急诊室
jízhěnshì
emergency room

病房
bìngfáng
ward

轮椅
lúnyǐ
wheelchair

CT扫描
CT sǎomiáo
scan

词汇 cíhuì · vocabulary

手术 shǒushù operation	出院 chūyuàn discharged	探视时间 tànshì shíjiān visiting hours	儿童病房 értóng bìngfáng children's ward	加护病房 jiāhù bìngfáng intensive care unit
收治的 shōuzhìde admitted	诊所 zhěnsuǒ clinic	产科病房 chǎnkē bìngfáng maternity ward	单人病房 dānrén bìngfáng private room	门诊病人 ménzhěn bìngrén outpatient

科室 kēshì • departments

耳鼻喉科
ěrbíhóukē
ENT

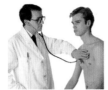

心脏病科
xīnzàngbìngkē
cardiology

整形外科
zhěngxíngwàikē
orthopaedics

妇科
fùkē
gynaecology

理疗科
lǐliáokē
physiotherapy

皮肤科
pífūkē
dermatology

儿科
érkē
paediatrics

放射科
fàngshèkē
radiology

外科
wàikē
surgery

产科
chǎnkē
maternity

精神科
jīngshénkē
psychiatry

眼科
yǎnkē
ophthalmology

词汇 cíhuì • vocabulary

神经科 shénjīngkē **neurology**	泌尿科 mìniàokē **urology**	内分泌科 nèifēnmìkē **endocrinology**	病理科 bìnglǐkē **pathology**	结果 jiéguǒ **result**
肿瘤科 zhǒngliúkē **oncology**	矫形外科 jiǎoxíngwàikē **plastic surgery**	转诊 zhuǎnzhěn **referral**	检查 jiǎnchá **test**	专科医生 zhuānkē yīshēng **consultant**

牙医 yáyī · dentist

牙齿 yáchǐ · tooth

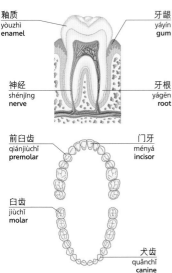

釉质
yòuzhì
enamel

牙龈
yáyín
gum

神经
shénjīng
nerve

牙根
yágēn
root

前臼齿
qiánjiùchǐ
premolar

门牙
ményá
incisor

臼齿
jiùchǐ
molar

犬齿
quǎnchǐ
canine

词汇 cíhuì · vocabulary

牙痛 yátòng toothache	牙钻 yázuàn drill
牙菌斑 yájūnbān plaque	牙线 yáxiàn dental floss
龋齿 qǔchǐ decay	拔牙 báyá extraction
填充物 tiánchōngwù filling	齿冠 chǐguān crown

检查 jiǎnchá · checkup

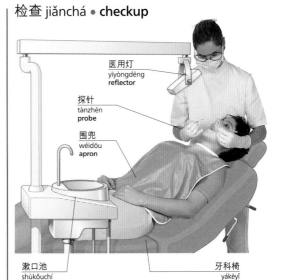

医用灯
yīyòngdēng
reflector

探针
tànzhēn
probe

围兜
wéidōu
apron

漱口池
shùkǒuchí
basin

牙科椅
yákēyǐ
dentist's chair

用牙线洁齿
yòng yáxiàn jiéchǐ
floss (v)

刷牙
shuāyá
brush (v)

畸齿矫正器
jīchǐ jiǎozhèngqì
braces

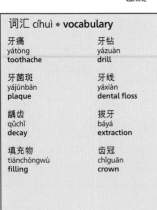

X光
X guāng
dental x-ray

牙片
yápiàn
x-ray film

假牙
jiǎyá
dentures

配镜师 pèijìngshī · optician

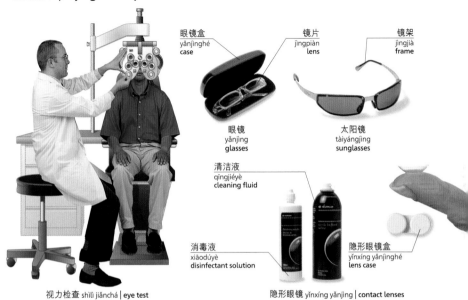

眼镜盒
yǎnjìnghé
case

镜片
jìngpiàn
lens

镜架
jìngjià
frame

眼镜
yǎnjìng
glasses

太阳镜
tàiyángjìng
sunglasses

清洁液
qīngjiéyè
cleaning fluid

隐形眼镜盒
yǐnxíng yǎnjìnghé
lens case

消毒液
xiāodúyè
disinfectant solution

视力检查 shìlì jiǎnchá | eye test

隐形眼镜 yǐnxíng yǎnjìng | contact lenses

眼睛 yǎnjīng · eye

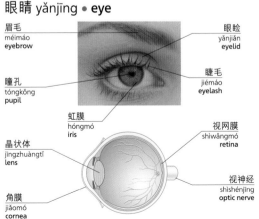

眉毛
méimáo
eyebrow

眼睑
yǎnjiǎn
eyelid

瞳孔
tóngkǒng
pupil

睫毛
jiémáo
eyelash

虹膜
hóngmó
iris

视网膜
shìwǎngmó
retina

晶状体
jīngzhuàngtǐ
lens

视神经
shìshénjīng
optic nerve

角膜
jiǎomó
cornea

词汇 cíhuì · vocabulary

视力 shìlì vision	散光 sǎnguāng astigmatism
屈光度 qūguāngdù diopter	远视 yuǎnshì long sight
眼泪 yǎnlèi tear	近视 jìnshì short sight
白内障 báinèizhàng cataract	双光的 shuāngguāngde bifocal

怀孕 huáiyùn · **pregnancy**

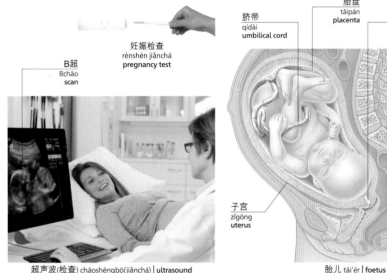

B超
Bchāo
scan

妊娠检查
rènshèn jiǎnchá
pregnancy test

脐带
qídài
umbilical cord

胎盘
tāipán
placenta

子宫颈
zǐgōngjǐng
cervix

子宫
zǐgōng
uterus

超声波(检查) chāoshēngbō(jiǎnchá) | ultrasound

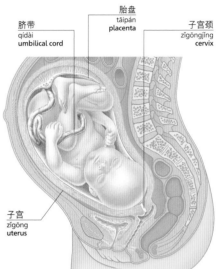

胎儿 tāi'ér | foetus

词汇 cíhuì · **vocabulary**

排卵 páiluǎn ovulation	出生前 chūshēngqián antenatal	宫缩 gōngsuō contraction	扩张术 kuòzhāngshù dilation	分娩 fēnmiǎn delivery	臀位分娩 túnwèifēnmiǎn breech birth
怀孕 huáiyùn conception	胚胎 pēitāi embryo	破羊水 pòyángshuǐ break waters (v)	硬膜外麻醉 yìngmó wài mázuì epidural	出生 chūshēng birth	早产的 zǎochǎnde premature
怀孕的 huáiyùnde pregnant	子宫 zǐgōng womb	羊水 yángshuǐ amniotic fluid	外阴切开术 wàiyīn qiēkāishù episiotomy	流产 liúchǎn miscarriage	妇科医生 fùkē yīshēng gynaecologist
待产的 dàichǎnde expectant	怀孕三个月 huáiyùnsāngèyuè trimester	羊水穿刺诊断 yángshuǐ chuāncì zhěnduàn amniocentesis	剖腹产 pōufùchǎn caesarean section	缝合 fénghé stitches	产科医生 chǎnkē yīshēng obstetrician

分娩 fēnmiǎn • childbirth

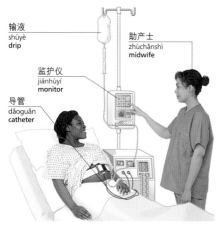

输液
shūyè
drip

助产士
zhùchǎnshì
midwife

监护仪
jiānhùyí
monitor

导管
dǎoguǎn
catheter

引产 yǐnchǎn | induce labour (v)

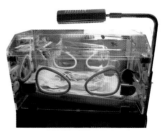

育婴箱 yùyīngxiāng | incubator

出生时体重 chūshēngshí tǐzhòng | birth weight

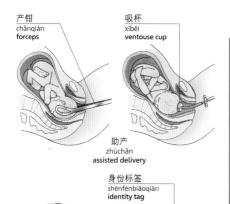

产钳
chǎnqián
forceps

吸杯
xībēi
ventouse cup

助产
zhùchǎn
assisted delivery

身份标签
shēnfènbiāoqiān
identity tag

新生儿 xīnshēng'ér | newborn baby

哺乳 bǔrǔ • nursing

吸乳器
xīrǔqì
breast pump

哺乳胸罩
bǔrǔ xiōngzhào
nursing bra

喂母乳
wèi mǔrǔ
breastfeed (v)

乳垫
rǔdiàn
pads

替代疗法 tìdài liáofǎ • alternative therapy

瑜伽姿势
yújiāzīshì
yoga pose

垫子
diànzi
mat

瑜伽 yújiā | **yoga**

按摩
ànmó
massage

指压按摩
zhǐyā ànmó
shiatsu

脊柱按摩法
jǐzhù ànmófǎ
chiropractic

整骨疗法
zhěnggǔ liáofǎ
osteopathy

足底反射疗法
zúdǐ fǎnshè liáofǎ
reflexology

冥想
míngxiǎng
meditation

顾问
gùwèn
counsellor

灵气疗法
língqì liáofǎ
reiki

针灸
zhēnjiǔ
acupuncture

集体治疗
jítǐ zhìliáo
group therapy

印度草药疗法
yìndù cǎoyào liáofǎ
ayurveda

催眠疗法
cuīmián liáofǎ
hypnotherapy

精油
jīngyóu
essential oils

本草疗法
běncǎo liáofǎ
herbalism

芳香疗法
fāngxiāng liáofǎ
aromatherapy

顺势疗法
shùnshì liáofǎ
homeopathy

指压疗法
zhǐyā liáofǎ
acupressure

治疗师
zhìliáoshī
therapist

精神疗法
jīngshén liáofǎ
psychotherapy

词汇 cíhuì • vocabulary

营养品 yíngyǎngpǐn **supplement**	自然疗法 zìrán liáofǎ **naturopathy**	放松 fàngsōng **relaxation**	药草 yàocǎo **herb**
水疗 shuǐliáo **hydrotherapy**	风水 fēngshuǐ **feng shui**	压力 yālì **stress**	水晶疗法 shuǐjīng liáofǎ **crystal healing**

家居 jiājū
home

房屋 fángwū · house

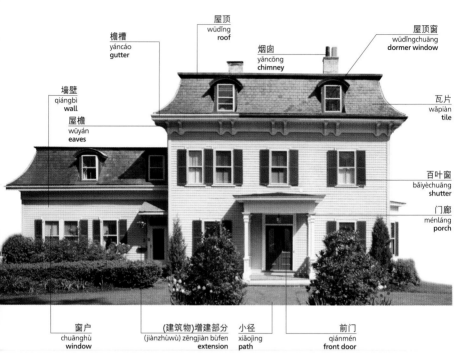

檐槽
yáncáo
gutter

屋顶
wūdǐng
roof

烟囱
yāncōng
chimney

屋顶窗
wūdǐngchuāng
dormer window

墙壁
qiángbì
wall

屋檐
wūyán
eaves

瓦片
wǎpiàn
tile

百叶窗
bǎiyèchuāng
shutter

门廊
ménláng
porch

窗户
chuānghù
window

(建筑物)增建部分
(jiànzhùwù) zēngjiàn bùfen
extension

小径
xiǎojìng
path

前门
qiánmén
front door

词汇 cíhuì · vocabulary

独立式 dúlìshì **detached**	房客 fángkè **tenant**	车库 chēkù **garage**	信箱 xìnxiāng **letterbox**	防盗警报 fángdào jǐngbào **burglar alarm**	租用 zūyòng **rent (v)**
半独立式 bàndúlìshì **semidetached**	平房 píngfáng **bungalow**	阁楼 gélóu **attic**	门廊灯 ménlángdēng **porch light**	庭院 tíngyuàn **courtyard**	房租 fángzū **rent**
连栋房屋 liándòngfángwū **townhouse**	地下室 dìxiàshì **basement**	房间 fángjiān **room**	房东 fángdōng **landlord**	楼层 lóucéng **floor**	连排式 liánpáishì **terraced**

入口 rùkǒu • entrance

扶手
fúshǒu
hand rail

楼梯平台
lóutī píngtái
landing

楼梯栏杆
lóutī lángān
banister

楼梯
lóutī
staircase

门厅
méntīng
hallway

门铃
ménlíng
doorbell

门垫
méndiàn
doormat

门环
ménhuán
door knocker

门链
ménliàn
door chain

钥匙
yàoshi
key

锁
suǒ
lock

门闩
ménshuān
bolt

公寓 gōngyù • flat

阳台
yángtái
balcony

公寓楼
gōngyùlóu
block of flats

对讲器
duìjiǎngqì
intercom

电梯
diàntī
lift

室内系统 shìnèi xìtǒng • internal systems

扇叶
shànyè
blade

风扇
fēngshàn
fan

暖器片
nuǎnqìpiàn
radiator

电暖器
diànnuǎnqì
heater

对流式电暖器
duìliúshì diànnuǎnqì
convector heater

电 diàn • electricity

节能灯泡
jiénéng dēngpào
energy-saving bulb

接地
jièdì
earthing

插片
chāpiàn
pin

插头 chātóu | **plug**

零线
língxiàn
neutral

火线
huǒxiàn
live

电线 diànxiàn | **wires**

词汇 cíhuì • vocabulary

电压 diànyā **voltage**	保险丝 bǎoxiǎnsī **fuse**	插座 chāzuò **socket**	直流电 zhíliúdiàn **direct current**	停电 tíngdiàn **power cut**
安培 ānpéi **amp**	保险盒 bǎoxiǎnhé **fuse box**	开关 kāiguān **switch**	变压器 biànyāqì **transformer**	供电系统 gōngdiàn xìtǒng **mains supply**
电力 diànlì **power**	发电机 fādiànjī **generator**	交流电 jiāoliúdiàn **alternating current**	电表 diànbiǎo **electricity meter**	

管道装置 guǎndào zhuāngzhì · **plumbing**

洗涤槽 xǐdícáo · **sink**

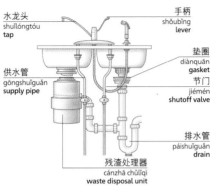

水龙头
shuǐlóngtóu
tap

手柄
shǒubǐng
lever

垫圈
diànquān
gasket

供水管
gōngshuǐguǎn
supply pipe

节门
jiémén
shutoff valve

排水管
páishuǐguǎn
drain

残渣处理器
cánzhā chǔlǐqì
waste disposal unit

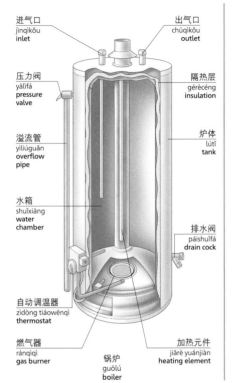

进气口
jìnqìkǒu
inlet

出气口
chūqìkǒu
outlet

压力阀
yālìfá
pressure valve

隔热层
gérècéng
insulation

溢流管
yìliúguǎn
overflow pipe

炉体
lútǐ
tank

水箱
shuǐxiāng
water chamber

排水阀
páishuǐfá
drain cock

自动调温器
zìdòng tiáowēnqì
thermostat

燃气器
ránqìqì
gas burner

锅炉
guōlú
boiler

加热元件
jiārè yuánjiàn
heating element

抽水马桶 chōushuǐ mǎtǒng · **toilet**

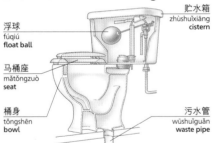

贮水箱
zhùshuǐxiāng
cistern

浮球
fúqiú
float ball

马桶座
mǎtǒngzuò
seat

桶身
tǒngshēn
bowl

污水管
wūshuǐguǎn
waste pipe

垃圾处理 lājīchǔlǐ · **waste disposal**

瓶子
píngzi
bottle

盖子
gàizi
lid

踏板
tàbǎn
pedal

垃圾回收箱
lājī huíshōuxiāng
recycling bin

垃圾桶
lājītǒng
rubbish bin

分类箱
fēnlèixiāng
sorting unit

有机废物
yǒujī fèiwù
organic waste

起居室 qǐjūshì • **living room**

壁灯
bìdēng
wall light

壁炉
bìlú
fireplace

天花板
tiānhuābǎn
ceiling

花瓶
huāpíng
vase

靠垫
kàodiàn
cushion

灯
dēng
lamp

茶几
chájī
coffee table

沙发
shāfā
sofa

地板
dìbǎn
floor

画框
huàkuàng
frame

窗帘
chuānglián
curtain

窗幔
chuāngmàn
net curtain

画
huà
painting

百叶窗
bǎiyèchuāng
Venetian blind

卷帘
juǎnlián
roller blind

装饰脚线
zhuāngshì jiǎoxiàn
moulding

扶手椅
fúshǒuyǐ
armchair

书架
shūjià
bookshelf

沙发床
shāfāchuáng
sofa bed

地毯
dìtǎn
rug

书房 shūfáng | study

餐厅 cāntīng • **dining room**

胡椒粉
húijiāofěn
pepper

盐
yán
salt

餐桌
cānzhuō
table

陶瓷餐具
táocí cānjù
crockery

餐具
cānjù
cutlery

椅子
yǐzi
chair

椅背
yǐbèi
back

座位
zuòwèi
seat

椅子腿
yǐzituǐ
leg

词汇 cíhuì • **vocabulary**

摆桌子 bǎizhuōzi lay the table (v)	**饿** è hungry	**午餐** wǔcān lunch	**饱** bǎo full	**主人** zhǔrén host
上菜 shàngcài serve (v)	**桌布** zhuōbù tablecloth	**晚餐** wǎncān dinner	**一份** yīfèn portion	**女主人** nǚzhǔrén hostess
吃 chī eat (v)	**早餐** zǎocān breakfast	**餐具垫** cānjùdiàn place mat	**饭菜** fàncài meal	**客人** kèrén guest

请再给我加一些，好吗？
qǐng zàigěi wǒ jiā yìxiē, hǎoma?
Can I have some more, please?

我吃饱了，谢谢。
wǒ chībǎole, xièxie.
I've had enough, thank you.

很好吃。
hěn hǎochī.
That was delicious.

餐具 cānjù · crockery and cutlery

马克杯
mǎkèbēi
mug

咖啡杯
kāfēibēi
coffee cup

茶杯
chábēi
teacup

茶匙
cháchí
teaspoon

盘子
pánzi
plate

碗
wǎn
bowl

咖啡壶
kāfēihú
cafetière

茶壶
cháhú
teapot

带柄水壶
dàibǐngshuǐhú
jug

蛋杯
dànbēi
egg cup

酒杯
jiǔbēi
wine glass

平底玻璃杯
píngdǐbōlibēi
tumbler

玻璃器皿
bōlí qìmǐn
glassware

餐巾套环
cānjīn tàohuán
napkin ring

甜点盘
tiándiǎnpán
side plate

正餐用盘
zhèngcān
yòngpán
dinner plate

汤盘
tāngpán
soup bowl

汤匙
tāngchí
soup spoon

餐叉
cānchā
fork

餐巾
cānjīn
napkin

餐具摆放
cānjù bǎifàng
place setting

餐匙
cānchí
spoon

餐刀
cāndāo
knife

厨房 chúfáng • kitchen

抽油烟机
chōuyóuyānjī
extractor

搁架
gējià
shelves

防溅挡板
fángjiàn dǎngbǎn
splashback

陶瓷炉台
táocí lútái
ceramic hob

水龙头
shuǐlóngtóu
tap

操作台
cāozuòtái
worktop

洗涤槽
xǐdícáo
sink

烤箱
kǎoxiāng
oven

抽屉
chōutì
drawer

橱柜
chúguì
cabinet

厨房电器 chúfáng diànqì • appliances

搅拌容器
jiǎobànróngqì
mixing bowl

盖子
gàizi
lid

微波炉
wēibōlú
microwave oven

刀片
dāopiàn
blade

电水壶
diànshuǐhú
kettle

烤面包机
kǎomiànbāojī
toaster

食品加工器
shípǐn jiāgōngqì
food processor

搅拌器
jiǎobànqì
blender

洗碗机
xǐwǎnjī
dishwasher

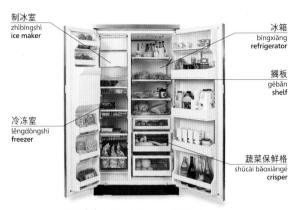

制冰室
zhìbīngshì
ice maker

冷冻室
lěngdòngshì
freezer

冰箱
bīngxiāng
refrigerator

搁板
gēbǎn
shelf

蔬菜保鲜格
shūcài bǎoxiāngé
crisper

双门冰箱 shuāngmén bīngxiāng | fridge-freezer

词汇 cíhuì • vocabulary

餐具沥水架 cānjù lìshuǐjià **draining board**	冷冻 lěngdòng **freeze (v)**
火炉 huǒlú **burner**	解冻 jiědòng **defrost (v)**
炉盘 lúpán **hob**	蒸 zhēng **steam (v)**
垃圾桶 lājītǒng **rubbish bin**	炒 chǎo **sauté (v)**

烹饪 pēngrèn • cooking

削皮
xuēpí
peel (v)

切片
qiēpiàn
slice (v)

擦碎
cāsuì
grate (v)

注水
zhùshuǐ
pour (v)

搅拌
jiǎobàn
mix (v)

搅打
jiǎodǎ
whisk (v)

煮沸
zhǔfèi
boil (v)

煎
jiān
fry (v)

擀
gǎn
roll (v)

搅动
jiǎodòng
stir (v)

文火烧，煨，炖
wénhuǒ shāo, wēi, dùn
simmer (v)

沸水煮
fèishuǐzhǔ
poach (v)

烘制
hōngzhì
bake (v)

烤制
kǎozhì
roast (v)

烧烤
shāokǎo
grill (v)

厨具 chújù • kitchenware

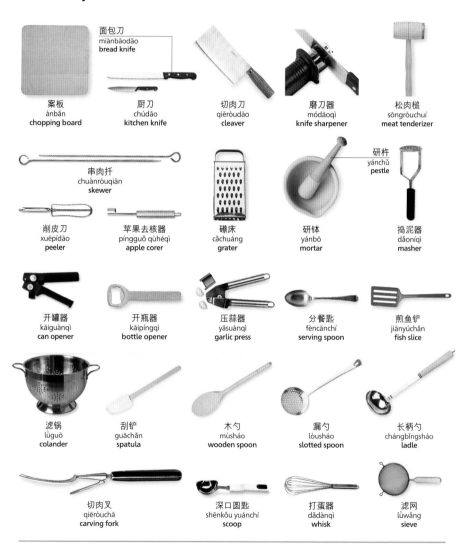

面包刀
miànbāodāo
bread knife

案板
ànbǎn
chopping board

厨刀
chúdāo
kitchen knife

切肉刀
qiēròudāo
cleaver

磨刀器
módāoqì
knife sharpener

松肉槌
sōngròuchuí
meat tenderizer

串肉扦
chuànròuqiān
skewer

研杵
yánchǔ
pestle

削皮刀
xuēpídāo
peeler

苹果去核器
píngguǒ qùhéqì
apple corer

礤床
cǎchuáng
grater

研钵
yánbō
mortar

捣泥器
dǎoníqì
masher

开罐器
kāiguànqì
can opener

开瓶器
kāipíngqì
bottle opener

压蒜器
yāsuànqì
garlic press

分餐匙
fēncānchí
serving spoon

煎鱼铲
jiānyúchǎn
fish slice

滤锅
lǜguō
colander

刮铲
guāchǎn
spatula

木勺
mùsháo
wooden spoon

漏勺
lòusháo
slotted spoon

长柄勺
chángbǐngsháo
ladle

切肉叉
qiēròuchā
carving fork

深口圆匙
shēnkǒu yuánchí
scoop

打蛋器
dǎdànqì
whisk

滤网
lǜwǎng
sieve

锅盖
guōgài
lid

不粘锅
bùzhānguō
non-stick

煎锅
jiānguō
frying pan

长柄深平底锅
chángbǐng shēn píngdǐguō
saucepan

烤架盘
kǎojiàpán
grill pan

炒锅
chǎoguō
wok

陶制炖锅
táozhìdùnguō
earthenware dish

玻璃
bōlí
glass

耐热
nàirè
ovenproof

搅拌碗
jiǎobànwǎn
mixing bowl

舒芙蕾模子
shūfúléi múzi
soufflé dish

烘烤菜肴盘
hōngkǎo càiyáopán
gratin dish

干酪蛋糕模
gānlào dàngāomú
ramekin

砂锅
shāguō
casserole dish

蛋糕制作 dàngāo zhìzuò • baking cakes

秤
chèng
scales

量壶
liánghú
measuring jug

蛋糕烤模
dàngāo kǎomú
cake tin

馅饼烤模
xiànbǐng kǎomú
pie tin

奶油蛋糕烤模
nǎiyóudàngāo kǎomú
flan tin

面粉刷 miànfěnshuā
pastry brush

擀面杖 gǎnmiànzhàng | rolling pin

蛋糕裱花袋 dàngāo
biǎohuādài | piping bag

松饼烤盘
sōngbǐng kǎopán
muffin tray

烤盘
kǎopán
baking tray

冷却架
lěngquèjià
cooling rack

烤箱手套
kǎoxiāng shǒutào
oven glove

围裙
wéiqún
apron

卧室 wòshì • **bedroom**

衣橱
yīchú
wardrobe

床头灯
chuángtóudēng
bedside lamp

床头板
chuángtóubǎn
headboard

床头柜
chuángtóuguì
bedside table

五斗橱
wǔdǒuchú
chest of drawers

抽屉
chōutì
drawer

床
chuáng
bed

床垫
chuángdiàn
mattress

床罩
chuángzhào
bedspread

枕头
zhěntou
pillow

暖水袋
nuǎnshuǐdài
hot-water bottle

时钟收音机
shízhōng shōuyīnjī
clock radio

闹钟
nàozhōng
alarm clock

纸巾盒
zhǐjīnhé
box of tissues

衣架
yījià
coat hanger

床上用品 chuángshàng yòngpǐn • bed linen

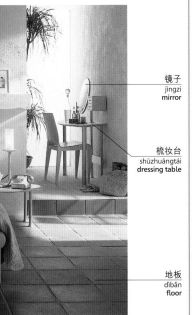

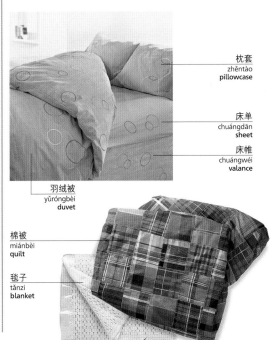

镜子
jìngzi
mirror

梳妆台
shūzhuāngtái
dressing table

地板
dìbǎn
floor

枕套
zhěntào
pillowcase

床单
chuángdān
sheet

床帷
chuángwéi
valance

羽绒被
yǔróngbèi
duvet

棉被
miánbèi
quilt

毯子
tǎnzi
blanket

词汇 cíhuì • vocabulary

单人床 dānrénchuáng **single bed**	床脚板 chuángjiǎobǎn **footboard**	失眠 shīmián **insomnia**	醒来 xǐnglái **wake up (v)**	设定闹钟 shèdìng nàozhōng **set the alarm (v)**
双人床 shuāngrénchuáng **double bed**	弹簧床面 tánhuáng chuángmiàn **bedspring**	上床睡觉 shàngchuáng shuìjiào **go to bed (v)**	起床 qǐchuáng **get up (v)**	打鼾 dǎhān **snore (v)**
电热毯 diànrètǎn **electric blanket**	地毯 dìtǎn **carpet**	入睡 rùshuì **go to sleep (v)**	整理床铺 zhěnglǐ chuángpù **make the bed (v)**	内嵌式衣橱 nèiqiànshì yīchú **built-in wardrobe**

浴室 yùshì • bathroom

毛巾架
máojīnjià
towel rail

淋浴隔门
línyù gémén
shower door

冷水龙头
lěngshuǐ lóngtóu
cold tap

热水龙头
rèshuǐ lóngtóu
hot tap

淋浴喷头
línyù pēntóu
shower head

洗手池
xǐshǒuchí
washbasin

塞子
sāizi
plug

淋浴
línyù
shower

地漏
dìlòu
drain

马桶座
mǎtǒngzuò
toilet seat

抽水马桶
chōushuǐ mǎtǒng
toilet

马桶刷
mǎtǒngshuā
toilet brush

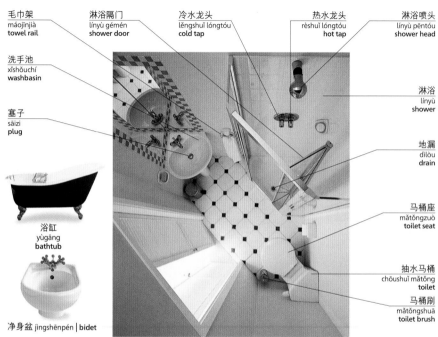

浴缸
yùgāng
bathtub

净身盆 jìngshēnpén | bidet

词汇 cíhuì • vocabulary

家用药箱
jiāyòng yàoxiāng
medicine cabinet

浴室防滑垫
yùshì fánghuádiàn
bath mat

卫生纸
wèishēngzhǐ
toilet roll

淋浴隔帘
línyù gélián
shower curtain

洗淋浴
xǐlínyù
take a shower (v)

洗澡
xǐzǎo
take a bath (v)

口腔卫生 kǒuqiāng wèishēng • dental hygiene

牙刷
yáshuā
toothbrush

牙线
yáxiàn
dental floss

牙膏
yágāo
toothpaste

漱口液
shùkǒuyè
mouthwash

海绵
hǎimián
sponge

浮石
fúshí
pumice stone

背刷
bèishuā
back brush

除臭剂
chúchòujì
deodorant

肥皂盒
féizàohé
soap dish

沐浴乳
mùyùrǔ
shower gel

肥皂
féizào
soap

面霜
miànshuāng
face cream

泡泡浴液
pàopào yùyè
bubble bath

擦手巾
cāshǒujīn
hand towel

浴巾
yùjīn
bath towel

毛巾
máojīn
towels

润肤露
rùnfūlù
body lotion

爽身粉
shuǎngshēnfěn
talcum powder

浴袍
yùpáo
bathrobe

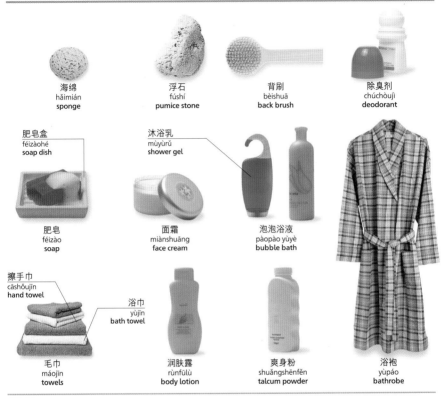

剃须 tìxū • **shaving**

电动剃须刀
diàndòng tìxūdāo
electric razor

剃须泡沫
tìxúpàomò
shaving foam

一次性剃须刀
yícìxìng tìxūdāo
disposable razor

剃刀刀片
tìdāo dāopiàn
razor blade

须后水
xūhòushuǐ
aftershave

育婴室 yùyīngshì • nursery

婴儿护理 yīng'ér hùlǐ • baby care

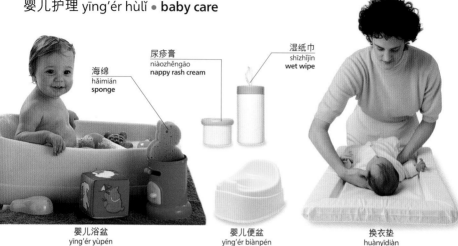

海绵
hǎimián
sponge

尿疹膏
niàozhěngāo
nappy rash cream

湿纸巾
shīzhǐjīn
wet wipe

婴儿浴盆
yīng'ér yùpén
baby bath

婴儿便盆
yīng'ér biànpén
potty

换衣垫
huànyīdiàn
changing mat

睡眠 shuìmián • sleeping

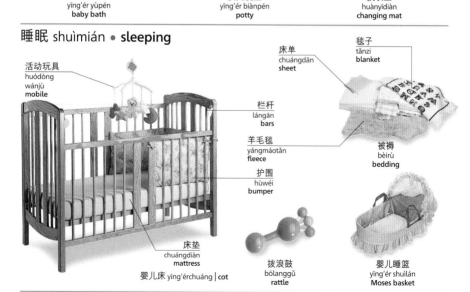

活动玩具
huódòng wánjù
mobile

床单
chuángdān
sheet

毯子
tǎnzi
blanket

栏杆
lángān
bars

羊毛毯
yángmáotǎn
fleece

被褥
bèirù
bedding

护围
hùwéi
bumper

床垫
chuángdiàn
mattress

婴儿床 yīng'érchuáng | cot

拨浪鼓
bōlanggǔ
rattle

婴儿睡篮
yīng'ér shuìlán
Moses basket

游戏 yóuxì • playing

娃娃
wáwa
doll

长毛绒玩具
chángmáoróng wánjù
soft toy

娃娃屋
wáwawū
doll's house

玩具屋
wánjùwū
playhouse

泰迪熊
tàidíxíong
teddy bear

玩具
wánjù
toy

球
qiú
ball

玩具篮
wánjùlán
toy basket

游戏围栏
yóuxì wéilán
playpen

安全 ānquán • safety

儿童安全锁
értóng ānquánsuǒ
child lock

婴儿监视器
yīng'ér jiānshìqì
baby monitor

楼梯门栏
lóutī ménlán
stair gate

饮食 yǐnshí • eating

高脚椅
gāojiǎoyǐ
high chair

奶嘴
nǎizuǐ
teat

婴儿杯
yīng'érbēi
drinking cup

奶瓶
nǎipíng
bottle

外出 wàichū • going out

折叠式婴儿车
zhédiéshì yīng'érchē
pushchair

卧式婴儿车
wòshìyīng'érchē
pram

遮阳蓬
zhēyángpéng
hood

手提式婴儿床
shǒutíshì yīng'érchuáng
carrycot

尿布
niàobù
nappy

婴儿衣物袋
yīng'ér yīwùdài
changing bag

婴儿吊带
yīng'ér diàodài
baby sling

洗衣间 xǐyījiān · **utility room**

洗涤 xǐdí · **laundry**

脏衣物
zāngyīwù
dirty washing

干净衣物
gānjìng yīwù
clean clothes

洗衣篮
xǐyīlán
laundry basket

洗衣机
xǐyījī
washing machine

洗衣干衣机
xǐyī gānyījī
washer-dryer

滚筒式烘干机
gǔntǒngshì hōnggānjī
tumble dryer

衣物篮
yīwùlán
linen basket

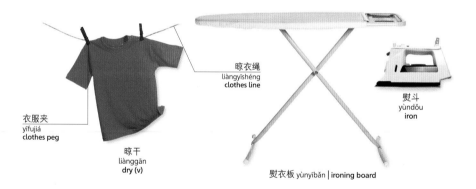

晾衣绳
liàngyīshéng
clothes line

衣服夹
yīfujiá
clothes peg

晾干
liànggān
dry (v)

熨斗
yùndǒu
iron

熨衣板 yùnyībǎn | ironing board

词汇 cíhuì · **vocabulary**

装入 zhuāngrù load (v)	**甩干** shuǎigān spin (v)	**熨烫** yùntàng iron (v)	**洗衣机怎么用?** xǐyījī zěnmeyòng? How do I operate the washing machine?
漂洗 piǎoxǐ rinse (v)	**甩干机** shuǎigānjī spin dryer	**织物柔顺剂** zhīwù róushùnjì fabric conditioner	**如何设定洗染色/白色衣物?** rúhé shèdìng xǐ rǎnsè/báisè yīwù? What is the setting for coloureds/whites?

清洁用具 qīngjiéyòngjù · cleaning equipment

吸管
xīguǎn
suction hose

短柄扫帚
duǎnbǐng sàozhou
brush

簸箕
bòji
dust pan

漂白剂
piǎobáijì
bleach

水桶
shuǐtǒng
bucket

去污粉
qùwūfěn
powder

洗涤液
xǐdíyè
liquid

抹布
mābù
duster

吸尘器
xīchénqì
vacuum cleaner

拖把
tuōbǎ
mop

清洁剂
qīngjiéjì
detergent

上光剂
shàngguāngjì
polish

扫除 sǎochú · activities

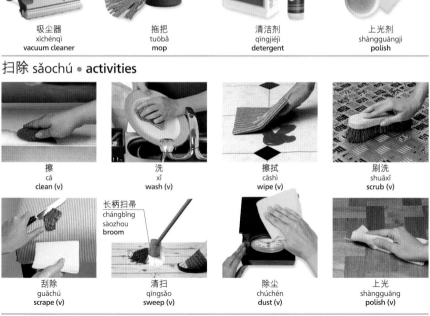

擦
cā
clean (v)

洗
xǐ
wash (v)

擦拭
cāshì
wipe (v)

刷洗
shuāxǐ
scrub (v)

刮除
guāchú
scrape (v)

长柄扫帚
chángbǐng
sàozhou
broom

清扫
qīngsǎo
sweep (v)

除尘
chúchén
dust (v)

上光
shàngguāng
polish (v)

工作间 gōngzuòjiān • workshop

钻夹头
zuànjiátóu
chuck

先端部钻头
xiānduānbù
zuàntóu
drill bit

电池盒
diànchíhé
battery pack

镂花锯
lòuhuājù
jigsaw

充电式电钻
chōngdiànshì diànzuàn
cordless drill

电钻
diànzuàn
electric drill

胶枪
jiāoqiāng
glue gun

夹钳
jiáqián
clamp

刃
rèn
blade

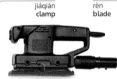

台钳
táiqián
vice

打磨机
dǎmójī
sander

圆锯
yuánjù
circular saw

工作台
gōngzuòtái
workbench

木材胶
mùcáijiāo
wood glue

工具架
gōngjùjià
tool rack

槽刨
cáopáo
router

手摇曲柄钻
shǒuyáo
qūbǐngzuàn
bit brace

刨花
bàohuā
wood shavings

电源箱延长线
diànyuánxiāng
yánchángxiàn
extension lead

技艺 jìyì · techniques

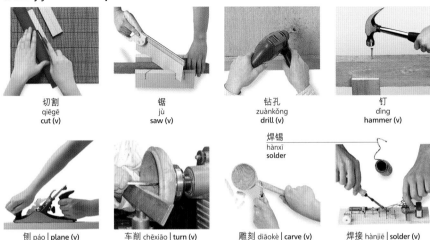

切割	锯	钻孔	钉
qiēgē	jù	zuànkǒng	dìng
cut (v)	**saw (v)**	**drill (v)**	**hammer (v)**

焊锡
hànxī
solder

刨 páo | plane (v)　　车削 chēxiāo | turn (v)　　雕刻 diāokè | carve (v)　　焊接 hànjiē | solder (v)

材料 cáiliào · materials

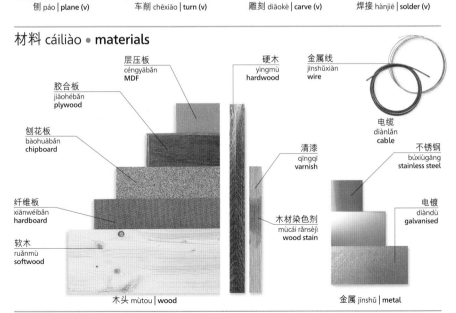

层压板
céngyābǎn
MDF

胶合板
jiāohébǎn
plywood

刨花板
bàohuābǎn
chipboard

纤维板
xiānwéibǎn
hardboard

软木
ruǎnmù
softwood

硬木
yìngmù
hardwood

金属线
jīnshǔxiàn
wire

电缆
diànlǎn
cable

清漆
qīngqī
varnish

不锈钢
búxiùgāng
stainless steel

木材染色剂
mùcái rǎnsèjì
wood stain

电镀
diàndù
galvanised

木头 mùtou | wood

金属 jīnshǔ | metal

工具箱 gōngjùxiāng • toolbox

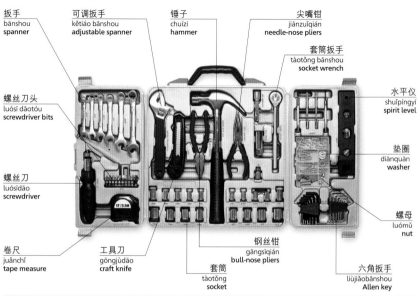

扳手
bānshou
spanner

可调扳手
kětiáo bānshou
adjustable spanner

锤子
chuízi
hammer

尖嘴钳
jiānzuǐqián
needle-nose pliers

套筒扳手
tàotǒng bānshou
socket wrench

水平仪
shuǐpíngyí
spirit level

螺丝刀头
luósī dāotóu
screwdriver bits

垫圈
diànquān
washer

螺丝刀
luósīdāo
screwdriver

螺母
luómǔ
nut

卷尺
juǎnchǐ
tape measure

工具刀
gōngjùdāo
craft knife

套筒
tàotǒng
socket

钢丝钳
gāngsīqián
bull-nose pliers

六角扳手
liùjiǎobānshou
Allen key

钻头 zuàntóu • drill bits

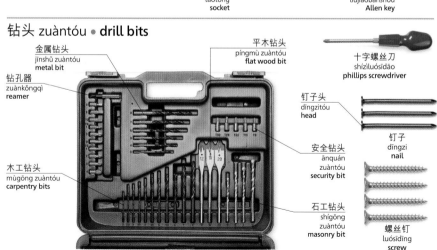

金属钻头
jīnshǔ zuàntóu
metal bit

平木钻头
píngmù zuàntóu
flat wood bit

十字螺丝刀
shízìluósīdāo
phillips screwdriver

钻孔器
zuànkǒngqì
reamer

钉子头
dīngzitóu
head

安全钻头
ānquán
zuàntóu
security bit

钉子
dīngzi
nail

木工钻头
mùgōng zuàntóu
carpentry bits

石工钻头
shígōng
zuàntóu
masonry bit

螺丝钉
luósīdīng
screw

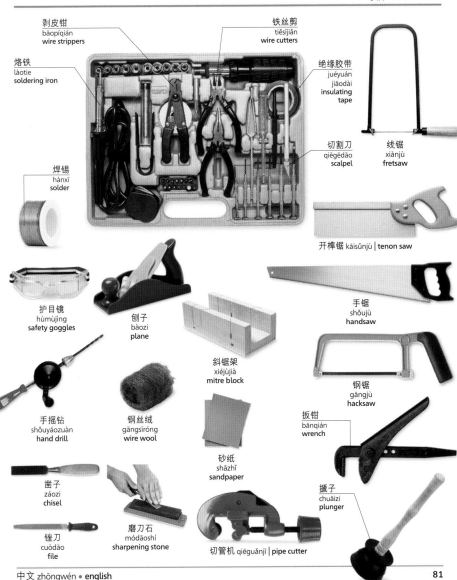

剥皮钳
bāopíqián
wire strippers

铁丝剪
tiěsījiǎn
wire cutters

烙铁
làotie
soldering iron

绝缘胶带
juéyuán
jiāodài
insulating
tape

切割刀
qiēgēdāo
scalpel

线锯
xiànjù
fretsaw

焊锡
hànxī
solder

开榫锯 kāisǔnjù | tenon saw

护目镜
hùmùjìng
safety goggles

刨子
bàozi
plane

手锯
shǒujù
handsaw

斜锯架
xiéjùjià
mitre block

钢锯
gāngjù
hacksaw

手摇钻
shǒuyáozuàn
hand drill

钢丝绒
gāngsīróng
wire wool

扳钳
bānqián
wrench

砂纸
shāzhǐ
sandpaper

凿子
záozi
chisel

撅子
chuāizi
plunger

锉刀
cuòdāo
file

磨刀石
módāoshí
sharpening stone

切管机 qiēguǎnjī | pipe cutter

装修 zhuāngxiū • **decorating**

剪刀
jiǎndāo
scissors

工艺刀
gōngyìdāo
craft knife

铅锤线
qiānchuíxiàn
plumb line

刮刀
guādāo
scraper

装修工
zhuāngxiūgōng
decorator

壁纸
bìzhǐ
wallpaper

折梯
zhétī
stepladder

裱糊刷
biǎohúshuā
wallpaper brush

裱糊台
biǎohútái
pasting table

上浆刷
shàngjiāngshuā
pasting brush

壁纸黏合剂
bìzhǐ niánhéjì
wallpaper paste

桶
tǒng
bucket

贴壁纸 tiēbìzhǐ | wallpaper (v)

铲掉 chǎndiào | strip (v)

抹 mǒ | fill (v)

用砂纸打磨 yòng shāzhǐ dǎmó
sand (v)

粉刷 fěnshuā | plaster (v)

贴(墙纸) tiē(qiángzhǐ) | hang (v)

铺砖 pūzhuān | tile (v)

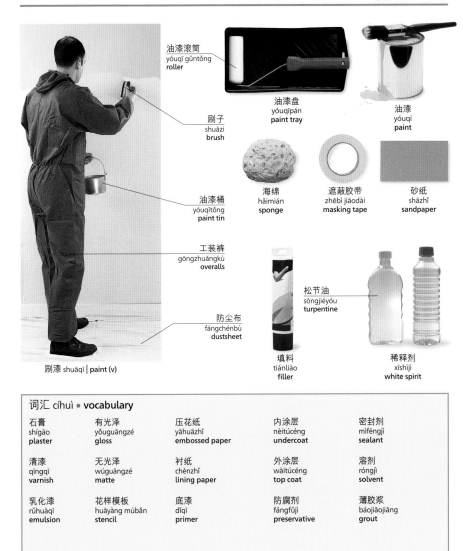

油漆滚筒
yóuqī gǔntǒng
roller

油漆盘
yóuqīpán
paint tray

油漆
yóuqī
paint

刷子
shuāzi
brush

海绵
hǎimián
sponge

遮蔽胶带
zhēbì jiāodài
masking tape

砂纸
shāzhǐ
sandpaper

油漆桶
yóuqītǒng
paint tin

工装裤
gōngzhuāngkù
overalls

松节油
sōngjiéyóu
turpentine

防尘布
fángchénbù
dustsheet

填料
tiánliào
filler

稀释剂
xīshìjì
white spirit

刷漆 shuāqī | paint (v)

词汇 cíhuì • vocabulary

石膏	有光泽	压花纸	内涂层	密封剂
shígāo	yǒuguāngzé	yāhuāzhǐ	nèitúcéng	mìfēngjì
plaster	**gloss**	**embossed paper**	**undercoat**	**sealant**
清漆	无光泽	衬纸	外涂层	溶剂
qīngqī	wúguāngzé	chènzhǐ	wàitúcéng	róngjì
varnish	**matte**	**lining paper**	**top coat**	**solvent**
乳化漆	花样模板	底漆	防腐剂	薄胶浆
rǔhuàqī	huāyàng múbǎn	dǐqī	fángfǔjì	báojiāojiāng
emulsion	**stencil**	**primer**	**preservative**	**grout**

花园 huāyuán • garden

花园风格 huāyuánfēnggé • garden styles

屋顶花园
wūdǐng huāyuán
roof garden

吊篮
diàolán
hanging basket

内院 nèiyuàn | patio garden

岩石园
yánshíyuán
rock garden

花格屏 huāgépíng | trellis

庭院 tíngyuàn | courtyard

法式花园 fǎshì huāyuán | formal garden

乡间花园
xiāngjiān huāyuán
cottage garden

香草花园
xiāngcǎo huāyuán
herb garden

水景花园
shuǐjǐng huāyuán
water garden

藤架
téngjià
pergola

石面路
shímiànlù
paving

小径
xiǎojìng
path

肥料堆
féiliàoduī
compost heap

门
mén
gate

花坛
huātán
flowerbed

棚屋
péngwū
shed

草坪
cǎopíng
lawn

温室
wēnshì
greenhouse

池塘
chítáng
pond

篱笆
líba
fence

树篱
shùlí
hedge

拱门
gǒngmén
arch

菜圃
càipǔ
vegetable
garden

绿草带
lǜcǎodài
herbaceous border

土壤 tǔrǎng • soil

表层土
biǎocéngtǔ
topsoil

沙土
shātǔ
sand

石灰石
shíhuīshí
chalk

淤泥
yūní
silt

黏土
niántǔ
clay

露台甲板
lùtáijiǎbǎn
decking

喷泉 pēnquán | fountain

花园植物 huāyuánzhíwù · garden plants

植物种类 zhíwùzhǒnglèi · types of plants

一年生(植物)
yìniánshēng (zhíwù)
annual

二年生(植物)
èrniánshēng (zhíwù)
biennial

多年生(植物)
duōniánshēng (zhíwù)
perennial

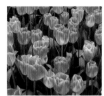
球茎植物
qiújīng zhíwù
bulb

蕨类植物
juélèi zhíwù
fern

灯心草
dēngxīncǎo
rush

竹子
zhúzi
bamboo

杂草
zácǎo
weeds

药草
yàocǎo
herb

水生植物
shuǐshēng zhíwù
water plant

树
shù
tree

落叶(植物)
luòyè (zhíwù)
deciduous

棕榈
zōnglǘ
palm

针叶树
zhēnyèshù
conifer

常绿(植物)
chánglǜ (zhíwù)
evergreen

剪型植物
jiǎnxíngzhíwù
topiary

高山植物
gāoshān zhíwù
alpine

肉质植物
ròuzhì zhíwù
succulent

仙人掌
xiānrénzhǎng
cactus

盆栽植物
pénzāi zhíwù
potted plant

阴地植物
yīndì zhíwù
shade plant

攀缘植物
pānyuán
zhíwù
climber

开花灌木
kāihuā guànmù
flowering shrub

地被植物
dìbèi zhíwù
ground cover

葡匐植物
púfú zhíwù
creeper

观赏(植物)
guānshǎng
(zhíwù)
ornamental

草
cǎo
grass

园艺工具 yuányì gōngjù • garden tools

搂草耙
lōucǎopá
lawn rake

堆肥
duīféi
compost

种子
zhǒngzi
seeds

骨粉
gǔfěn
bone meal

铲
chǎn
spade

叉
chā
fork

长柄修篱剪
chángbǐng xiūlíjiǎn
long-handled shears

耙子
pázi
rake

锄头
chútou
hoe

碎石
suìshí
gravel

草袋
cǎodài
grass bag

马达
mǎdá
motor

把手
bǎshou
handle

浅底篮
qiǎndǐlán
trug

防护盘
fánghùpán
shield

支架
zhījià
stand

剪草器
jiǎncǎoqì
trimmer

剪草机
jiǎncǎojī
lawnmower

独轮手推车
dúlún shǒutuīchē
wheelbarrow

手叉
shǒuchā
hand fork

移植铲
yízhíchǎn
trowel

刃
rèn
blade

修篱剪
xiūlíjiǎn
shears

手锯
shǒujù
handsaw

修枝剪
xiūzhījiǎn
secateurs

育苗盘
yùmiáopán
seed tray

杀虫剂
shāchóngjì
pesticide

园艺手套
yuányì shǒutào
gardening gloves

合股线
hégǔxiàn
twine

园艺标签
yuányìbiāoqiān
labels

捆绑细丝
kǔnbǎng xìsī
twist ties

固枝环
gùzhīhuán
ring ties

支撑杆
zhīchēnggān
canes

筛子
shāizǐ
sieve

花盆
huāpén
plant pot

橡胶靴
xiàngjiāoxuē
rubber boots

浇灌 jiāoguàn • watering

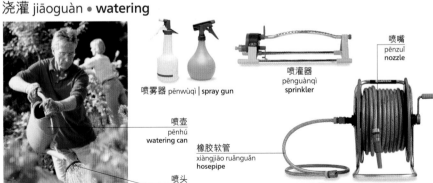

喷雾器 pēnwùqì | spray gun

喷灌器
pēnguànqì
sprinkler

喷嘴
pēnzuǐ
nozzle

喷壶
pēnhú
watering can

橡胶软管
xiàngjiāo ruǎnguǎn
hosepipe

喷头
pēntóu
rose

水管车 shuǐguǎnchē | hose reel

园艺 yuányì · gardening

草地
cǎodì
lawn

花坛
huātán
flowerbed

割草机
gēcǎojī
lawnmower

树篱
shùlí
hedge

树木支桩
shùmù zhīzhuāng
stake

割草 gēcǎo | mow (v)

铺草皮
pūcǎopí
turf (v)

扎孔透气
zhākǒngtòuqì
spike (v)

耙
pá
rake (v)

修枝
xiūzhī
trim (v)

挖
wā
dig (v)

播种
bōzhǒng
sow (v)

土表施肥
tǔbiǎo shīféi
top dress (v)

浇水
jiāoshuǐ
water (v)

支撑杆
zhīchēnggān
cane

整枝
zhěngzhī
train (v)

摘除枯花
zhāichú kūhuā
deadhead (v)

喷水
pēnshuǐ
spray (v)

插条
chātiáo
cutting

嫁接
jiàjiē
graft (v)

繁殖
fánzhí
propagate (v)

修剪
xiūjiǎn
prune (v)

用杆支撑
yònggān zhīchēng
stake (v)

移植
yízhí
transplant (v)

清除杂草
qīngchú zácǎo
weed (v)

加护盖物
jiā hùgàiwù
mulch (v)

收获
shōuhuò
harvest (v)

词汇 cíhuì • vocabulary

栽培 zāipéi cultivate (v)	园艺设计 yuányì shèjì landscape (v)	施肥 shīféi fertilize (v)	筛 shāi sieve (v)	有机(栽培)的 yǒujī(zāipéi)de organic	秧苗 yāngmiáo seedling	底土 dǐtǔ subsoil
护理 hùlǐ tend (v)	把…种于盆内 bǎ…zhòng yú pénnèi pot up (v)	采摘 cǎizhāi pick (v)	松土 sōngtǔ aerate (v)	排水 páishuǐ drainage	肥料 féiliào fertilizer	除草剂 chúcǎojì weedkiller

服务 fúwù
services

急救 jíjiù • emergency services

救护车 jiùhùchē • ambulance

救护车 jiùhùchē | ambulance

担架
dānjià
stretcher

急救人员 jíjiù rényuán | paramedic

警察 jǐngchá • police

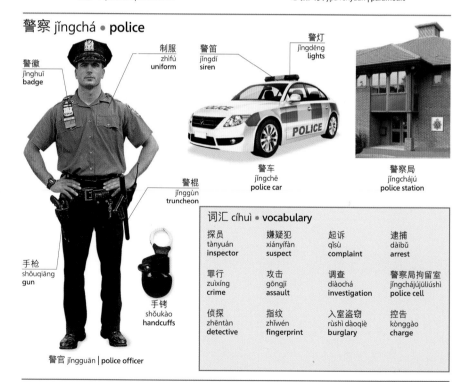

警徽
jǐnghuī
badge

制服
zhìfú
uniform

警笛
jǐngdí
siren

警灯
jǐngdēng
lights

警棍
jǐnggùn
truncheon

手枪
shǒuqiāng
gun

手铐
shǒukào
handcuffs

警官 jǐngguān | police officer

警车
jǐngchē
police car

警察局
jǐngchájú
police station

词汇 cíhuì • vocabulary

探员 tànyuán inspector	嫌疑犯 xiányífàn suspect	起诉 qǐsù complaint	逮捕 dàibǔ arrest
罪行 zuìxíng crime	攻击 gōngjī assault	调查 diàochá investigation	警察局拘留室 jǐngchájújūliúshì police cell
侦探 zhēntàn detective	指纹 zhǐwén fingerprint	入室盗窃 rùshì dàoqiè burglary	控告 kònggào charge

消防队 xiāofángduì · fire brigade

烟
yān
smoke

水龙带
shuǐlóngdài
hose

头盔
tóukuī
helmet

吊篮
diàolán
cradle

水柱
shuǐzhù
water jet

消防队员
xiāofángduìyuán
firefighters

悬臂
xuánbì
boom

消防梯
xiāofángtī
ladder

驾驶室
jiàshǐshì
cab

火情 huǒqíng | fire

消防站
xiāofángzhàn
fire station

消防通道
xiāofángtōngdào
fire escape

消防车
xiāofángchē
fire engine

烟雾报警器
yānwù bàojǐngqì
smoke alarm

火灾警报器
huǒzāi jǐngbàoqì
fire alarm

消防斧
xiāofángfǔ
axe

灭火器
mièhuǒqì
fire extinguisher

消防栓
xiāofángshuān
hydrant

我需要警察/消防队/救护车。 wǒ xūyào jǐngchá/xiāofángduì/ jiùhùchē. **I need the police/fire brigade/ ambulance.**	在…有火情。 zài…yǒu huǒqíng. **There's a fire at …**	发生了事故。 fāshēngle shìgù. **There's been an accident.**	报警！ bàojǐng! **Call the police!**

银行 yínháng • bank

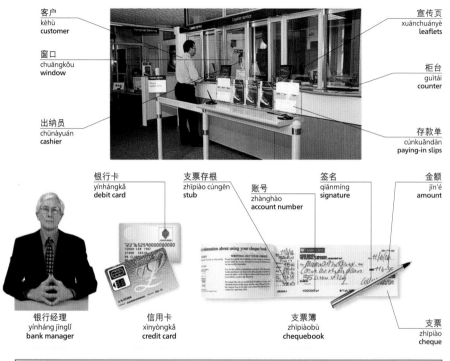

客户
kèhù
customer

窗口
chuāngkǒu
window

出纳员
chūnàyuán
cashier

宣传页
xuānchuányè
leaflets

柜台
guìtái
counter

存款单
cúnkuǎndān
paying-in slips

银行卡
yínhángkǎ
debit card

支票存根
zhīpiào cúngēn
stub

账号
zhànghào
account number

签名
qiānmíng
signature

金额
jīn'é
amount

银行经理
yínháng jīnglǐ
bank manager

信用卡
xìnyòngkǎ
credit card

支票簿
zhīpiàobù
chequebook

支票
zhīpiào
cheque

词汇 cíhuì • vocabulary

储蓄 chǔxù savings	抵押贷款 dǐyā dàikuǎn mortgage	付款 fùkuǎn payment	存入 cúnrù pay in (v)	活期存款账户 huóqīcúnkuǎn zhànghù current account
税 shuì tax	透支 tòuzhī overdraft	直接借记 zhíjiē jièjì direct debit	银行手续费 yínháng shǒuxùfèi bank charge	储蓄账户 chǔxù zhànghù savings account
贷款 dàikuǎn loan	利率 lìlǜ interest rate	取款单 qǔkuǎndān withdrawal slip	银行转账 yínháng zhuǎnzhàng bank transfer	密码 mìmǎ PIN

硬币
yìngbì
coin

纸币
zhǐbì
note

屏幕
píngmù
screen

按键区
ànjiànqū
keypad

插卡口
chākǎkǒu
card slot

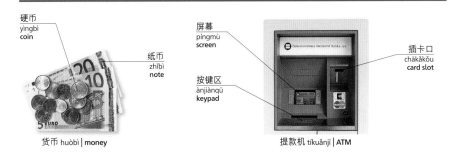

货币 huòbì | money

提款机 tíkuǎnjī | ATM

外币 wàibì • foreign currency

外币兑换处
wàibì duìhuànchù
bureau de change

旅行支票
lǚxíng zhīpiào
traveller's cheque

汇率
huìlǜ
exchange rate

金融 jīnróng • finance

股票价格
gǔpiào jiàgé
share price

股票经纪人
gǔpiào jīngjìrén
stockbroker

投资顾问
tóuzī gùwèn
financial advisor

证券交易所 zhèngquàn jiāoyìsuǒ
stock exchange

通讯 tōngxùn • communications

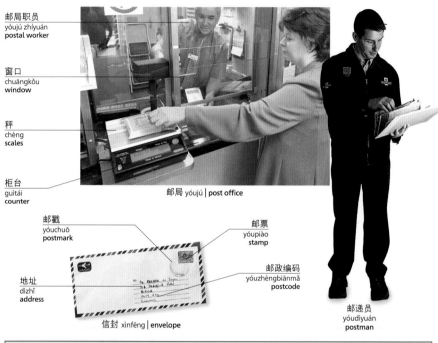

邮局职员
yóujú zhíyuán
postal worker

窗口
chuāngkǒu
window

秤
chèng
scales

柜台
guìtái
counter

邮局 yóujú | **post office**

邮戳
yóuchuō
postmark

邮票
yóupiào
stamp

邮政编码
yóuzhèngbiānmǎ
postcode

地址
dìzhǐ
address

信封 xìnfēng | **envelope**

邮递员
yóudìyuán
postman

词汇 cíhuì • vocabulary

信 xìn **letter**	寄信人地址 jìxìnrén dìzhǐ **return address**	递送 dìsòng **delivery**	易损坏 yìsǔnhuài **fragile**	勿折 wùzhé **do not bend (v)**
航空邮件 hángkōng yóujiàn **by airmail**	签名 qiānmíng **signature**	汇票 huìpiào **postal order**	邮袋 yóudài **mailbag**	此面向上 cǐmiàn xiàngshàng **this way up**
挂号邮件 guàhào yóujiàn **registered post**	(从邮筒中)取信 (cóng yóutǒng zhōng) qǔxìn **collection**	邮资 yóuzī **postage**	电报 diànbào **telegram**	

邮筒
yóutǒng
postbox

信箱
xìnxiāng
letterbox

包裹
bāoguǒ
parcel

速递
sùdì
courier

电话 diànhuà • telephone

话机
huàjī
handset

机座
jīzuò
base station

无绳电话
wúshéng diànhuà
cordless phone

答录机
dálùjī
answering machine

可视电话
kěshìdiànhuà
video phone

电话亭
diànhuàtíng
telephone box

智能手机
zhìnéng shǒujī
smartphone

移动电话
yídòng diànhuà
mobile phone

按键区
ànjiànqū
keypad

听筒
tīngtǒng
receiver

退币口
tuìbìkǒu
coin return

付费电话
fùfèi diànhuà
payphone

词汇 cíhuì • vocabulary

电话号码查询台
diànhuàhào mǎ cháxúntái
directory enquiries

对方付费电话
duìfāng fùfèi diànhuà
reverse charge call

拨号
bōhào
dial (v)

应用
yìngyòng
app

接听电话
jiētīng diànhuà
answer (v)

短信
duǎnxìn
text (SMS)

语音讯息
yǔyīn xùnxī
voice message

密码
mìmǎ
passcode

接线员
jiēxiànyuán
operator

占线
zhànxiàn
engaged/busy

断线
duànxiàn
disconnected

你能告诉我...的号码吗?
nǐ néng gàosù wǒ...de hàomǎ ma?
Can you give me the number for ...?

...的拨叫号码是多少?
...de bōjiào hàomǎ shì duōshǎo?
What is the dialling code for ...?

请短信通知我
qǐng duǎnxìn tōngzhī wǒ
Text me!

旅馆 lǚguǎn · hotel
大厅 dàtīng · lobby

留言
liúyán
messages

客人
kèrén
guest

房间钥匙
fángjiān yàoshi
room key

分类架
fēnlèijià
pigeonhole

接待员
jiēdàiyuán
receptionist

登记簿
dēngjìbù
register

柜台
guìtái
counter

接待总台 jiēdài zǒngtái | reception

行李
xíngli
luggage

行李车
xínglǐchē
trolley

搬运工 bānyùngōng | porter

电梯 diàntī | lift

房间号码
fángjiān hàomǎ
room number

房间 fángjiān · rooms

单人间
dānrénjiān
single room

双人间
shuāngrénjiān
double room

双床间
shuāngchuángjiān
twin room

专用浴室
zhuānyòngyùshì
private bathroom

服务 fúwù • services

客房清洁服务
kèfáng qīngjié fúwù
maid service

洗衣服务
xǐyī fúwù
laundry service

早餐盘
zǎocānpán
breakfast tray

房间送餐服务 fángjiān sòngcān fúwù | room service

小冰箱
xiǎobīngxiāng
minibar

餐厅
cāntīng
restaurant

健身房
jiànshēnfáng
gym

游泳池
yóuyǒngchí
swimming pool

词汇 cíhuì • vocabulary

提供住宿和早餐
tígōng zhùsù hé zǎocān
bed and breakfast

供应三餐
gōngyìng sāncān
full board

半食宿
bànshísù
half board

有空房间吗?
yǒu kōng fángjiān ma?
Do you have any vacancies?

我预定了房间。
wǒ yùdìngle fángjiān.
I have a reservation.

我想要一个单人间。
wǒ xiǎngyào yīgè dānrénjiān,
I'd like a single room.

我要一个房间,住三天。
wǒ yào yīgèfángjiān, zhù sāntiān.
I'd like a room for three nights.

住一晚多少钱?
zhù yīwǎn duōshǎoqián?
What is the charge per night?

我什么时候得腾房?
wǒ shénme shíhou děi téng fáng?
When do I have to vacate the room?

购物 gòuwù
shopping

购物中心 gòuwùzhōngxīn • **shopping centre**

大厅
dàtīng
atrium

招牌
zhāopái
sign

电梯
diàntī
lift

三层
sāncéng
second floor

二层
èrcéng
first floor

自动扶梯
zìdòng fútī
escalator

一层
yīcéng
ground floor

顾客
gùkè
customer

词汇 cíhuì • **vocabulary**

儿童用品部
értóng yòngpǐnbù
children's department

箱包部
xiāngbāobù
luggage department

鞋靴部
xiéxuēbù
shoe department

购物指南
gòuwù zhǐnán
store directory

售货员
shòuhuòyuán
sales assistant

客户服务
kèhù fúwù
customer services

更衣室
gēngyīshì
changing rooms

婴儿间
yīng'érjiān
baby changing facilities

卫生间
wèishēngjiān
toilets

这个多少钱?
zhège duōshǎo qián?
How much is this?

我可以换一件吗?
wǒ kěyǐ huàn yíjiàn ma?
May I exchange this?

百货商店 bǎihuò shāngdiàn · department store

男装
nánzhuāng
menswear

女装
nǚzhuāng
womenswear

女用内衣
nǚyòng nèiyī
lingerie

香水
xiāngshuǐ
perfumery

美容用品
měiróng yòngpǐn
beauty

家用纺织品
jiāyòng fǎngzhīpǐn
linen

家具
jiājù
home furnishings

缝纫用品
féngrèn yòngpǐn
haberdashery

厨房用品
chúfáng yòngpǐn
kitchenware

瓷器
cíqì
china

电子产品
diànzǐ chǎnpǐn
electrical goods

灯具
dēngjù
lighting

体育用品
tǐyù yòngpǐn
sports

玩具
wánjù
toys

文具
wénjù
stationery

食品
shípǐn
food hall

超级市场 chāojí shìchǎng • supermarket

过道
guòdào
aisle

货架
huòjià
shelf

传送带
chuánsòngdài
conveyer belt

收银员
shōuyínyuán
cashier

促销海报
cùxiāo hǎibào
offers

收款台 shōukuǎntái | checkout

顾客
gùkè
customer

收款机
shōukuǎnjī
till

购物袋
gòuwùdài
shopping bag

食品杂货
shípǐn záhuò
groceries

提手
tíshǒu
handle

条形码
tiáoxíngmǎ
bar code

购物车 gòuwùchē | trolley

购物篮 gòuwùlán | basket

条形码扫描器 tiáoxíngmǎ
sǎomiáoqì | scanner

烘烤食品
hōngkǎo shípǐn
bakery

乳制品
rǔzhìpǐn
dairy

早餐麦片
zǎocān màipiàn
breakfast cereals

罐装食品
guànzhuāng shípǐn
tinned food

甜食
tiánshí
confectionery

蔬菜
shūcài
vegetables

水果
shuǐguǒ
fruit

肉禽
ròuqín
meat and poultry

鱼
yú
fish

熟食
shúshí
deli

冷冻食品
lěngdòng shípǐn
frozen food

方便食品
fāngbiàn shípǐn
convenience food

饮料
yǐnliào
drinks

家庭日用品
jiātíng rìyòngpǐn
household products

化妆品
huàzhuāngpǐn
toiletries

婴儿用品
yīng'ér yòngpǐn
baby products

家用电器
jiāyòng diànqì
electrical goods

宠物饲料
chǒngwù sìliào
pet food

杂志 zázhì | magazines

药店 yàodiàn · chemist

牙齿护理
yáchǐ hùlǐ
dental care

妇女保健
fùnǚ bǎojiàn
feminine hygiene

除臭剂
chúchòujì
deodorants

维生素
wéishēngsù
vitamins

药剂室
yàojìshì
dispensary

药剂师
yàojìshī
pharmacist

止咳药
zhǐkéyào
cough medicine

草药
cǎoyào
herbal remedies

皮肤护理
pífū hùlǐ
skin care

晒后护肤液
shàihòu hùfūyè
aftersun

防晒霜
fángshàishuāng
sunscreen

防晒液
fángshàiyè
sunblock

驱虫剂
qūchóngjì
insect repellent

湿纸巾
shīzhǐjīn
wet wipe

纸巾
zhǐjīn
tissue

卫生巾
wèishēngjīn
sanitary towel

卫生棉条
wèishēng miántiáo
tampon

卫生护垫
wèishēng hùdiàn
panty liner

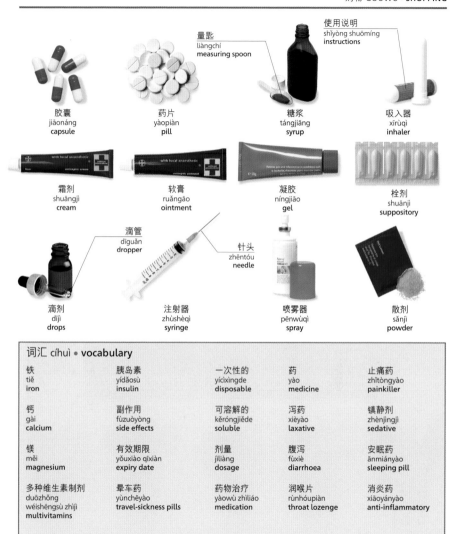

量匙
liàngchí
measuring spoon

使用说明
shǐyòng shuōmíng
instructions

胶囊
jiāonáng
capsule

药片
yàopiàn
pill

糖浆
tángjiāng
syrup

吸入器
xīrùqì
inhaler

霜剂
shuāngjì
cream

软膏
ruǎngāo
ointment

凝胶
níngjiāo
gel

栓剂
shuānjì
suppository

滴管
dīguǎn
dropper

针头
zhēntóu
needle

滴剂
dījì
drops

注射器
zhùshèqì
syringe

喷雾器
pēnwùqì
spray

散剂
sǎnjì
powder

词汇 cíhuì • vocabulary

铁 tiě iron	胰岛素 yídǎosù insulin	一次性的 yícìxìngde disposable	药 yào medicine	止痛药 zhǐtòngyào painkiller
钙 gài calcium	副作用 fùzuòyòng side effects	可溶解的 kěróngjiěde soluble	泻药 xièyào laxative	镇静剂 zhènjìngjì sedative
镁 měi magnesium	有效期限 yǒuxiào qīxiàn expiry date	剂量 jìliàng dosage	腹泻 fùxiè diarrhoea	安眠药 ānmiányào sleeping pill
多种维生素制剂 duōzhǒng wéishēngsù zhìjì multivitamins	晕车药 yùnchēyào travel-sickness pills	药物治疗 yàowù zhìliáo medication	润喉片 rùnhóupiàn throat lozenge	消炎药 xiāoyányào anti-inflammatory

花店 huādiàn • florist

花
huā
flowers

百合
bǎihé
lily

洋槐
yánghuái
acacia

康乃馨
kāngnǎixin
carnation

盆栽植物
pénzāi zhíwù
pot plant

剑兰
jiànlán
gladiolus

鸢尾
yuānwěi
iris

雏菊
chújú
daisy

菊花
júhuā
chrysanthemum

满天星
mǎntiānxing
gypsophila

紫罗兰
zǐluólán
stocks

非洲菊
fēizhōujú
gerbera

叶簇
yècù
foliage

玫瑰
méiguī
rose

小苍兰
xiǎocānglán
freesia

插花 chāhuā • arrangements

花瓶
huāpíng
vase

兰花
lánhuā
orchid

牡丹
mǔdān
peony

花束
huāshù
bunch

茎
jīng
stem

黄水仙
huángshuǐxiān
daffodil

花苞
huābāo
bud

包装纸
bāozhuāngzhǐ
wrapping

郁金香 yùjīnxiāng | tulip

缎带
duàndài
ribbon

花束
huāshù
bouquet

干花
gānhuā
dried flowers

盆花 pénhuā | potpourri

花环 huāhuán | wreath

花环
huāhuán
garland

我能附上留言吗?
wǒ néng fùshàng liúyán ma?
Can I attach a message?

能帮我包一下吗?
néng bāng wǒ bāo yíxià ma?
Can I have them wrapped?

能不能将它们送到...?
néngbùnéng jiāng tāmen
sòngdào...?
Can you send them to ...?

这些花能开多久?
zhèxiē huā néng kāi duōjiǔ?
How long will these last?

这些花香吗?
zhèxiē huā xiāng ma?
Are they fragrant?

我想买一束...
wǒ xiǎng mǎi yíshù...
Can I have a bunch of ... please.

报刊亭 bàokāntíng • newsagent

香烟
xiāngyān
cigarettes

烟盒
yānhé
packet of cigarettes

邮票
yóupiào
stamps

明信片
míngxinpiàn
postcard

连环画
liánhuánhuà
comic

杂志
zázhì
magazine

报纸
bàozhǐ
newspaper

吸烟 xīyān • smoking

烟草
yāncǎo
tobacco

打火机
dǎhuǒjī
lighter

烟嘴
yānzuǐ
stem

烟锅
yānguō
bowl

烟斗
yāndǒu
pipe

雪茄
xuějiā
cigar

糖果店 tángguǒdiàn · confectioner

巧克力盒
qiǎokèlìhé
box of chocolates

零食
língshí
snack bar

薯片
shǔpiàn
crisps

甜食店 tiánshídiàn | **sweet shop**

词汇 cíhuì · vocabulary

牛奶巧克力
niúnǎiqiǎokèlì
milk chocolate

焦糖
jiāotáng
caramel

黑巧克力
hēiqiǎokèlì
plain chocolate

松露巧克力
sōnglùqiǎokèlì
truffle

白巧克力
báiqiǎokèlì
white chocolate

饼干
bǐnggān
biscuit

杂拌糖果
zábàntángguǒ
pick and mix

硬糖
yìngtáng
boiled sweets

糖果 tángguǒ · confectionery

巧克力
qiǎokèlì
chocolate

块状巧克力板
kuàizhuàng qiǎokèlìbǎn
chocolate bar

糖果
tángguǒ
sweets

棒棒糖
bàngbàngtáng
lollipop

太妃糖 tàifēitáng | **toffee**

奶油杏仁糖
nǎiyóuxìngréntáng | **nougat**

棉花软糖
miánhuāruǎntáng
marshmallow

薄荷糖
bòhétáng
mint

口香糖
kǒuxiāngtáng
chewing gum

软心豆粒糖
ruǎnxīndòulìtáng
jellybean

果味橡皮糖
guǒwèixiàngpítáng
fruit gum

甘草糖
gāncǎotáng
liquorice

其他店铺 qítā diànpù • **other shops**

面包店
miànbāodiàn
baker's

糕点店
gāodiǎndiàn
cake shop

肉铺
ròupù
butcher's

水产店
shuǐchǎndiàn
fishmonger's

蔬菜水果店
shūcàishuǐguǒdiàn
greengrocer's

食品杂货店
shípǐnzáhuòdiàn
grocer's

鞋店
xiédiàn
shoe shop

五金店
wǔjīndiàn
hardware shop

古董店
gǔdǒngdiàn
antique shop

礼品店
lǐpǐndiàn
gift shop

旅行社
lǚxíngshè
travel agent's

首饰店
shǒushìdiàn
jeweller's

书店
shūdiàn
book shop

音像店
yīnxiàngdiàn
record shop

酒类专卖店
jiǔlèizhuānmàidiàn
off licence

宠物商店
chǒngwùshāngdiàn
pet shop

家具店
jiājùdiàn
furniture shop

时装店
shízhuāngdiàn
boutique

词汇 cíhuì • vocabulary

房地产商
fángdìchǎnshāng
estate agent's

园艺用品店
yuányì yòngpǐndiàn
garden centre

干洗店
gānxǐdiàn
dry cleaner's

投币式自动洗衣店
tóubìshì zìdòngxǐyīdiàn
launderette

照相器材店
zhàoxiàng qìcáidiàn
camera shop

绿色食品店
lǜsèshípǐndiàn
health food shop

艺术品店
yìshùpǐndiàn
art shop

旧货商店
jiùhuò shāngdiàn
second-hand shop

裁缝店
cáifengdiàn
tailor's

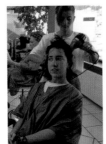

美发厅
měifàtīng
hairdresser's

市场 shìchǎng | market

食物 shíwù
food

肉 ròu ● meat

羊羔肉
gāoyángròu
lamb

肉店老板
ròudiànlǎobǎn
butcher

吊肉钩
diàoròugōu
meat hook

秤
chèng
scales

磨刀器
módāoqì
knife sharpener

熏肉
xūnròu
bacon

香肠
xiāngcháng
sausages

肝脏
gānzàng
liver

词汇 cíhuì ● vocabulary

猪肉 zhūròu **pork**	野味肉 yěwèiròu **venison**	下水 xiàshuǐ **offal**	放养的 fàngyǎngde **free range**	熟肉 shúròu **cooked meat**
牛肉 niúròu **beef**	兔肉 tùròu **rabbit**	腌制的 yānzhide **cured**	有机(饲养)的 yǒujī(sìyǎng)de **organic**	白肉 (指家禽肉、鱼肉等) báiròu (zhǐjiāqínròu, yúròuděng) **white meat**
小牛肉 xiǎoniúròu **veal**	牛舌 niúshé **tongue**	熏制的 xūnzhide **smoked**	瘦肉 shòuròu **lean meat**	红肉(指牛肉、猪肉和羊肉) hóngròu (zhǐniúròu, zhūròuhéyángròu) **red meat**

切块 qiēkuài • cuts

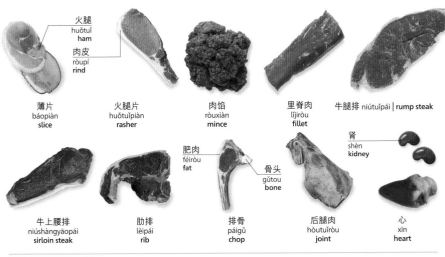

火腿
huǒtuǐ
ham

肉皮
ròupí
rind

薄片
báopiàn
slice

火腿片
huǒtuǐpiàn
rasher

肉馅
ròuxiàn
mince

里脊肉
lǐjǐròu
fillet

牛腿排 niútuǐpái | rump steak

肥肉
féiròu
fat

骨头
gǔtou
bone

肾
shèn
kidney

牛上腰排
niúshàngyāopái
sirloin steak

肋排
lèipái
rib

排骨
páigǔ
chop

后腿肉
hòutuǐròu
joint

心
xīn
heart

禽肉 qínròu • poultry

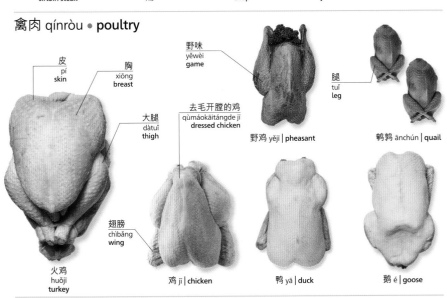

皮
pí
skin

胸
xiōng
breast

野味
yěwèi
game

腿
tuǐ
leg

大腿
dàtuǐ
thigh

去毛开膛的鸡
qùmáokāitángde jī
dressed chicken

野鸡 yějī | pheasant

鹌鹑 ānchún | quail

翅膀
chìbǎng
wing

火鸡
huǒjī
turkey

鸡 jī | chicken

鸭 yā | duck

鹅 é | goose

鱼 yú • fish

去皮虾
qùpíxiā
peeled prawns

冰
bīng
ice

羊鱼
yángyú
red mullet

大比目鱼片
dàbǐmùyúpiàn
halibut fillets

虹鳟鱼
hóngzūnyú
rainbow trout

鳐鱼翅
yáoyúchì
skate wings

水产店
shuǐchǎndiàn
fishmonger's

安康鱼
ānkāngyú
monkfish

鲭鱼
qīngyú
mackerel

鳟鱼
zūnyú
trout

剑鱼
jiànyú
swordfish

鳎鱼
tǎyú
Dover sole

柠檬鲽
níngméngdié
lemon sole

黑线鳕
hēixiànxuě
haddock

沙丁鱼
shādīngyú
sardine

鳐鱼
yáoyú
skate

牙鳕
yáxuě
whiting

海鲈
hǎilú
sea bass

鲑鱼 guīyú | salmon

鳕鱼
xuěyú
cod

鲷鱼
diāoyú
sea bream

金枪鱼
jīnqiāngyú
tuna

海鲜 hǎixiān · seafood

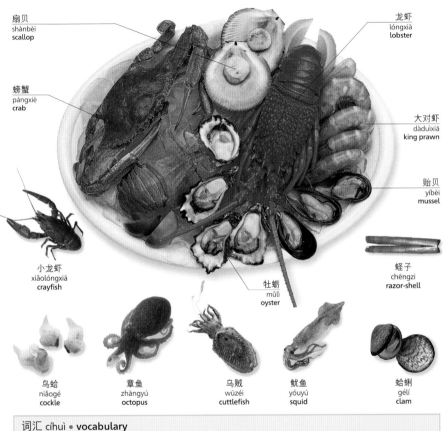

扇贝
shànbèi
scallop

龙虾
lóngxiā
lobster

螃蟹
pángxiè
crab

大对虾
dàduìxiā
king prawn

贻贝
yíbèi
mussel

小龙虾
xiǎolóngxiā
crayfish

牡蛎
mǔlì
oyster

蛏子
chēngzi
razor-shell

鸟蛤
niǎogé
cockle

章鱼
zhāngyú
octopus

乌贼
wūzéi
cuttlefish

鱿鱼
yóuyú
squid

蛤蜊
gélí
clam

词汇 cíhuì · vocabulary

冷冻的 lěngdòngde frozen	盐渍的 yánzìde salted	熏制的 xūnzhìde smoked	去鳞的 qùlínde descaled	去骨鱼片 qùgǔyúpiàn fillet	腰肉 yāoròu loin	尾部 wěibù tail	骨头 gǔtou bone	鳞片 línpiàn scale
新鲜 xīnxiān fresh	处理干净的 chǔlǐgān jìngde cleaned	去皮的 qùpíde skinned	去骨的 qùgǔde boned	切片的 qiēpiànde filleted	鱼片 yúpiàn steak	能帮我把它收拾干净吗? néng bāng wǒ bǎ tā shōushi gānjìng ma? Will you clean it for me?		

蔬菜1 shūcàiyī · **vegetables 1**

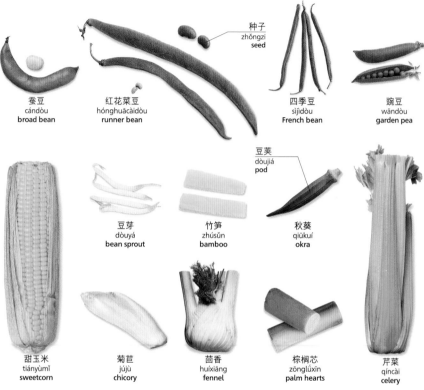

种子
zhǒngzi
seed

蚕豆
cándòu
broad bean

红花菜豆
hónghuācàidòu
runner bean

四季豆
sìjìdòu
French bean

豌豆
wāndòu
garden pea

豆荚
dòujiá
pod

豆芽
dòuyá
bean sprout

竹笋
zhúsǔn
bamboo

秋葵
qiūkuí
okra

甜玉米
tiányùmǐ
sweetcorn

菊苣
jújù
chicory

茴香
huíxiāng
fennel

棕榈芯
zōnglǘxīn
palm hearts

芹菜
qíncài
celery

词汇 cíhuì · **vocabulary**

叶 yè **leaf**	小花 xiǎohuā **floret**	尖 jiān **tip**	有机(栽培)的 yǒujī(zāipéi)de **organic**	这儿卖有机蔬菜吗？ zhè'er mài yǒujīshūcài ma? **Do you sell organic vegetables?**
菜梗 càigěng **stalk**	果仁 guǒrén **kernel**	芯 xīn **heart**	塑料袋 sùliàodài **plastic bag**	这些是当地产的吗？ zhèxiē shì dāngdìchǎnde ma? **Are these grown locally?**

芝麻菜
zhīmacài
rocket

豆瓣菜
dòubàncài
watercress

红球菊苣
hóngqiújújù
radicchio

抱子甘蓝
bàozǐgānlán
Brussels sprout

甜叶菜
tiányècài
Swiss chard

羽衣甘蓝
yǔyīgānlán
kale

酸模
suānmó
sorrel

苦苣
kǔjù
endive

蒲公英
púgōngyīng
dandelion

菠菜
bōcài
spinach

球茎甘蓝
qiújīnggānlán
kohlrabi

油菜
yóucài
pak-choi

莴苣
wōjù
lettuce

西兰花
xīlánhuā
broccoli

卷心菜
juǎnxīncài
cabbage

嫩圆白菜
nènyuánbáicài
spring greens

蔬菜2 shūcài'èr • vegetables 2

萝卜，芜菁
luóbo, wújīng
turnip

朝鲜蓟
cháoxiānjì
artichoke

小红萝卜
xiǎohóngluóbo
radish

花椰菜，菜花
huāyēcài, càihuā
cauliflower

芦笋
lúsǔn
asparagus

马铃薯
mǎlíngshǔ
potato

西葫芦
xīhúlu
marrow

洋葱
yángcōng
onion

甜椒
tiánjiāo
pepper

辣椒
làjiāo
chilli

甜玉米
tiányùmǐ
sweetcorn

词汇 cíhuì • vocabulary

樱桃番茄 yīngtáofānqié cherry tomato	块根芹 kuàigēnqín celeriac	冷冻的 lěngdòngde frozen	苦 kǔ bitter	请给我一公斤马铃薯。 qǐng gěi wǒ yì gōngjīn mǎlíngshǔ. **Can I have one kilo of potatoes please?**
胡萝卜 húluóbo carrot	芋头 yùtou taro root	生 shēng raw	硬 yìng firm	每公斤多少钱? měi gōngjīn duōshǎo qián? **What's the price per kilo?**
面包果 miànbāoguǒ breadfruit	木薯 mùshǔ cassava	辣 là hot (spicy)	果肉 guǒròu flesh	那些叫什么? nàxiē jiào shénme? **What are those called?**
嫩马铃薯 nènmǎlíngshǔ new potato	荸荠 bíqí water chestnut	甜 tián sweet	根 gēn root	

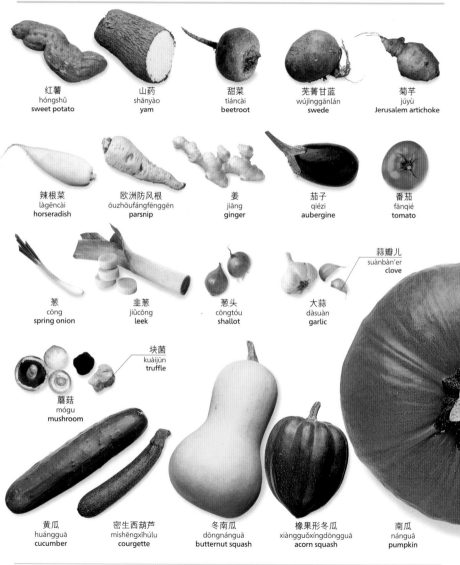

红薯
hóngshǔ
sweet potato

山药
shānyào
yam

甜菜
tiáncài
beetroot

芜菁甘蓝
wújīnggānlán
swede

菊芋
júyù
Jerusalem artichoke

辣根菜
làgēncài
horseradish

欧洲防风根
ōuzhōufángfēnggēn
parsnip

姜
jiāng
ginger

茄子
qiézi
aubergine

番茄
fānqié
tomato

葱
cōng
spring onion

韭葱
jiǔcōng
leek

葱头
cōngtóu
shallot

大蒜
dàsuàn
garlic

蒜瓣儿
suànbàn'er
clove

块菌
kuàijūn
truffle

蘑菇
mógu
mushroom

黄瓜
huángguā
cucumber

密生西葫芦
mìshēngxīhúlu
courgette

冬南瓜
dōngnánguā
butternut squash

橡果形冬瓜
xiàngguǒxíngdōngguā
acorn squash

南瓜
nánguā
pumpkin

水果1 shuǐguǒyī · fruit 1

柑橘类水果 gānjúlèishuǐguǒ · citrus fruit

橙子
chéngzi
orange

细皮小柑橘
xìpíxiǎogānjú
clementine

牙买加丑橘
yámǎijiāchǒujú
ugli fruit

海绵层
hǎimiáncéng
pith

葡萄柚
pútáoyòu
grapefruit

橘瓣儿
júbànr
segment

无核蜜橘
wúhémìjú
satsuma

橘子
júzi
tangerine

外皮
wàipí
zest

酸橙
suānchéng
lime

柠檬
níngméng
lemon

金橘
jīnjú
kumquat

有核水果 yǒuhéshuǐguǒ · stone fruit

桃
táo
peach

油桃
yóutáo
nectarine

杏
xìng
apricot

李子
lǐzi
plum

樱桃
yīngtáo
cherry

苹果
píngguǒ
apple

梨
lí
pear

果篮 guǒlán | basket of fruit

浆果和甜瓜 jiāngguǒ hé tiánguā · **berries and melons**

草莓
cǎoméi
strawberry

覆盆子
fùpénzǐ
raspberry

甜瓜
tiánguā
melon

葡萄
pútáo
grapes

黑莓
hēiméi
blackberry

红醋栗
hóngcùlì
redcurrant

瓜皮
guāpí
rind

蔓越橘
mànyuèjú
cranberry

黑醋栗
hēicùlì
blackcurrant

瓜籽
guāzǐ
seed

蓝莓
lánméi
blueberry

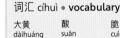

白醋栗
báicùlì
white currant

瓜瓤
guāráng
flesh

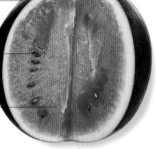

西瓜
xīguā
watermelon

罗甘莓
luógānméi
loganberry

醋栗
cùlì
gooseberry

词汇 cíhuì · **vocabulary**

大黄 dàihuáng **rhubarb**	酸 suān **sour**	脆 cuì **crisp**	汁液 zhīyè **juice**	它们熟吗? tāmen shú ma? **Are they ripe?**
纤维 xiānwéi **fibre**	新鲜 xīnxiān **fresh**	烂 làn **rotten**	核 hé **core**	我可以尝一个吗? wǒ kěyǐ cháng yígè ma? **Can I try one?**
甜 tián **sweet**	多汁 duōzhī **juicy**	果肉 guǒròu **pulp**	无核 wúhé **seedless**	它们能放多久? tāmen néng fàng duōjiǔ? **How long will they keep?**

水果2 shuǐguǒ • fruit 2

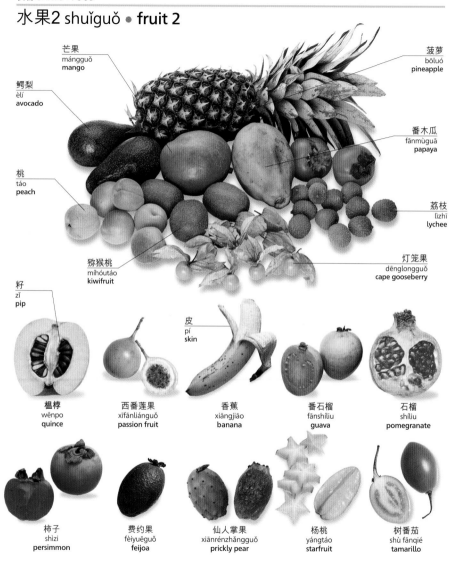

芒果
mángguǒ
mango

鳄梨
èlí
avocado

桃
táo
peach

籽
zǐ
pip

狝猴桃
míhóutáo
kiwifruit

菠萝
bōluó
pineapple

番木瓜
fānmùguā
papaya

荔枝
lìzhī
lychee

灯笼果
dēnglóngguǒ
cape gooseberry

皮
pí
skin

榅桲
wēnpo
quince

西番莲果
xīfānliánguǒ
passion fruit

香蕉
xiāngjiāo
banana

番石榴
fānshíliu
guava

石榴
shíliu
pomegranate

柿子
shìzi
persimmon

费约果
fèiyuēguǒ
feijoa

仙人掌果
xiānrénzhǎngguǒ
prickly pear

杨桃
yángtáo
starfruit

树番茄
shù fānqié
tamarillo

坚果和干果 jiānguǒ hé gānguǒ · nuts and dried fruit

松子
sōngzǐ
pine nut

开心果
kāixīnguǒ
pistachio

腰果
yāoguǒ
cashew nut

花生
huāshēng
peanut

榛子
zhēnzi
hazelnut

巴西果
bāxīguǒ
brazil nut

美洲山核桃
měizhōushānhétao
pecan

杏仁
xìngrén
almond

核桃
hétao
walnut

栗子
lìzi
chestnut

澳洲坚果
àozhōujiānguǒ
macadamia

无花果
wúhuāguǒ
fig

椰枣
yēzǎo
date

梅干
méigān
prune

壳
ké
shell

无核葡萄干
wúhépútáogān
sultana

葡萄干
pútáogān
raisin

无核小葡萄干
wúhéxiǎopútáogān
currant

果肉
guǒròu
flesh

椰子
yēzi
coconut

词汇 cíhuì · vocabulary

未熟的 wèishúde **green**	硬 yìng **hard**	果仁 guǒrén **kernel**	盐渍的 yánzìde **salted**	烘烤的 hōngkǎode **roasted**	去壳的 qùkéde **shelled**	蜜饯 mìjiàn **candied fruit**
成熟的 chéngshúde **ripe**	软 ruǎn **soft**	脱水的 tuōshuǐde **desiccated**	生 shēng **raw**	应季的 yìngjìde **seasonal**	完整 wánzhěng **whole**	热带水果 rèdàishuǐguǒ **tropical fruit**

谷物及豆类 gǔwùjídòulèi • grains and pulses

谷物 gǔwù • grains

小麦
xiǎomài
wheat

燕麦
yànmài
oats

大麦
dàmài
barley

小米
xiǎomǐ
millet

玉米
yùmǐ
corn

奎奴亚藜
kuínúyàlí
quinoa

词汇 cíhuì • vocabulary

种子 zhǒngzi **seed**	香 xiāng **fragranced**	易烹调的 yìpēngtiáode **easy cook**
外壳 wàiké **husk**	谷类食品 gǔlèishípǐn **cereal**	长粒 chánglì **long-grain**
谷粒 gǔlì **kernel**	整粒 zhěnglì **wholegrain**	短粒 duǎnlì **short-grain**
干燥 gānzào **dry**	浸泡 jìnpào **soak (v)**	
新鲜 xīnxiān **fresh**		

米 mǐ • rice

白米
báimǐ
white rice

糙米
cāomǐ
brown rice

菰米
gūmǐ
wild rice

布丁米
bùdīngmǐ
pudding rice

加工过的谷物 jiāgōngguòde gǔwù • processed grains

蒸粗麦粉
zhēngcūmàifěn
couscous

碎粒小麦
suìlìxiǎomài
cracked wheat

粗粒小麦粉
cūlìxiǎomàifěn
semolina

麦麸
màifū
bran

豆类 dòulèi · **pulses**

棉豆
miándòu
butter beans

菜豆
càidòu
haricot beans

红芸豆
hóngyúndòu
red kidney beans

赤豆
chìdòu
adzuki beans

蚕豆
cándòu
broad beans

大豆
dàdòu
soya beans

黑眼豆
hēiyǎndòu
black-eyed beans

斑豆
bāndòu
pinto beans

绿豆
lǜdòu
mung beans

小(粒)菜豆
xiǎo(lì)càidòu
flageolet beans

褐色小扁豆
hèsèxiǎobiǎndòu
brown lentils

红豆
hóngdòu
red lentils

青豆
qīngdòu
green peas

鹰嘴豆
yīngzuǐdòu
chickpeas

干豌豆瓣
gānwāndòubàn
split peas

种子 zhǒngzi · **seeds**

南瓜籽
nánguāzǐ
pumpkin seed

芥菜籽
jiècàizǐ
mustard seed

葛缕子籽
gělǚzǐzǐ
caraway

芝麻籽
zhīmazǐ
sesame seed

向日葵籽
xiàngrìkuízǐ
sunflower seed

香草和香辛料 xiāngcǎo hé xiāngxīnliào ● herbs and spices

香辛料 xiāngxīnliào ● spices

香子兰 xiāngzǐlán | vanilla

肉豆蔻
ròudòukòu
nutmeg

肉豆蔻衣
ròudòukòuyī
mace

姜黄根
jiānghuánggēn
turmeric

枯茗，小茴香
kūmíng, xiǎohuíxiāng
cumin

香料包
xiāngliàobāo
bouquet garni

多香果
duōxiāngguǒ
allspice

胡椒粒
hújiāolì
peppercorn

葫芦巴
húlúbā
fenugreek

辣椒末
làjiāomò
chilli

颗粒状
kēlizhuàng
whole

压碎的
yāsuìde
crushed

藏红花
zànghónghuā
saffron

小豆蔻
xiǎodòukòu
cardamom

咖喱粉
gālífěn
curry powder

磨碎的
mósuìde
ground

辣椒粉
làjiāofěn
paprika

片状
piànzhuàng
flakes

大蒜
dàsuàn
garlic

中文 zhōngwén ● english

香草 xiāngcǎo • herbs

桂皮
guìpí
sticks

肉桂
ròuguì
cinnamon

茴香
huíxiāng
fennel

茴香籽
huíxiāngzǐ
fennel seeds

月桂叶
yuèguìyè
bay leaf

欧芹
ōuqín
parsley

柠檬草
níngméngcǎo
lemon grass

丁香
dīngxiāng
cloves

八角，大料
bājiǎo, dàliào
star anise

细香葱
xixiāngcōng
chives

薄荷
bòhe
mint

百里香
bǎilǐxiāng
thyme

鼠尾草
shǔwěicǎo
sage

龙蒿
lónghāo
tarragon

墨角兰
mòjiǎolán
marjoram

罗勒
luólè
basil

姜
jiāng
ginger

牛至
niúzhì
oregano

香菜
xiāngcài
coriander

蒔萝
shíluó
dill

迷迭香
mídiéxiāng
rosemary

瓶装食品 píngzhuāngshípǐn • bottled foods

软木塞
ruǎnmùsāi
cork

葵花籽油
kuíhuāzǐyóu
sunflower oil

核桃油
hétaoyóu
walnut oil

葡萄籽油
pútáozǐyóu
grapeseed oil

杏仁油
xìngrényóu
almond oil

芝麻油
zhīmayóu
sesame seed oil

榛仁油
zhēnrényóu
hazelnut oil

橄榄油
gǎnlǎnyóu
olive oil

油
yóu
oils

香草
xiāngcǎo
herbs

香油
xiāngyóu
flavoured oil

甜酱 tiánjiàng • sweet spreads

广口瓶
guǎngkǒupíng
jar

蜜脾
mìpí
honeycomb

固体蜂蜜
gùtǐfēngmì
set honey

柠檬酱
níngméngjiàng
lemon curd

覆盆子酱
fùpénzǐjiàng
raspberry jam

橘子酱
júzijiàng
marmalade

液体蜂蜜
yètǐfēngmì
clear honey

枫糖浆
fēngtángjiàng
maple syrup

酱料和调味品 jiàngliàohétiáowèipǐn •
sauces and condiments

苹果醋
píngguǒcù
cider vinegar

香脂醋
xiāngzhīcù
balsamic vinegar

瓶
píng
bottle

蛋黄酱
dànhuángjiàng
mayonnaise

酸辣酱
suānlàjiàng
chutney

麦芽醋
màiyácù
malt vinegar

酒醋
jiǔcù
wine vinegar

醋
cù
vinegar

番茄酱
fānqiéjiàng
ketchup

调味汁
tiáowèizhī
sauce

英式芥末酱
yīngshì jièmojiàng
English mustard

法式芥末酱
fǎshì jièmojiàng
French mustard

颗粒芥末酱
kēlì jièmojiàng
wholegrain mustard

花生酱
huāshēngjiàng
peanut butter

巧克力酱
qiǎokèlìjiàng
chocolate spread

密封瓶
mìfēngpíng
preserving jar

罐装水果
guànzhuāngshuǐguǒ
preserved fruit

词汇 cíhuì • vocabulary

玉米油
yùmǐyóu
corn oil

花生油
huāshēngyóu
groundnut oil

植物油
zhíwùyóu
vegetable oil

菜籽油
càizǐyóu
rapeseed oil

冷榨油
lěngzhàyóu
cold-pressed oil

乳制品 rǔzhìpǐn • dairy produce

奶酪 nǎilào • cheese

碎奶酪
suìnǎilào
grated cheese

奶酪皮
nǎilàopí
rind

半硬奶酪
bànyìngnǎilào
semi-hard cheese

硬奶酪
yìngnǎilào
hard cheese

半软奶酪
bànruǎnnǎilào
semi-soft cheese

白干酪
báigānlào
cottage cheese

奶油干酪
nǎiyóugānlào
cream cheese

蓝纹奶酪
lánwénnǎilào
blue cheese

软奶酪
ruǎnnǎilào
soft cheese

鲜奶酪 xiānnǎilào | fresh cheese

奶 nǎi • milk

全脂奶
quánzhīnǎi
whole milk

半脱脂牛奶
bàntuōzhī niúnǎi
semi-skimmed milk

脱脂牛奶
tuōzhī niúnǎi
skimmed milk

奶盒
nǎihé
milk carton

山羊奶
shānyángnǎi
goat's milk

炼乳
liànrǔ
condensed milk

牛奶 niúnǎi | cow's milk

黄油
huángyóu
butter

人造黄油
rénzàohuángyóu
margarine

奶油
nǎiyóu
cream

稀奶油
xīnǎiyóu
single cream

高脂肪奶油
gāozhīfángnǎiyóu
double cream

掼奶油
guànnǎiyóu
whipped cream

酸奶油
suānnǎiyóu
sour cream

酸奶
suānnǎi
yoghurt

冰激凌
bīngjīlíng
ice cream

蛋 dàn • eggs

蛋黄
dànhuáng
yolk

蛋白
dànbái
egg white

蛋壳
dànké
shell

蛋杯
dànbēi
egg cup

煮鸡蛋 zhǔjīdàn I boiled egg

鸡蛋
jīdàn
hen's egg

鸭蛋
yādàn
duck egg

鹅蛋
édàn
goose egg

鹌鹑蛋
ānchúndàn
quail egg

词汇 cíhuì • vocabulary

已经过巴氏消毒的 yǐ jīngguò bāshìxiāodúde **pasteurized**	奶昔 nǎixī **milkshake**	盐渍的 yánzìde **salted**	绵羊奶 miányángnǎi **sheep's milk**	乳糖 rǔtáng **lactose**	均质 jūnzhì **homogenized**
未经过巴氏消毒的 wèi jīngguò bāshìxiāodúde **unpasteurized**	冻酸奶 dòngsuānnǎi **frozen yoghurt**	无盐的 wúyánde **unsalted**	酪乳 làorǔ **buttermilk**	不含脂肪的 bùhánzhīfángde **fat free**	奶粉 nǎifěn **powdered milk**

面包和面粉 miànbāo hé miànfěn • breads and flours

切片面包
qiēpiànmiànbāo
sliced bread

罂粟籽
yīngsùzǐ
poppy seeds

黑面包
hēimiànbāo
rye bread

棍子面包
gùnzimiànbāo
baguette

面包店 miànbāodiàn | bakery

制作面包 zhìzuò miànbāo • making bread

精白面粉
jīngbáimiànfěn
white flour

黑麦面粉
hēimàimiànfěn
brown flour

全麦面粉
quánmàimiànfěn
wholemeal flour

酵母
jiàomǔ
yeast

筛撒 shāisǎ | sift (v)

生面团
shēng
miàntuán
dough

搅拌 jiǎobàn | mix (v)

和面 huómiàn | knead (v)

烘制 hōngzhì | bake (v)

面包皮
miànbāopí
crust

面包块
miànbāokuài
loaf

切片
qiēpiàn
slice

白面包
báimiànbāo
white bread

黑面包
hēimiànbāo
brown bread

全麦面包
quánmàimiànbāo
wholemeal bread

麸皮面包
fūpímiànbāo
granary bread

玉米面包
yùmǐmiànbāo
corn bread

苏打面包
sūdámiànbāo
soda bread

酸面包
suānmiànbāo
sourdough bread

薄干脆饼
báogǎncuìbǐng
flatbread

硬面包圈，百吉饼
yìngmiànbāoquān, bǎijíbǐng
bagel

软面包片
ruǎnmiànbāopiàn **I bap**

小面包
xiǎomiànbāo **I roll**

葡萄干面包
pútáogānmiànbāo
fruit bread

撒籽面包
sǎzǐmiànbāo
seeded bread

印度式面包
yìndùshìmiànbāo
naan bread

皮塔饼
pítǎbǐng
pitta bread

薄脆饼干
báocuìbǐnggān
crispbread

词汇 cíhuì · vocabulary

高筋面粉 gāojīnmiànfěn **strong flour**	发起 fāqǐ **rise (v)**	发酵 fājiào **prove (v)**	面包屑 miànbāoxiè **breadcrumbs**	切片机 qiēpiànjī **slicer**
自发粉 zìfāfěn **self-raising flour**	中筋面粉 zhōngjīnmiànfěn **plain flour**	浇糖 jiāotáng **glaze (v)**	细长形面包 xìchángxíngmiànbāo **flute**	面包师 miànbāoshī **baker**

糕点 gāodiǎn • cakes and desserts

长条奶油夹心点心
chángtiáo nǎiyóu jiāxīn diǎnxīn
éclair

奶油
nǎiyóu
cream

夹心
jiāxīn
filling

花结酥皮
huājiésūpí
choux pastry

千层饼
qiāncéngbǐng
puff pastry

夹心酥
jiāxīnsū
filo pastry

水果蛋糕
shuǐguǒ dàngāo
fruit cake

水果馅饼
shuǐguǒ xiànbǐng
fruit tart

蛋白甜饼
dànbái tiánbǐng
meringue

外覆巧克力
wàifù qiǎokèlì
chocolate coated

松饼
sōngbǐng
muffin

松糕
sōnggāo
sponge cake

蛋糕 dàngāo | cakes

词汇 cíhuì • vocabulary

奶油蛋糕 nǎiyóu dàngāo crème pâtissière	小圆蛋糕 xiǎoyuán dàngāo bun	面团 miàntuán pastry	米饭布丁 mǐfàn bùdīng rice pudding	我可以吃一片吗? wǒ kěyǐ chī yīpiàn ma? May I have a slice please?
巧克力蛋糕 qiǎokèlì dàngāo chocolate cake	蛋奶糕 dànnǎigāo custard	切片 qiēpiàn slice	庆祝会 qìngzhùhuì celebration	

巧克力脆片
qiǎokèlì cuìpiàn
chocolate chip

指形饼干
zhǐxíng bǐnggān
sponge fingers

果仁巧克力脆饼
guǒrén qiǎokèlì
cuìbǐng
Florentine

蜜饯布丁
mìjiàn bùdīng
trifle

饼干 bǐnggān | biscuits

奶油冻，慕思
nǎiyóudòng, mùsī
mousse

果汁冰糕
guǒzhī bīnggāo
sorbet

奶油馅饼
nǎiyóu xiànbǐng
cream pie

焦糖蛋奶
jiāotáng dànnǎi
crème caramel

庆祝蛋糕 qìngzhù dàngāo • celebration cakes

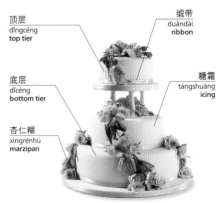

顶层
dǐngcéng
top tier

缎带
duàndài
ribbon

底层
dǐcéng
bottom tier

糖霜
tángshuāng
icing

杏仁糊
xìngrénhú
marzipan

婚礼蛋糕 hūnlǐ dàngāo | wedding cake

装饰
zhuāngshì
decoration

生日蜡烛
shēngrì làzhú
birthday candles

吹熄
chuīxī
blow out (v)

生日蛋糕 shēngrì dàngāo | birthday cake

熟食店 shúshídiàn • delicatessen

辣香肠
làxiāngcháng
spicy sausage

油
yóu
oil

醋
cù
vinegar

生肉
shēngròu
uncooked meat

柜台
guìtái
counter

果酱饼
guǒjiàngbǐng
flan

肉酱
ròujiàng
pâté

萨拉米香肠
sàlāmǐ
xiāngcháng
salami

意大利辣香肠
yìdàlìlà
xiāngcháng
pepperoni

莫泽雷勒干酪
mòzéléilè gānlào
mozzarella

布里干酪
bùlǐ gānlào
Brie

山羊奶酪
shānyáng nǎilào
goat's cheese

切达干酪
qiēdá gānlào
cheddar

帕尔马干酪
pà'ěrmǎ gānlào
Parmesan

卡门贝干酪
kǎménbèi gānlào
Camembert

外皮
wàipí
rind

伊丹奶酪
yīdānnǎilào
Edam

蒙切各干酪
méngqiēgè gānlào
Manchego

西式馅饼，派
xīshì xiànbǐng, pài
pies

黑橄榄
hēigǎnlǎn
black olive

辣椒
làjiāo
chilli

酱
jiàng
sauce

小圆面包
xiǎoyuán miànbāo
bread roll

熟肉
shúròu
cooked meat

绿橄榄
lǜgǎnlǎn
green olive

火腿
huǒtuǐ
ham

三明治柜台 sānmíngzhì guìtái | **sandwich counter**

熏鱼
xūnyú
smoked fish

马槟榔
mǎbīngláng
capers

西班牙香肠
xībānyáxiāngcháng
chorizo

意大利熏火腿
yìdàlì xūnhuǒtuǐ
prosciutto

填馅橄榄
tiánxiàn gǎnlǎn
stuffed olive

词汇 cíhuì • vocabulary

油渍 yóuzì **in oil**	调味汁浸泡的 tiáowèizhījìnpàode **marinated**	熏制的 xūnzhìde **smoked**
卤制 lǔzhì **in brine**	盐渍的 yánzìde **salted**	风干的 fēnggānde **cured**

请拿一个号。
qǐng ná yīgè hào.
Take a number please.

我能尝尝吗？
wǒ néng chángchang ma?
Can I try some of that please?

请来6片。
qǐng lái liùpiàn.
May I have six slices of that please?

饮料 yǐnliào · drinks

水 shuǐ · water

瓶装水
píngzhuāng shuǐ
bottled water

碳酸(饮料)
tànsuān (yǐnliào)
sparkling

非碳酸(饮料)
fēitànsuān(yǐnliào)
still

自来水
zìlái shuǐ
tap water

奎宁水
kuíníng shuǐ
tonic water

苏打水
sūdá shuǐ
soda water

矿泉水 kuàngquán shuǐ | mineral water

热饮 rèyǐn · hot drinks

茶包
chábāo
teabag

茶叶
cháyè
loose leaf tea

茶
chá
tea

咖啡豆
kāfēidòu
beans

咖啡末
kāfēimò
ground coffee

咖啡
kāfēi
coffee

热巧克力
rèqiǎokèlì
hot chocolate

麦芽饮料
màiyáyǐnliào
malted drink

软(不含酒精的)饮料 ruǎn (bùhán jiǔjīngde) yǐnliào · **soft drinks**

吸管
xīguǎn
straw

番茄汁
fānqiézhī
tomato juice

葡萄汁
pútáozhī
grape juice

柠檬水
níngméng shuǐ
lemonade

橘子水
júzi shuǐ
orangeade

可乐
kělè
cola

含酒精饮料 hán jiǔjīng yǐnliào • alcoholic drinks

杜松子酒
dùsōngzǐjiǔ | **gin**

罐
guàn
can

啤酒
píjiǔ
beer

苹果酒
píngguǒjiǔ
cider

苦啤酒
kǔpíjiǔ
bitter

浓烈黑啤酒
nóngliè hēipíjiǔ
stout

伏特加酒
fútèjiājiǔ | **vodka**

威士忌 wēishìjì | **whisky**

朗姆酒
lǎngmǔjiǔ
rum

白兰地
báilándì
brandy

波尔图葡萄酒
bōěrtú pútáojiǔ
port

无糖份的
wútángfènde
dry

雪利酒
xuělìjiǔ
sherry

堪培利酒
kānpéilìjiǔ
Campari

玫瑰红
méiguīhóng
rosé

白
bái
white

红
hóng
red

利口酒
lìkǒujiǔ
liqueur

龙舌兰酒
lóngshélánjiǔ
tequila

香槟酒
xiāngbīnjiǔ
champagne

葡萄酒 pútáojiǔ | **wine**

LES CHAMPS CLOS
SANCERRE
1994

Bourgue

外出就餐 wàichū jiùcān
eating out

咖啡馆 kāfēiguǎn · café

菜单
càidān
menu

遮阳篷
zhēyángpéng
awning

遮阳伞
zhēyángsǎn
umbrella

露天咖啡座
lùtiān kāfēizuò
terrace café

侍者
shìzhě
waiter

咖啡机
kāfēijī
coffee machine

桌子
zhuōzi
table

路边咖啡座 lùbiān kāfēizuò | pavement café

快餐店 kuàicāndiàn | snack bar

咖啡 kāfēi · coffee

牛奶咖啡
niúnǎi kāfēi
white coffee

黑咖啡
hēikāfēi
black coffee

可可粉
kěkěfěn
cocoa powder

泡沫
pàomò
froth

过滤式咖啡
guòlùshì kāfēi
filter coffee

意式浓缩咖啡
yìshìnóngsuō kāfēi
espresso

卡布奇诺咖啡
kǎbùqínuò kāfēi
cappuccino

冰咖啡
bīngkāfēi
iced coffee

中文 zhōngwén · english

茶 chá • tea

草药茶
cǎoyàochá
herbal tea

菊花茶
júhuāchá
camomile tea

绿茶
lǜchá
green tea

奶茶
nǎichá
tea with milk

红茶
hóngchá
black tea

柠檬茶
níngméngchá
tea with lemon

薄荷茶
bòhéchá
mint tea

冰茶
bīngchá
iced tea

果汁和奶昔 guǒzhī hé nǎixī • juices and milkshakes

橘子汁
júzizhī
orange juice

苹果汁
píngguǒzhī
apple juice

菠萝汁
bōluózhī
pineapple juice

番茄汁
fānqiézhī
tomato juice

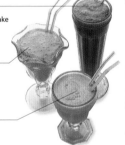
巧克力奶昔
qiǎokèlì nǎixī
chocolate milkshake

草莓奶昔
cǎoméi nǎixī
strawberry
milkshake

咖啡奶昔
kāfēi nǎixī
coffee milkshake

食物 shíwù • food

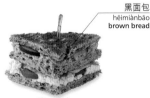
黑面包
hēimiànbāo
brown bread

烤三明治
kǎosānmíngzhì
toasted sandwich

沙拉
shālā
salad

一勺量
yìsháoliàng
scoop

冰激凌
bīngjīlíng
ice cream

油酥点心
yóusūdiǎnxīn
pastry

酒吧 jiǔbā • bar

玻璃杯
bōlibēi
glasses

量杯
liángbēi
optic

收款机
shōukuǎnjī
till

酒保
jiǔbǎo
bartender

啤酒龙头
píjiǔ lóngtóu
beer tap

咖啡机
kāfēijī
coffee machine

冰桶
bīngtǒng
ice bucket

酒吧椅
jiǔbāyǐ
bar stool

烟灰缸
yānhuīgāng
ashtray

杯垫
bēidiàn
coaster

吧台
bātái
bar counter

开瓶器
kāipíngqì
bottle opener

摇杆
yáogǎn
lever

拔塞钻 básāizuàn | corkscrew

夹钳
jiáqián
tongs

搅拌棒
jiǎobànbàng
stirrer

量杯
liángbēi
measure

鸡尾酒调制器 jīwěijiǔ tiáozhìqì
cocktail shaker

中文 zhōngwén · english

水罐
shuǐguàn
pitcher

冰块
bīngkuài
ice cube

奎宁杜松子酒
kuíníng dùsōngzǐjiǔ
gin and tonic

加水威士忌
jiāshuǐ wēishìjì
scotch and water

加可乐朗姆酒
jiākělè lǎngmǔjiǔ
rum and cola

加橙汁伏特加酒
jiāchéngzhī fútèjiājiǔ
vodka and orange

马提尼酒
mǎtíníjiǔ
martini

鸡尾酒
jīwěijiǔ
cocktail

葡萄酒
pútáojiǔ
wine

啤酒 píjiǔ | **beer**

双份
shuāngfèn
double

单份
dānfèn
single

冰和柠檬
bīng hé níngméng
ice and lemon

一小杯
yì xiǎobēi
a shot

量杯
liángbēi
measure

不加冰
bù jiābīng
without ice

加冰
jiābīng
with ice

酒吧小吃 jiǔbā xiǎochī · **bar snacks**

腰果
yāoguǒ
cashew nuts

杏仁
xìngrén
almonds

花生
huāshēng
peanuts

炸薯片 zháshǔpiàn | **crisps**

坚果 jiānguǒ | **nuts**

橄榄 gǎnlǎn | **olives**

餐馆 cānguǎn • restaurant

餐具摆放
cānjù bǎifàng
table setting

助厨
zhùchú
commis chef

主厨
zhǔchú
chef

玻璃杯
bōlibēi
glass

托盘
tuōpán
tray

厨房 chúfáng | kitchen

侍者 shìzhě | waiter

词汇 cíhuì • vocabulary

晚餐菜单 wǎncān càidān **evening menu**	**特色菜** tèsècài **specials**	**价格** jiàgé **price**	**小费** xiǎofèi **tip**	**自助餐** zìzhùcān **buffet**	**盐** yán **salt**
酒单 jiǔdān **wine list**	**按菜单点菜** àn càidān diǎncài **à la carte**	**账单** zhàngdān **bill**	**含服务费** hán fúwùfèi **service included**	**酒吧** jiǔbā **bar**	**胡椒粉** hújiāofěn **pepper**
午餐菜单 wǔcān càidān **lunch menu**	**甜食小车** tiánshí xiǎochē **sweet trolley**	**收据** shōujù **receipt**	**不含服务费** bùhán fúwùfèi **service not included**	**客人** kèrén **customer**	

菜单
càidān
menu

儿童套餐
értóng tàocān
child's meal

点菜 diǎncài | order (v)

付账 fùzhàng | pay (v)

菜肴 càiyáo • courses

开胃酒
kāiwèijiǔs
apéritif

头盘
tóupán
starter

汤
tāng
soup

主菜
zhǔcài
main course

配菜
pèicài
side order

餐后甜点 cānhòu tiándiǎn
dessert

咖啡 kāfēi
coffee

要一张两人桌。
yào yīzhāng liǎngrénzhuō.
A table for two please.

能让我看看菜单/酒单吗?
néng ràng wǒ kànkan càidān/jiǔdān ma?
Can I see the menu/wine list please?

有固定价格菜单吗?
yǒu gùdìng jiàgé càidān ma?
Is there a fixed price menu?

有素食吗?
yǒu sùshí ma?
Do you have any vegetarian dishes?

请给我账单/收据。
qǐng gěi wǒ zhàngdān/shōujù.
Could I have the bill/a receipt please?

我们能分开结账吗?
wǒmen néng fēnkāi jiézhàng ma?
Can we pay separately?

请问卫生间在哪儿?
qǐngwèn wèishēngjiān zàinǎ'er?
Where are the toilets, please?

快餐 kuàicān · **fast food**

汉堡包
hànbǎobāo
burger

吸管
xīguǎn
straw

软饮料
ruǎn yǐnliào
soft drink

薯条
shǔtiáo
French fries

餐巾纸
cānjīnzhǐ
paper napkin

托盘
tuōpán
tray

汉堡套餐 hànbǎotàocān | **burger meal**

词汇 cíhuì · **vocabulary**

比萨饼店
bǐsàbǐngdiàn
pizza parlour

快餐店
kuàicāndiàn
burger bar

菜单
càidān
menu

店内用餐
diànnèi yòngcān
eat-in

外带
wàidài
take-away

重新加热
chóngxīn jiārè
re-heat (v)

番茄酱
fānqiéjiàng
tomato sauce

我带走吃。
wǒ dàizǒu chī.
Can I have that to go please?

你们提供送餐服务吗?
nǐmen tígōng sòngcānfúwù ma?
Do you deliver?

比萨饼
bǐsàbǐng
pizza

价目表
jiàmùbiǎo
price list

罐装饮料
guànzhuāng yǐnliào
canned drink

送餐 sòngcān | **home delivery**

食品摊 shípǐntān | **street stall**

小圆面包
xiǎoyuán
miànbāo
bun

芥末
jièmo
mustard

香肠
xiāngcháng
sausage

汉堡包
hànbǎobāo
hamburger

鸡肉汉堡
jīròu hànbǎo
chicken burger

蔬菜汉堡
shūcài hànbǎo
veggie burger

热狗 règǒu | **hot dog**

三明治
sānmíngzhì
sandwich

总汇三明治
zǒnghuì sānmíngzhì
club sandwich

馅
xiàn
filling

单片三明治
dānpiàn sānmíngzhì
open sandwich

菜卷
càijuǎn
wrap

酱
jiàng
sauce

开胃的
kāiwèide
savoury

甜味的
tiánwèide
sweet

装饰配料
zhuāngshìpèiliào
topping

烤肉串
kǎoròuchuàn
kebab

鸡块
jīkuài
chicken nuggets

薄饼卷 báobǐngjuǎn | **crêpes**

鱼和薯条
yú hé shǔtiáo
fish and chips

肋排
lèipái
ribs

炸鸡
zhájī
fried chicken

比萨饼
bǐsàbǐng
pizza

早餐 zǎocān • breakfast

牛奶
niúnǎi
milk

谷类食品
gǔlèishípǐn
cereal

果酱
guǒjiàng
jam

干果
gānguǒ
dried fruit

火腿
huǒtuǐ
ham

奶酪
nǎilào
cheese

薄脆饼干
báocuìbǐnggān
crispbread

自助早餐
zìzhùzǎocān
breakfast buffet

橘子酱
júzijiàng
marmalade

肉酱
ròujiàng
pâté

黄油
huángyóu
butter

果汁
guǒzhī
fruit juice

咖啡
kāfēi
coffee

热巧克力
rèqiǎokèlì
hot chocolate

羊角面包
yángjiǎo miànbāo
croissant

茶
chá
tea

早餐桌 zǎocānzhuō | breakfast table

饮料 yǐnliào | drinks

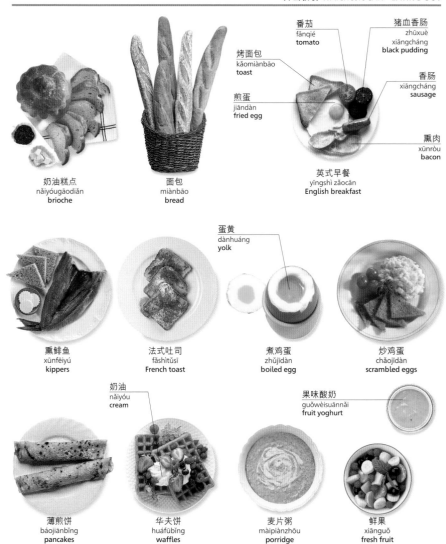

番茄
fānqié
tomato

猪血香肠
zhūxuè
xiāngcháng
black pudding

烤面包
kǎomiànbāo
toast

香肠
xiāngcháng
sausage

煎蛋
jiāndàn
fried egg

熏肉
xūnròu
bacon

英式早餐
yīngshì zǎocān
English breakfast

奶油糕点
nǎiyóugāodiǎn
brioche

面包
miànbāo
bread

蛋黄
dànhuáng
yolk

熏鲱鱼
xūnfēiyú
kippers

法式吐司
fǎshìtǔsī
French toast

煮鸡蛋
zhǔjīdàn
boiled egg

炒鸡蛋
chǎojīdàn
scrambled eggs

奶油
nǎiyóu
cream

果味酸奶
guǒwèisuānnǎi
fruit yoghurt

薄煎饼
báojiānbǐng
pancakes

华夫饼
huáfūbǐng
waffles

麦片粥
màipiànzhōu
porridge

鲜果
xiānguǒ
fresh fruit

正餐 zhèngcān · **dinner**

汤 tāng | soup

肉汤 ròutāng | broth

炖菜 dùncài | stew

咖喱 gālí | curry

烤肉 kǎoròu | roast

馅饼 xiànbǐng | pie

蛋奶酥 dànnǎisū | soufflé

烤肉串 kǎoròuchuàn
kebab

肉丸 ròuwán | meatballs

煎蛋饼 jiāndànbǐng
omelette

面条
miàntiáo
noodles

炒菜 chǎocài | stir-fry

意大利面食 yìdàlì miànshí
pasta

米饭 mǐfàn | rice

什锦沙拉 shíjǐnshālā
mixed salad

蔬菜沙拉 shūcàishālā
green salad

调味汁 tiáowèizhī | dressing

烹调手法 pēngtiáo shǒufǎ · techniques

装馅 zhuāngxiàn | stuffed

浇汁 jiāozhī | in sauce

烤制 kǎozhì | grilled

调味汁浸泡的
tiáowèizhījìnpàode | marinated

水煮 shuǐzhǔ | poached

捣成糊状 dǎochénghúzhuàng
mashed

烘制 hōngzhì | baked

煎制 jiānzhì | pan fried

炒制 chǎozhì | fried

腌渍 yānzì | pickled

熏制 xūnzhì | smoked

油炸 yóuzhá | deep-fried

枫糖浸泡 fēngtángjìnpào
in syrup

调味 tiáowèi | dressed

清蒸 qīngzhēng | steamed

风干 fēnggān | cured

学习 xuéxí
study

学校 xuéxiào • school

白板
báibǎn
whiteboard

老师
lǎoshī
teacher

书包
shūbāo
school bag

学生
xuéshēng
pupil

课桌
kèzhuō
desk

教室 jiàoshì | classroom

女生
nǚshēng
schoolgirl

男生
nánshēng
schoolboy

词汇 cíhuì • vocabulary

历史 lìshǐ **history**	自然科学 zìránkēxué **science**	物理 wùlǐ **physics**
语言 yǔyán **languages**	艺术 yìshù **art**	化学 huàxué **chemistry**
文学 wénxué **literature**	音乐 yīnyuè **music**	生物学 shēngwùxué **biology**
地理 dìlǐ **geography**	数学 shùxué **maths**	体育 tǐyù **physical education**

学习活动 xuéxí huódòng • activities

读 dú | read (v)

写 xiě | write (v)

拼写 pīnxiě | spell (v)

画 huà | draw (v)

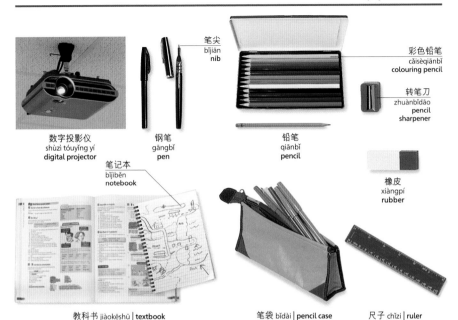

笔尖
bǐjiān
nib

彩色铅笔
cǎisèqiānbǐ
colouring pencil

转笔刀
zhuànbǐdāo
pencil sharpener

数字投影仪
shùzì tóuyǐng yí
digital projector

钢笔
gāngbǐ
pen

铅笔
qiānbǐ
pencil

橡皮
xiàngpí
rubber

笔记本
bǐjìběn
notebook

教科书 jiàokēshū | textbook

笔袋 bǐdài | pencil case

尺子 chǐzi | ruler

提问 tíwèn | question (v)

回答 huídá | answer (v)

讨论 tǎolùn | discuss (v)

学习 xuéxí | learn (v)

词汇 cíhuì • vocabulary

校长 xiàozhǎng head teacher	答案 dá'àn answer	评分 píngfēn grade
课 kè lesson	作业 zuòyè homework	年级 niánjí year
问题 wèntí question	考试 kǎoshì examination	字典 zìdiǎn dictionary
记笔记 jìbǐjì take notes (v)	作文 zuòwén essay	百科全书 bǎikēquánshū encyclopedia

数学 shùxué · **maths**

平面图形 píngmiàntúxíng · **shapes**

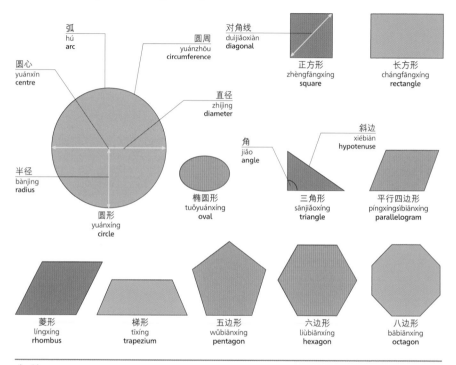

弧
hú
arc

圆周
yuánzhōu
circumference

圆心
yuánxīn
centre

直径
zhíjìng
diameter

对角线
duìjiǎoxiàn
diagonal

正方形
zhèngfāngxíng
square

长方形
chángfāngxíng
rectangle

半径
bànjìng
radius

圆形
yuánxíng
circle

椭圆形
tuǒyuánxíng
oval

角
jiǎo
angle

斜边
xiébiān
hypotenuse

三角形
sānjiǎoxíng
triangle

平行四边形
píngxíngsìbiānxíng
parallelogram

菱形
língxíng
rhombus

梯形
tīxíng
trapezium

五边形
wǔbiānxíng
pentagon

六边形
liùbiānxíng
hexagon

八边形
bābiānxíng
octagon

立体 lìtǐ · **solids**

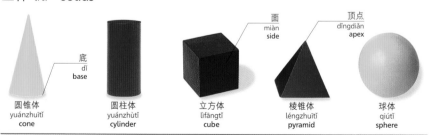

底
dǐ
base

面
miàn
side

顶点
dǐngdiǎn
apex

圆锥体
yuánzhuītǐ
cone

圆柱体
yuánzhùtǐ
cylinder

立方体
lìfāngtǐ
cube

棱锥体
léngzhuītǐ
pyramid

球体
qiútǐ
sphere

线 xiàn · **lines**

平直	平行	垂直	弯曲
píngzhí	píngxíng	chuízhí	wānqū
straight	**parallel**	**perpendicular**	**curved**

度量 dùliàng · **measurements**

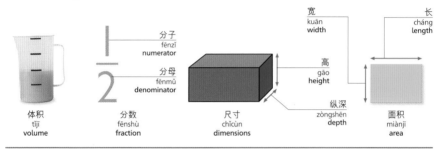

宽
kuān
width

长
cháng
length

分子
fēnzǐ
numerator

分母
fēnmǔ
denominator

高
gāo
height

纵深
zòngshēn
depth

体积	分数	尺寸	面积
tǐjī	fēnshù	chǐcùn	miànjī
volume	**fraction**	**dimensions**	**area**

学习用具 xuéxíyòngjù · **equipment**

三角板	量角器	直尺	圆规	计算器
sānjiǎobǎn	liángjiǎoqì	zhíchǐ	yuánguī	jìsuànqì
set square	**protractor**	**ruler**	**compass**	**calculator**

词汇 cíhuì · **vocabulary**

几何	正	倍	等于	加	乘	等式
jǐhé	zhèng	bèi	děngyú	jiā	chéng	děngshì
geometry	**plus**	**times**	**equals**	**add (v)**	**multiply (v)**	**equation**

算术	负	除以	计数	减	除	百分比
suànshù	fù	chúyǐ	jìshù	jiǎn	chú	bǎifēnbǐ
arithmetic	**minus**	**divided by**	**count (v)**	**subtract (v)**	**divide (v)**	**percentage**

科学 kēxué · **science**

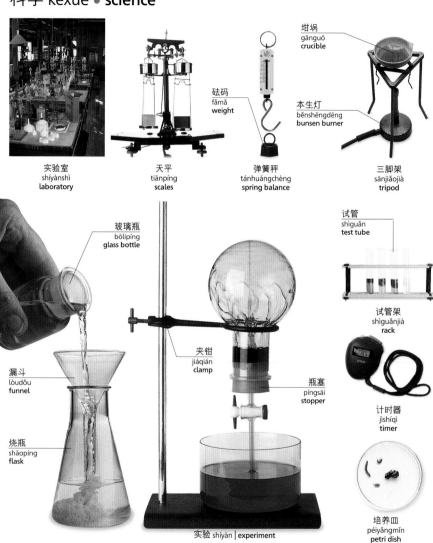

实验室
shíyànshì
laboratory

天平
tiānpíng
scales

砝码
fǎmǎ
weight

弹簧秤
tánhuángchèng
spring balance

坩埚
gānguō
crucible

本生灯
běnshēngdēng
bunsen burner

三脚架
sānjiǎojià
tripod

玻璃瓶
bōlípíng
glass bottle

试管
shìguǎn
test tube

试管架
shìguǎnjià
rack

夹钳
jiáqián
clamp

计时器
jìshíqì
timer

瓶塞
píngsāi
stopper

漏斗
lòudǒu
funnel

烧瓶
shāopíng
flask

培养皿
péiyǎngmǐn
petri dish

实验 shíyàn | experiment

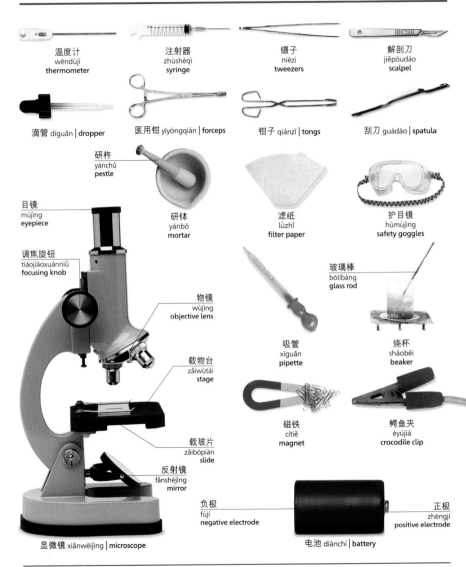

温度计
wēndùjì
thermometer

注射器
zhùshèqì
syringe

镊子
nièzi
tweezers

解剖刀
jiěpōudāo
scalpel

滴管 dīguǎn | dropper

医用钳 yīyòngqián | forceps

钳子 qiánzi | tongs

刮刀 guādāo | spatula

研杵
yánchǔ
pestle

目镜
mùjìng
eyepiece

研钵
yánbō
mortar

滤纸
lǜzhǐ
filter paper

护目镜
hùmùjìng
safety goggles

调焦旋钮
tiáojiāoxuánniǔ
focusing knob

玻璃棒
bōlíbàng
glass rod

物镜
wùjìng
objective lens

吸管
xīguǎn
pipette

烧杯
shāobēi
beaker

载物台
zàiwùtái
stage

载玻片
zàibōpiàn
slide

磁铁
cítiě
magnet

鳄鱼夹
èyújiá
crocodile clip

反射镜
fǎnshèjìng
mirror

负极
fùjí
negative electrode

正极
zhèngjí
positive electrode

显微镜 xiǎnwēijìng | microscope

电池 diànchí | battery

高等院校 gāoděngyuànxiào • college

招生办
zhāoshēngbàn
admissions

运动场
yùndòngchǎng
sports field

学生食堂
xuéshēngshítáng
refectory

学生宿舍
xuéshēngsùshè
hall of
residence

健康中心
jiànkāngzhōngxīn
health centre

校园 xiàoyuán | campus

词汇 cíhuì • vocabulary

借书证 jièshūzhèng library card	问询处 wènxúnchù enquiries	借出 jièchū loan
阅览室 yuèlǎnshì reading room	借入 jièrù borrow (v)	书 shū book
推荐书目 tuījiànshūmù reading list	预订 yùdìng reserve (v)	书名 shūmíng title
还书日期 huánshūrìqī return date	续借 xùjiè renew (v)	走廊 zǒuláng aisle

图书管理员
túshūguǎnlǐyuán
librarian

借书处
jièshūchù
loans desk

书架
shūjià
bookshelf

期刊
qīkān
periodical

杂志
zázhì
journal

图书馆 túshūguǎn | library

大学生
dàxuéshēng
undergraduate

讲师
jiǎngshī
lecturer

毕业生
bìyèshēng
graduate

学位袍
xuéwèipáo
robe

阶梯教室 jiētījiàoshì | lecture theatre

毕业典礼 bìyèdiǎnlǐ | graduation ceremony

高等专科学校 gāoděngzhuānkē xuéxiào · schools

模特
mótè
model

美术学院 měishùxuéyuàn
art college

音乐学院 yīnyuèxuéyuàn
music school

舞蹈学院 wǔdǎoxuéyuàn
dance academy

词汇 cíhuì · vocabulary

奖学金 jiǎngxuéjīn scholarship	研究 yánjiū research	(学位) 论文 (xuéwèi) lùnwén dissertation	医学 yīxué medicine	哲学 zhéxué philosophy
文凭 wénpíng diploma	硕士学位 shuòshìxuéwèi master's	系 xì department	动物学 dòngwùxué zoology	文学 wénxué literature
学位 xuéwèi degree	博士学位 bóshìxuéwèi doctorate	法律 fǎlǜ law	物理学 wùlǐxué physics	艺术史 yìshùshǐ history of art
研究生阶段的 yánjiūshēng jiēduànde postgraduate	论文 lùnwén thesis	工程学 gōngchéngxué engineering	政治学 zhèngzhìxué politics	经济学 jīngjìxué economics

工作 gōngzuò
work

办公室1 bàngōngshìyī • office 1

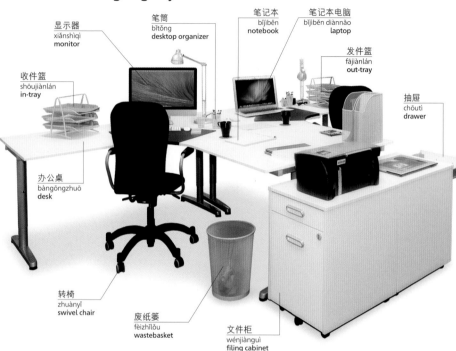

显示器
xiǎnshìqì
monitor

笔筒
bǐtǒng
desktop organizer

笔记本
bǐjìběn
notebook

笔记本电脑
bǐjìběn diànnǎo
laptop

发件篮
fājiànlán
out-tray

抽屉
chōuti
drawer

收件篮
shōujiànlán
in-tray

办公桌
bàngōngzhuō
desk

转椅
zhuànyǐ
swivel chair

废纸篓
fèizhǐlǒu
wastebasket

文件柜
wénjiànguì
filing cabinet

办公设备 bàngōngshèbèi • office equipment

纸盒
zhǐhé
paper tray

打印机 dǎyìnjī | printer

碎纸机 suìzhǐjī | shredder

词汇 cíhuì • vocabulary

打印
dǎyìn
print (v)

放大
fàngdà
enlarge (v)

复印
fùyìn
copy (v)

缩小
suōxiǎo
reduce (v)

我要复印。
wǒ yào fùyìn.
I need to make some copies.

办公用品 bàngōngyòngpǐn · office supplies

礼帖
lǐtiē
compliments slip

印有笺头的信纸
yìn yǒu jiāntóude xìnzhǐ
letterhead

信封
xìnfēng
envelope

文件盒
wénjiànhé
box file

标签
biāoqiān
tab

分隔页
fēngéyè
divider

带纸夹的笔记板
dài zhǐjiáde bǐjìbǎn
clipboard

便笺
biànjiān
note pad

悬挂式文件夹
xuánguàshì wénjiànjiā
hanging file

格式文件夹
géshì wénjiànjiā
concertina file

盒式文件夹
héshì wénjiànjiā
lever arch file

订书钉
dìngshūdīng
staples

透明胶带
tòumíngjiāodài
sticky tape

印台
yìntái
ink pad

备忘录
bèiwànglù
personal organizer

订书机
dìngshūjī
stapler

胶带架
jiāodàijià
tape dispenser

打孔器
dǎkǒngqì
hole punch

橡皮图章
xiàngpítúzhāng
rubber stamp

皮筋
píjīn
rubber band

强力纸夹
qiánglìzhǐjiá
bulldog clip

曲别针
qūbiézhēn
paper clip

图钉
túdīng
drawing pin

公告栏 gōnggàolán | notice board

办公室2 bàngōngshì'èr · office 2

活动挂图
huódòngguàtú
flip chart

会议记录
huìyìjìlù
minutes

挂图架
guàtújià
easel

报告
bàogào
report

经理
jīnglǐ
manager

提案
tí'àn
proposal

主管
zhǔguǎn
executive

会议 huìyì | meeting

词汇 cíhuì · vocabulary

会议室 huìyìshì meeting room	参加 cānjiā attend (v)
议程 yìchéng agenda	主持 zhǔchí chair (v)

什么时候开会?
shénme shíhou kāihuì?
What time is the meeting?

您几点上下班?
nín jǐdiǎn shàngxiàbān?
What are your office hours?

讲解人
jiǎngjiěrén
speaker

介绍 jièshào | presentation

商务 shāngwù • business

商人
shāngrén
businessman

女商人
nǔshāngrén
businesswoman

工作午餐 gōngzuòwǔcān | **business lunch**

商务旅行 shāngwùlǔxíng | **business trip**

日志 rìzhì | **diary**

约会
yuēhuì
appointment

总经理
zǒngjīnglǐ
managing director

客户
kèhù
client

商业交易 shāngyèjiāoyì | **business deal**

词汇 cíhuì • vocabulary

公司 gōngsī **company**	员工 yuángōng **staff**	会计部 kuàijìbù **accounts department**	法律事务部 fǎlǜshìwùbù **legal department**
总部，总公司 zǒngbù, zǒnggōngsī **head office**	薪水 xīnshuǐ **salary**	市场部 shìchǎngbù **marketing department**	客户服务部 kèhùfúwùbù **customer service department**
分部，分公司 fēnbù, fēngōngsī **branch**	工资单 gōngzīdān **payroll**	销售部 xiāoshòubù **sales department**	人力资源部 rénlìzīyuánbù **human resources department**

计算机 jìsuànjī • computer

打印机
dǎyìnjī
printer

屏幕
píngmù
screen

扫描仪
sǎomiáoyí
scanner

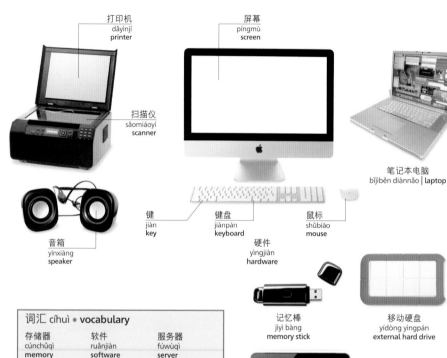

笔记本电脑
bǐjìběn diànnǎo | laptop

键
jiàn
key

键盘
jiànpán
keyboard

鼠标
shǔbiāo
mouse

硬件
yìngjiàn
hardware

音箱
yīnxiāng
speaker

记忆棒
jìyì bàng
memory stick

移动硬盘
yídòng yìngpán
external hard drive

词汇 cíhuì • vocabulary

存储器 cúnchǔqì memory	软件 ruǎnjiàn software	服务器 fúwùqì server
随机存储器 suíjī cúnchǔqì RAM	应用程序 yìngyòng chéngxù application	端口 duānkǒu port
字节 zìjié bytes	程序 chéngxù program	处理器 chǔlǐqì processor
系统 xìtǒng system	网络 wǎngluò network	电源线 diànyuánxiàn power cable

平板电脑
píngbǎn diànnǎo
tablet

智能手机
zhìnéng shǒujī
smartphone

桌面 zhuōmiàn · **desktop**

菜单栏
càidānlán
menubar

字体
zìtǐ
font

图标
túbiāo
icon

工具栏
gōngjùlán
toolbar

滚动条
gǔndòngtiáo
scrollbar

视窗
shìchuāng
window

桌面背景
zhuōmiàn bèijǐng
wallpaper

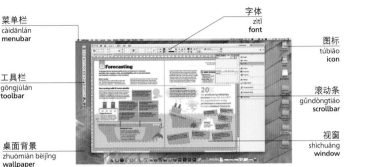

文件
wénjiàn
file

文件夹
wénjiànjiā
folder

回收站
huíshōuzhàn
trash

互联网 hùliánwǎng · **internet**

浏览器
liúlǎnqì
browser

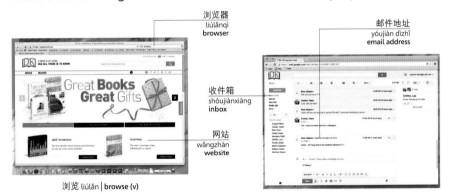

浏览 liúlǎn | browse (v)

电子邮件 diànzǐ yóujiàn · **email**

邮件地址
yóujiàn dìzhǐ
email address

收件箱
shōujiànxiāng
inbox

网站
wǎngzhàn
website

词汇 cíhuì · **vocabulary**

连接 liánjiē connect (v)	服务商 fúwùshāng service provider	登录 dēnglù log on (v)	下载 xiàzài download (v)	发送 fāsòng send (v)	保存 bǎocún save (v)
安装 ānzhuāng install (v)	电子邮件账户 diànzǐyóujiàn zhànghù email account	在线 zàixiàn online	附件 fùjiàn attachment	接收 jiēshōu receive (v)	搜索 sōusuǒ search (v)

媒体 méitǐ · media

电视演播室 diànshì yǎnbōshì · television studio

布景
bùjǐng
set

节目主持人
jiémùzhǔchírén
presenter

照明
zhàomíng
light

摄像机
shèxiàngjī
camera

摄像机升降器
shèxiàngjī shēngjiàngqì
camera crane

摄像师
shèxiàngshī
cameraman

词汇 cíhuì · vocabulary

频道 píndào channel	新闻 xīnwén news	新闻媒体 xīnwénméitǐ press	肥皂剧 féizàojù soap	动画片 dònghuàpiàn cartoon	直播 zhíbō live
节目编排 jiémùbiānpái programming	纪录片 jìlùpiàn documentary	电视连续剧 diànshì liánxùjù television series	游戏节目 yóuxìjiémù game show	录播 lùbō prerecorded	播放 bōfàng broadcast (v)

采访记者 cǎifǎngjìzhě
interviewer

记者 jìzhě | reporter

自动提示机 zìdòngtíshìjī
autocue

新闻播音员 xīnwénbōyīnyuán
newsreader

演员 yǎnyuán | actors

录音吊杆 lùyīndiàogān
sound boom

场记板 chǎngjìbǎn
clapper board

电影布景 diànyǐngbùjǐng
film set

无线电广播 wúxiàndiànguǎngbō · radio

录音师
lùyīnshī
sound technician

混音台
hùnyīntái
mixing desk

话筒
huàtǒng
microphone

录音室 lùyīnshì | recording studio

词汇 cíhuì · vocabulary

广播电台
guǎngbōdiàntái
radio station

中波
zhōngbō
medium wave

广播
guǎngbō
broadcast

频率
pínlǜ
frequency

波长
bōcháng
wavelength

音量
yīnliàng
volume

长波
chángbō
long wave

调音
tiáoyīn
tune (v)

短波
duǎnbō
short wave

流行音乐节目主持人
liúxíngyīnyuè jiémù
zhǔchírén
DJ

模拟收音机
mónǐ shōuyīnjī
analogue

数码收音机
shùmǎ shōuyīnjī
digital

法律 fǎlǜ · law

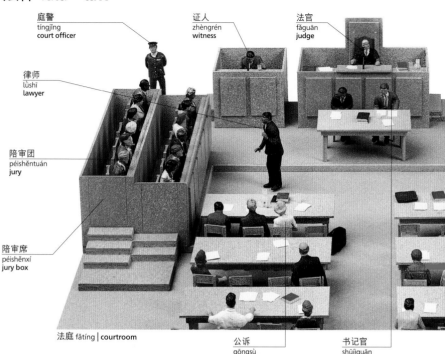

庭警
tíngjǐng
court officer

证人
zhèngrén
witness

法官
fǎguān
judge

律师
lǜshī
lawyer

陪审团
péishěntuán
jury

陪审席
péishěnxí
jury box

法庭 fǎtíng | courtroom

公诉
gōngsù
prosecution

书记官
shūjìguān
court official

词汇 cíhuì · vocabulary

律师事务所 lǜshīshìwùsuǒ **lawyer's office**	**传讯** chuánxùn **summons**	**传票** chuánpiào **writ**	**诉讼案件** sùsòng ànjiàn **court case**
法律咨询 fǎlǜzīxún **legal advice**	**陈辞** chéncí **statement**	**开庭日** kāitíngrì **court date**	**控告** kònggào **charge**
诉讼委托人 sùsòngwěituōrén **client**	**逮捕令** dàibǔlìng **warrant**	**抗辩** kàngbiàn **plea**	**被告** bèigào **accused**

速记员
sùjìyuán
stenographer

嫌疑犯
xiányífàn
suspect

被告人
bèigàorén
defendant

被告律师
bèigàolǜshī
defence

罪犯
zuìfàn
criminal

拼凑人像
pīncòurénxiàng | photofit

犯罪记录
fànzuìjìlù | criminal record

狱警 yùjǐng | prison guard

单人牢房
dānrénláofáng | cell

监狱 jiānyù | prison

词汇 cíhuì • vocabulary

证据 zhèngjù evidence	有罪 yǒuzuì guilty	保释金 bǎoshìjīn bail	我要见律师。 wǒ yào jiàn lǜshī. I want to see a lawyer.
判决 pànjué verdict	无罪释放 wúzuìshìfàng acquitted	上诉 shàngsù appeal	法院在哪儿? fǎyuàn zàinǎ'er? Where is the courthouse?
无罪 wúzuì innocent	判刑 pànxíng sentence	假释 jiǎshì parole	我可以保释吗? wǒ kěyǐ bǎoshì ma? Can I post bail?

农场1 nóngchǎngyī · farm 1

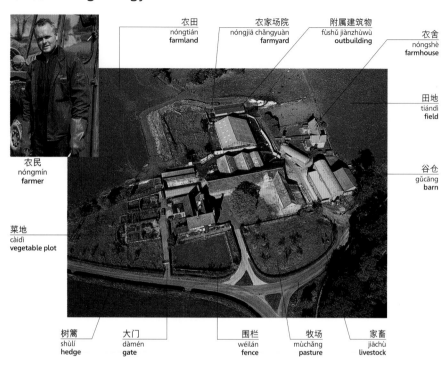

农田
nóngtián
farmland

农家场院
nóngjiā chǎngyuàn
farmyard

附属建筑物
fùshǔ jiànzhùwù
outbuilding

农舍
nóngshè
farmhouse

农民
nóngmín
farmer

田地
tiándì
field

谷仓
gǔcāng
barn

菜地
càidì
vegetable plot

树篱
shùlí
hedge

大门
dàmén
gate

围栏
wéilán
fence

牧场
mùchǎng
pasture

家畜
jiāchù
livestock

中耕机
zhōnggēngjī
cultivator

拖拉机 tuōlājī | tractor

联合收割机 liánhéshōugējī | combine harvester

中文 zhōngwén · english

农场类型 nóngchǎng lèixíng · types of farm

庄稼
zhuāngjia
crop

羊群
yángqún
flock

种植园
zhòngzhíyuán
arable farm

乳牛场
rǔniúchǎng
dairy farm

牧羊场
mùyángchǎng
sheep farm

养鸡场 yǎngjīchǎng
poultry farm

葡萄树
pútáoshù
vine

养猪场
yǎngzhūchǎng
pig farm

养鱼场
yǎngyúchǎng
fish farm

果园
guǒyuán
fruit farm

葡萄园
pútáoyuán
vineyard

农活 nónghuó · actions

犁
lí
furrow

犁地
lídì
plough (v)

播种
bōzhǒng
sow (v)

挤奶
jǐ'nǎi
milk (v)

饲养
sìyǎng
feed (v)

灌溉 guàngài | water (v)

收获 shōuhuò | harvest (v)

词汇 cíhuì · vocabulary

除草剂 chúcǎojì herbicide	牧群 mùqún herd	饲料槽 sìliàocáo trough
杀虫剂 shāchóngjì pesticide	筒仓 tǒngcāng silo	种植 zhòngzhí plant (v)

农场2 nóngchǎng'èr · farm 2

农作物 nóngzuòwù · crops

小麦
xiǎomài
wheat

玉米
yùmǐ
corn

大麦
dàmài
barley

油菜籽
yóucàizǐ
rapeseed

向日葵
xiàngrìkuí
sunflower

捆包
kǔnbāo
bale

干草
gāncǎo
hay

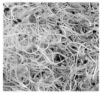

紫花苜蓿
zǐhuāmùxu
alfalfa

烟草
yāncǎo
tobacco

水稻
shuǐdào
rice

茶
chá
tea

咖啡
kāfēi
coffee

亚麻
yàmá
flax

甘蔗
gānzhe
sugarcane

棉花
miánhua
cotton

稻草人
dàocǎorén
scarecrow

家畜 jiāchù · livestock

小猪
xiǎozhū
piglet

牛犊
niúdú
calf

猪
zhū
pig

母牛
mǔniú
cow

公牛
gōngniú
bull

绵羊
miányáng
sheep

小山羊
xiǎoshānyáng
kid

马驹
mǎjū
foal

羊羔
yánggāo
lamb

山羊
shānyáng
goat

马
mǎ
horse

驴
lǘ
donkey

小鸡
xiǎojī
chick

小鸭
xiǎoyā
duckling

鸡
jī
chicken

公鸡
gōngjī
cockerel

火鸡
huǒjī
turkey

鸭
yā
duck

马厩
mǎjiù
stable

家畜圈
jiāchùjuàn
pen

鸡舍
jīshè
chicken coop

猪圈
zhūjuàn
pigsty

建筑 jiànzhù · **construction**

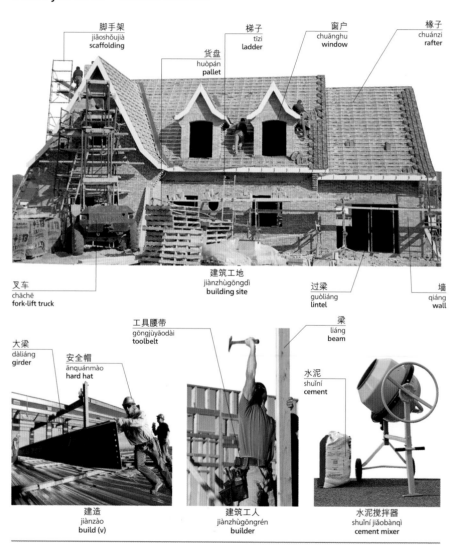

脚手架
jiǎoshǒujià
scaffolding

梯子
tīzi
ladder

窗户
chuānghu
window

椽子
chuánzi
rafter

货盘
huòpán
pallet

叉车
chāchē
fork-lift truck

建筑工地
jiànzhùgōngdì
building site

过梁
guòliáng
lintel

墙
qiáng
wall

工具腰带
gōngjùyāodài
toolbelt

梁
liáng
beam

大梁
dàliáng
girder

安全帽
ānquánmào
hard hat

水泥
shuǐní
cement

建造
jiànzào
build (v)

建筑工人
jiànzhùgōngrén
builder

水泥搅拌器
shuǐní jiǎobànqì
cement mixer

建筑材料 jiànzhù cáiliào · materials

砖
zhuān
brick

木材
mùcái
timber

瓦片
wǎpiàn
roof tile

煤渣砌块
méizhāqìkuài
breeze block

工具 gōngjù · tools

灰浆
huījiāng
mortar

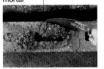

抹刀
mǒdāo
trowel

水准仪
shuǐzhǔnyí
spirit level

柄
bǐng
handle

大锤
dàchuí
sledgehammer

丁字镐
dīngzìgǎo
pickaxe

铁锹
tiěqiāo
shovel

(工程)机械 (gōngchéng) jīxiè · machinery

压路机
yālùjī
roadroller

翻斗卡车
fāndǒukǎchē
dumper truck

支座
zhīzuò
support

吊钩
diàogōu
hook

起重机 qǐzhòngjī I crane

道路施工 dàolùshīgōng · roadworks

柏油路面
bǎiyóulùmiàn
tarmac

锥形隔离墩
zhuīxínggélídūn
cone

风钻
fēngzuàn
pneumatic drill

重铺路面
chóngpū lùmiàn
resurfacing

挖掘机
wājuéjī
mechanical digger

职业1 zhíyèyī • **occupations 1**

木匠
mùjiàng
carpenter

电工
diàngōng
electrician

水暖工
shuǐnuǎngōng
plumber

建筑工人
jiànzhùgōngrén
builder

园丁
yuándīng
gardener

吸尘器
xīchénqì
vacuum cleaner

清洁工
qīngjiégōng
cleaner

机械师
jīxièshī
mechanic

屠户
túhù
butcher

美发师
měifàshī
hairdresser

鱼贩
yúfàn
fishmonger

蔬菜水果商
shūcài shuǐguǒshāng
greengrocer

花商
huāshāng
florist

理发师
lǐfàshī
barber

珠宝匠
zhūbǎojiàng
jeweller

售货员
shòuhuòyuán
shop assistant

房地产商
fángdìchǎnshāng
estate agent

配镜师
pèijìngshī
optician

口罩
kǒuzhào
mask

牙医
yáyī
dentist

医生
yīshēng
doctor

药剂师
yàojìshī
pharmacist

护士
hùshi
nurse

兽医
shòuyī
vet

农民
nóngmín
farmer

渔民
yúmín
fisherman

机枪
jīqiāng
machine gun

徽章
huīzhāng
identity badge

制服
zhìfú
uniform

保安
bǎo'ān
security guard

水手
shuǐshǒu
sailor

士兵
shìbīng
soldier

警察
jīngchá
policeman

消防队员
xiāofángduìyuán
fireman

职业2 zhíyè'èr • occupations 2

律师
lǜshī
lawyer

会计师
kuàijìshī
accountant

模型
móxíng
model

建筑师 jiànzhùshī | architect

科学家
kēxuéjiā
scientist

老师
lǎoshī
teacher

图书管理员
túshūguǎnlǐyuán
librarian

接待员
jiēdàiyuán
receptionist

邮袋
yóudài
mailbag

邮递员
yóudìyuán
postman

公共汽车司机
gōnggòngqìchē sījī
bus driver

卡车司机
kǎchē sījī
lorry driver

出租车司机
chūzūchē sījī
taxi driver

飞行员
fēixíngyuán
pilot

空中小姐
kōngzhōngxiǎojiě
air stewardess

旅行代理
lǚxíngdàilǐ
travel agent

厨师帽
chúshīmào
chef's hat

厨师
chúshī
chef

芭蕾舞裙
bālěiwǔqún
tutu

音乐家
yīnyuèjiā
musician

舞蹈演员
wǔdǎoyǎnyuán
dancer

女演员
nǚ yǎnyuán
actress

歌手
gēshǒu
singer

女侍者
nǚshìzhě
waitress

酒保
jiǔbǎo
bartender

运动员
yùndòngyuán
sportsman

雕塑家
diāosùjiā
sculptor

笔记
bǐjì
notes

画家
huàjiā
painter

摄影师
shèyǐngshī
photographer

新闻播音员
xīnwén bōyīnyuán
newsreader

新闻记者
xīnwén jìzhě
journalist

编辑
biānjí
editor

制图员
zhìtúyuán
designer

女缝纫师
nǚféngrènshī
seamstress

裁缝
cáiféng
tailor

交通运输 jiāotōngyùnshū
transport

道路 dàolù ● roads

高速公路
gāosùgōnglù
motorway

收费站
shōufèizhàn
toll booth

路面标志
lùmiànbiāozhì
road markings

主路入口
zhǔlùrùkǒu
slip road

单行道
dānxíngdào
one-way street

隔离带
gélídài
divider

交汇处
jiāohuìchù
junction

交通信号灯
jiāotōng
xìnhàodēng
traffic light

内车道
nèichēdào
inside lane

中央车道
zhōngyāngchēdào
middle lane

外车道
wàichēdào
outside lane

出口匝道
chūkǒuzādào
exit ramp

交通
jiāotōng
traffic

立交桥
lìjiāoqiáo
flyover

硬质路肩
yìngzhìlùjiān
hard shoulder

载重汽车
zàizhòngqìchē
lorry

中央分车带
zhōngyāng fēnchēdài
central reservation

高架桥下通道
gāojià qiáoxià tōngdào
underpass

求救电话
qiújiù diànhuà
emergency phone

残疾人停车处
cánjírén tíngchēchù
disabled parking

人行横道
rénxínghéngdào
pedestrian crossing

交通堵塞
jiāotōngdǔsè
traffic jam

卫星导航
wèixīng dǎoháng
satnav

停车计时收费器
tíngchē jìshí shōufèiqì
parking meter

交通警察
jiāotōng jǐngchá
traffic policeman

词汇 cíhuì · vocabulary

环岛
huándǎo
roundabout

绕行道路
ràoxíngdàolù
diversion

道路施工
dàolùshīgōng
roadworks

防撞护栏
fángzhuànghùlán
crash barrier

双程分隔车道
shuāngchéng
fēngéchēdào
dual carriageway

停车
tíngchē
park (v)

驾驶
jiàshǐ
drive (v)

倒车
dàochē
reverse (v)

超车
chāochē
overtake (v)

拖走
tuōzǒu
tow away (v)

这是去... 的路吗?
zhèshìqù... de lù ma?
Is this the road to ...?

哪里可以停车?
nǎli kěyǐ tíngchē?
Where can I park?

交通标志 jiāotōng biāozhì · road signs

禁行
jìnxíng
no entry

60

限速
xiànsù
speed limit

危险
wēixiǎn
hazard

禁止停车
jìnzhǐ tíngchē
no stopping

禁止右转
jìnzhǐ yòuzhuǎn
no right turn

公共汽车 gōnggòngqìchē · bus

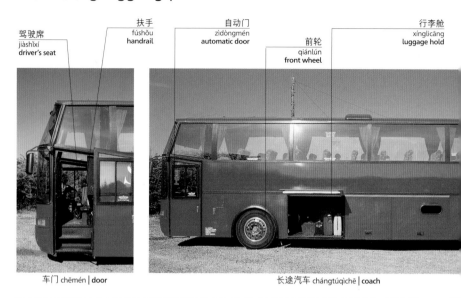

驾驶席
jiàshǐxí
driver's seat

扶手
fúshǒu
handrail

自动门
zìdòngmén
automatic door

前轮
qiánlún
front wheel

行李舱
xínglǐcāng
luggage hold

车门 chēmén | **door**

长途汽车 chángtúqìchē | **coach**

公共汽车种类 gōnggòngqìchē zhǒnglèi · types of buses

公交线路号
gōngjiāoxiànlùhào
route number

司机
sījī
driver

无轨电车
wúguǐdiànchē
trolley bus

双层公共汽车
shuāngcéng gōnggòngqìchē
double-decker bus

有轨电车
yǒuguǐdiànchē
tram

校车 xiàochē | **school bus**

后轮
hòulún
rear wheel

窗户
chuānghu
window

停车按钮
tíngchē ànniǔ
stop button

公共汽车票
gōnggòngqìchēpiào
bus ticket

铃
líng
bell

公共汽车总站
gōnggòngqìchē zǒngzhàn
bus station

公共汽车站
gōnggòngqìchēzhàn
bus stop

词汇 cíhuì • vocabulary

车费
chēfèi
fare

轮椅通道
lúnyǐ tōngdào
wheelchair access

时刻表
shíkèbiǎo
timetable

公共汽车候车亭
gònggqìchē hòuchētíng
bus shelter

您在... 停吗?
nín zài... tíng ma?
Do you stop at ...?

哪路车去...?
nǎlù chē qù...?
Which bus goes to ...?

小型公共汽车
xiǎoxíng gōnggòngqìchē
minibus

游览车 yóulǎnchē | tourist bus

班车 bānchē | shuttle bus

汽车1 qìchēyī • car 1

外部 wàibù • exterior

外后视镜
wàihòushìjìng
wing mirror

风挡
fēngdǎng
windscreen

内后视镜
nèihòushìjìng
rear-view mirror

雨刷
yǔshuā
windscreen wiper

车门
chēmén
door

引擎盖
yǐnqínggài
bonnet

行李箱
xínglixiāng
boot

转向灯
zhuànxiàngdēng
indicator

车牌
chēpái
licence plate

保险杠
bǎoxiǎngàng
bumper

前灯
qiándēng
headlight

车轮
chēlún
wheel

轮胎
lúntāi
tyre

行李
xíngli
luggage

车顶行李架
chēdǐng xínglijià
roof rack

尾部车门
wěibùchēmén
tailgate

安全带
ānquándài
seat belt

儿童座椅
értóngzuòyǐ
child seat

种类 zhǒnglèi · types

电动汽车
diàndòng qìchē
electric car

揭背式轿车
jiēbèishì jiàochē
hatchback

家庭轿车，三厢车
jiātíng jiàochē, sānxiāngchē
saloon

客货两用车
kèhuò liǎngyòngchē
estate

敞篷车
chǎngpéngchē
convertible

跑车
pǎochē
sports car

六座厢式车
liùzuò xiāngshìchē
people carrier

四轮驱动(车)
sìlúnqūdòng(chē)
four-wheel drive

老式汽车
lǎoshìqìchē
vintage

大型高级轿车
dàxínggāojí jiàochē
limousine

加油站 jiāyóuzhàn · petrol station

汽油泵
qìyóubèng
petrol pump

价格
jiàgé
price

加油处
jiāyóuchù
forecourt

词汇 cíhuì · vocabulary

油 yóu oil	含铅 hánqiān leaded	自动洗车站 zìdòngxǐchēzhàn car wash
汽油 qìyóu petrol	柴油 cháiyóu diesel	防冻液 fángdòngyè antifreeze
无铅 wúqiān unleaded	汽车修理站 qìchē xiūlǐzhàn garage	喷水器 pēnshuǐqì screenwash

请加满油。
qǐng jiāmǎn yóu.
Fill the tank, please.

汽车 2 qìchē'èr • car 2

内部 nèibù • interior

座椅头枕
zuòyǐ tóuzhěn
headrest

门锁
ménsuǒ
door lock

车门把手
chēmén
bǎshou
handle

后座
hòuzuò
back seat

扶手
fúshǒu
armrest

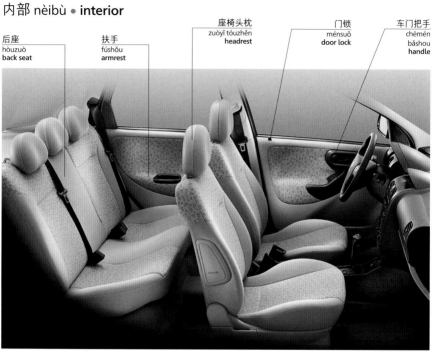

词汇 cíhuì • vocabulary

双门 shuāngmén **two-door**	四门 sìmén **four-door**	自动 zìdòng **automatic**	刹车 shāchē **brake**	加速器，油门 jiāsùqì, yóumén **accelerator**
三门 sānmén **three-door**	手动 shǒudòng **manual**	点火 diǎnhuǒ **ignition**	离合器 líhéqì **clutch**	空调 kōngtiáo **air conditioning**

您能告诉我去…的路吗?
nín néng gàosù wǒ qù…de lù ma?
Can you tell me the way to …?

停车场在哪里?
tíngchēchǎng zàinǎli?
Where is the car park?

这儿可以停车吗?
zhè'er kěyǐ tíngchē ma?
Can I park here?

操作装置 cāozuòzhuāngzhì · controls

方向盘
fāngxiàngpán
steering
wheel

喇叭
lǎba
horn

仪表盘
yíbiǎopán
dashboard

警示灯
jǐngshìdēng
hazard lights

卫星导航仪
wèixīng dǎohángyí
satellite navigation

左侧驾驶 zuǒcèjiàshǐ | left-hand drive

温度计
wēndùjì
temperature gauge

转速表
zhuànsùbiǎo
rev counter

车速表
chēsùbiǎo
speedometer

油量表
yóuliàngbiǎo
fuel gauge

汽车音响
qìchē
yīnxiǎng
car stereo

车灯开关
chēdēng kāiguān
lights switch

里程表
lǐchéngbiǎo
odometer

暖风开关
nuǎnfēng kāiguān
heater controls

安全气囊
ānquánqìnáng
air bag

变速杆
biànsùgǎn
gearstick

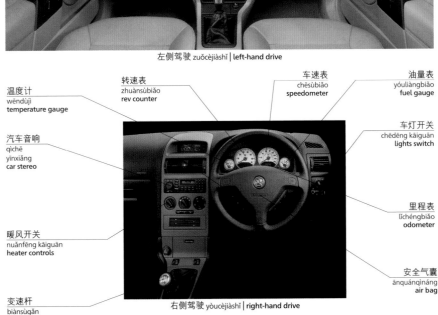

右侧驾驶 yòucèjiàshǐ | right-hand drive

汽车 3 qìchēsān • car 3

机械构造 jīxiègòuzào • mechanics

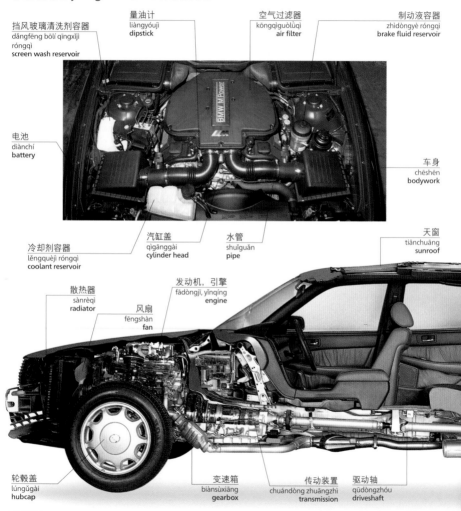

挡风玻璃清洗剂容器
dǎngfēng bōlí qīngxǐjì
róngqì
screen wash reservoir

量油计
liàngyóujì
dipstick

空气过滤器
kōngqìguòlǜqì
air filter

制动液容器
zhìdòngyè róngqì
brake fluid reservoir

电池
diànchí
battery

车身
chēshēn
bodywork

冷却剂容器
lěngquèjì róngqì
coolant reservoir

汽缸盖
qìgānggài
cylinder head

水管
shuǐguǎn
pipe

天窗
tiānchuāng
sunroof

散热器
sànrèqì
radiator

发动机, 引擎
fādòngjī, yǐnqíng
engine

风扇
fēngshàn
fan

轮毂盖
lúngǔgài
hubcap

变速箱
biànsùxiāng
gearbox

传动装置
chuándòng zhuāngzhì
transmission

驱动轴
qūdòngzhóu
driveshaft

爆胎 bàotāi · **puncture**

备用轮胎
bèiyòng lúntāi
spare tyre

换胎扳手
huàntāibānshǒu
wrench

固定螺母
gùdìngluómǔ
wheel nuts

千斤顶
qiānjīndǐng
jack

更换轮胎
gēnghuàn lúntāi
change a wheel (v)

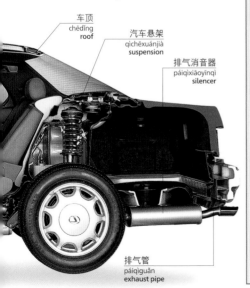

车顶
chēdǐng
roof

汽车悬架
qìchēxuánjià
suspension

排气消音器
páiqìxiāoyīnqì
silencer

排气管
páiqìguǎn
exhaust pipe

词汇 cíhuì · **vocabulary**

车祸
chēhuò
car accident

故障
gùzhàng
breakdown

保险
bǎoxiǎn
insurance

拖车
tuōchē
tow truck

机械师
jīxièshī
mechanic

胎压
tāiyā
tyre pressure

保险盒
bǎoxiǎnhé
fuse box

火花塞
huǒhuāsāi
spark plug

风扇皮带
fēngshànpídài
fan belt

油箱
yóuxiāng
petrol tank

点火定时
diǎnhuǒdìngshí
timing

涡轮增压器
wōlúnzēngyāqì
turbocharger

配电器
pèidiànqì
distributor

底盘
dǐpán
chassis

手刹车
shǒushāchē
handbrake

交流发电机
jiāoliúfādiànjī
alternator

轮轴皮带
lúnzhóupídài
cam belt

. . . .

我的车坏了。
wǒ de chē huàile.
I've broken down.

我的车发动不起来。
wǒ de chē fādòng bù qǐlái.
My car won't start.

摩托车 mótuōchē ● motorbike

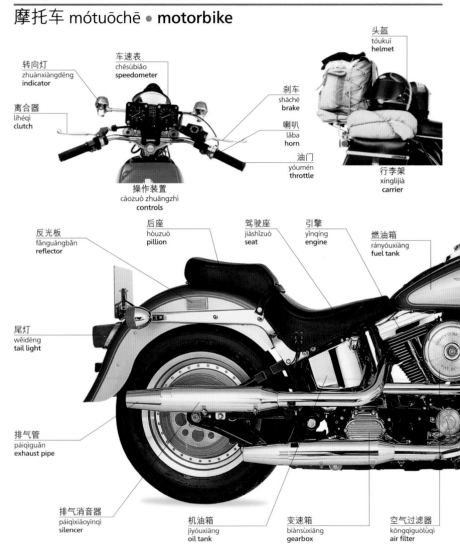

转向灯
zhuǎnxiàngdēng
indicator

车速表
chēsùbiǎo
speedometer

头盔
tóukuī
helmet

刹车
shāchē
brake

离合器
líhéqì
clutch

喇叭
lǎba
horn

油门
yóumén
throttle

操作装置
cāozuò zhuāngzhì
controls

行李架
xínglijià
carrier

反光板
fǎnguāngbǎn
reflector

后座
hòuzuò
pillion

驾驶座
jiàshǐzuò
seat

引擎
yǐnqíng
engine

燃油箱
rányóuxiāng
fuel tank

尾灯
wěidēng
tail light

排气管
páiqìguǎn
exhaust pipe

排气消音器
páiqìxiāoyīnqì
silencer

机油箱
jīyóuxiāng
oil tank

变速箱
biànsùxiāng
gearbox

空气过滤器
kōngqìguòlǜqì
air filter

皮衣
píyī
leathers

头盔面罩
tóukuīmiànzhào
visor

护膝
hùxī
knee pad

反光肩带
fǎnguāng jiāndài
reflector strap

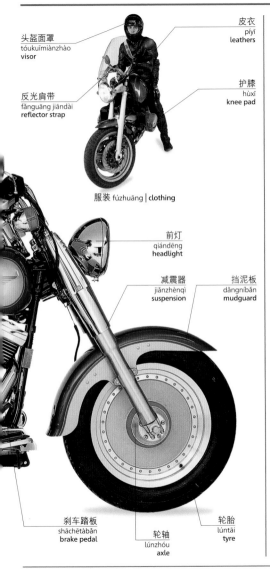

服装 fúzhuāng | clothing

前灯
qiándēng
headlight

减震器
jiǎnzhènqì
suspension

挡泥板
dǎngníbǎn
mudguard

刹车踏板
shāchētàbǎn
brake pedal

轮轴
lúnzhóu
axle

轮胎
lúntāi
tyre

种类 zhǒnglèi • types

赛车 sàichē | racing bike

风挡
fēngdǎng
windshield

旅行摩托 lǚxíngmótuō | tourer

越野摩托 yuèyěmótuō | dirt bike

支架
zhījià
stand

小轮摩托 xiǎolúnmótuō | scooter

自行车 zìxíngchē · **bicycle**

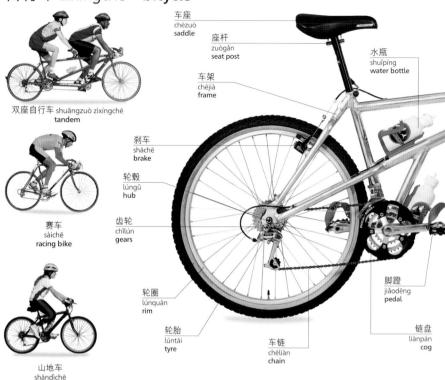

车座
chēzuò
saddle

座杆
zuògǎn
seat post

水瓶
shuǐpíng
water bottle

车架
chējià
frame

刹车
shāchē
brake

轮毂
lúngǔ
hub

齿轮
chǐlún
gears

轮圈
lúnquān
rim

轮胎
lúntāi
tyre

车链
chēliàn
chain

脚蹬
jiǎodēng
pedal

链盘
liànpán
cog

双座自行车 shuāngzuò zìxíngchē
tandem

赛车
sàichē
racing bike

山地车
shāndìchē
mountain bike

旅行车
lǚxíngchē
touring bike

公路车
gōnglùchē
road bike

头盔
tóukuī
helmet

自行车道 zìxíngchēdào | **cycle lane**

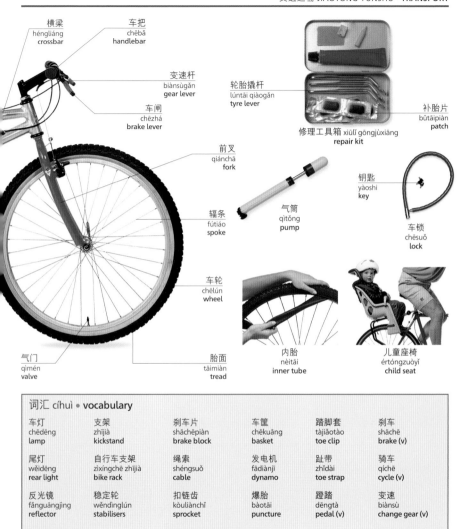

横梁
héngliáng
crossbar

车把
chēbǎ
handlebar

变速杆
biànsùgǎn
gear lever

车闸
chēzhá
brake lever

轮胎撬杆
lúntāi qiàogǎn
tyre lever

补胎片
bǔtāipiàn
patch

修理工具箱 xiūlǐ gōngjùxiāng
repair kit

前叉
qiánchā
fork

辐条
fútiáo
spoke

气筒
qìtǒng
pump

钥匙
yàoshi
key

车锁
chēsuǒ
lock

车轮
chēlún
wheel

气门
qìmén
valve

胎面
tāimiàn
tread

内胎
nèitāi
inner tube

儿童座椅
értóngzuòyǐ
child seat

词汇 cíhuì • vocabulary

车灯 chēdēng **lamp**	支架 zhījià **kickstand**	刹车片 shāchēpiàn **brake block**	车筐 chēkuāng **basket**	踏脚套 tàjiǎotào **toe clip**	刹车 shāchē **brake (v)**
尾灯 wěidēng **rear light**	自行车支架 zìxíngchē zhījià **bike rack**	绳索 shéngsuǒ **cable**	发电机 fādiànjī **dynamo**	趾带 zhǐdài **toe strap**	骑车 qíchē **cycle (v)**
反光镜 fǎnguāngjìng **reflector**	稳定轮 wěndìnglún **stabilisers**	扣链齿 kòuliànchǐ **sprocket**	爆胎 bàotāi **puncture**	蹬踏 dēngtà **pedal (v)**	变速 biànsù **change gear (v)**

列车 lièchē · **train**

客车厢
kèchēxiāng
carriage

站台
zhàntái
platform

手推车
shǒutuīchē
trolley

站台号
zhàntáihào
platform number

旅客
lǚkè
commuter

火车站 huǒchēzhàn | train station

列车种类 lièchē zhǒnglèi · **types of train**

蒸汽机车
zhēngqìjīchē
steam train

火车头
huǒchētóu
engine

驾驶室
jiàshǐshì
driver's cab

铁轨
tiěguǐ
rail

柴油机车 cháiyóujīchē | diesel train

电力机车
diànlìjīchē
electric train

高速列车
gāosùlièchē
high-speed train

单轨列车
dānguǐlièchē
monorail

地铁
dìtiě
underground train

有轨电车
yǒuguǐdiànchē
tram

货车
huòchē
freight train

行李架
xínglǐjià
luggage rack

车窗
chēchuāng
window

轨道
guǐdào
track

检票口 jiǎnpiàokǒu | **ticket barrier**

门
mén
door

座位
zuòwèi
seat

车厢隔间
chēxiānggéjiān
compartment

扩音器
kuòyīnqì
public address system

列车时刻表
lièchē
shíkèbiǎo
timetable

车票
chēpiào
ticket

餐车 cānchē | **dining car**

卧铺车厢
wòpùchēxiāng
sleeping compartment

车站大厅 chēzhàndàtīng | **concourse**

词汇 cíhuì · vocabulary

铁路网
tiělùwǎng
rail network

地铁线路图
dìtiě xiànlùtú
underground map

售票处
shòupiàochù
ticket office

载电轨
zàidiànguǐ
live rail

城际列车
chéngjì lièchē
inter-city train

晚点
wǎndiǎn
delay

检票员
jiǎnpiàoyuán
ticket inspector

信号
xìnhào
signal

上下班高峰期
shàngxiàbān gāofēngqī
rush hour

车费
chēfèi
fare

换乘
huànchéng
change (v)

紧急刹车闸
jǐnjí shāchēzhá
emergency lever

飞机 fēijī · aircraft

班机 bānjī · airliner

机头
jītóu
nose

驾驶舱
jiàshǐcāng
cockpit

引擎
yǐnqíng
engine

机身
jīshēn
fuselage

机翼
jīyì
wing

尾翼
wěiyì
tail

方向舵
fāngxiàngduò
rudder

舱门
cāngmén
exit

头部机轮
tóubùjīlún
nosewheel

起落架
qǐluòjià
landing gear

副翼
fùyì
aileron

垂直尾翼
chuízhíwěiyì
fin

水平尾翼
shuǐpíngwěiyì
tailplane

机舱 jīcāng · cabin

紧急出口
jǐnjí chūkǒu
emergency exit

空乘人员
kōngchéng rényuán
flight attendant

头顶锁柜
tóudǐng suǒguì
overhead locker

通风口
tōngfēngkǒu
air vent

窗户
chuānghu
window

阅读灯
yuèdúdēng
reading light

座位
zuòwèi
seat

排
pái
row

搁板
gēbǎn
tray-table

扶手
fúshǒu
armrest

走廊
zǒuláng
aisle

椅背
yǐbèi
seat back

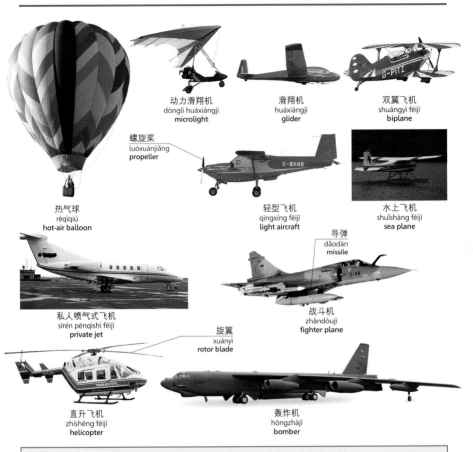

动力滑翔机
dònglì huáxiángjī
microlight

滑翔机
huáxiángjī
glider

双翼飞机
shuāngyì fēijī
biplane

螺旋桨
luóxuánjiǎng
propeller

G-BNHB

热气球
rèqìqiú
hot-air balloon

轻型飞机
qīngxíng fēijī
light aircraft

水上飞机
shuǐshàng fēijī
sea plane

导弹
dǎodàn
missile

私人喷气式飞机
sīrén pēnqìshì fēijī
private jet

战斗机
zhàndòujī
fighter plane

旋翼
xuányì
rotor blade

直升飞机
zhíshēng fēijī
helicopter

轰炸机
hōngzhàjī
bomber

词汇 cíhuì · vocabulary

飞行员 fēixíngyuán **pilot**	起飞 qǐfēi **take off (v)**	着陆 zhuólù **land (v)**	经济舱 jīngjìcāng **economy class**	手提行李 shǒutíxíngli **hand luggage**
副驾驶员 fùjiàshǐyuán **co-pilot**	飞行 fēixíng **fly (v)**	高度 gāodù **altitude**	商务舱 shāngwùcāng **business class**	安全带 ānquándài **seat belt**

机场 jīchǎng · airport

停机坪
tíngjīpíng
apron

行李拖车
xínglituōchē
baggage trailer

候机楼
hòujīlóu
terminal

服务车
fúwùchē
service vehicle

登机通道
dēngjītōngdào
jetway

班机 bānjī I airliner

词汇 cíhuì · vocabulary

跑道 pǎodào **runway**	航班号 hángbānhào **flight number**	行李传送带 xíngli chuánsòngdài **carousel**	假日 jiàrì **holiday**
国际航线 guójì hángxiàn **international flight**	入境检查 rùjìngjiǎnchá **immigration**	安全 ānquán **security**	办理登机手续 bànlǐ dēngjī shǒuxù **check in (v)**
国内航线 guónèi hángxiàn **domestic flight**	海关 hǎiguān **customs**	X光行李检查机 Xguāng xíngli jiǎnchájī **x-ray machine**	控制塔 kòngzhìtǎ **control tower**
联运 liányùn **connection**	超重行李 chāozhòng xíngli **excess baggage**	假日指南 jiàrì zhǐnán **holiday brochure**	订机票 dìngjīpiào **book a flight (v)**

手提行李
shǒutí xíngli
hand luggage

(大件)行李
(dàjiàn) xíngli
luggage

行李推车
xíngli tuīchē
trolley

办理登机手续处
bànlǐ dēngjī shǒuxùchù
check-in desk

签证
qiānzhèng
visa

护照 hùzhào **I passport**

护照检查处
hùzhào jiǎncháchù
passport control

登机牌
dēngjīpái
boarding pass

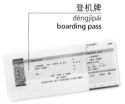

机票
jīpiào
ticket

登机门号
dēngjīménhào
gate number

出发
chūfā
departures

候机大厅
hòujīdàtīng
departure lounge

目的地
mùdìdì
destination

抵达
dǐdá
arrivals

信息屏
xìnxīpíng
information screen

免税商店
miǎnshuì shāngdiàn
duty-free shop

领取行李处
lǐngqǔ xínglichù
baggage reclaim

出租车站
chūzūchēzhàn
taxi rank

租车处
zūchēchù
car hire

船 chuán · ship

雷达
léidá
radar

无线电天线
wúxiàndiàn tiānxiàn
radio antenna

甲板
jiǎbǎn
deck

烟囱
yāncōng
funnel

后甲板
hòujiǎbǎn
quarterdeck

船首
chuánshǒu
prow

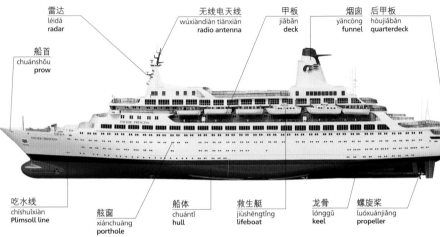

吃水线
chīshuǐxiàn
Plimsoll line

舷窗
xiánchuāng
porthole

船体
chuántǐ
hull

救生艇
jiùshēngtǐng
lifeboat

龙骨
lónggǔ
keel

螺旋桨
luóxuánjiǎng
propeller

远洋客轮 yuǎnyángkèlún I ocean liner

驾驶台
jiàshǐtái
bridge

轮机舱
lúnjīcāng
engine room

客舱
kècāng
cabin

船上厨房
chuánshàng chúfáng
galley

词汇 cíhuì · vocabulary

船坞
chuánwù
dock

卷扬机
juǎnyángjī
windlass

港口
gǎngkǒu
port

船长
chuánzhǎng
captain

舷梯
xiántī
gangway

快艇
kuàitǐng
speedboat

锚
máo
anchor

划桨船
huájiǎngchuán
rowing boat

岸边缆桩
ànbiānlǎnzhuāng
bollard

独木舟
dúmùzhōu
canoe

其他船型 qítāchuánxíng ● **other ships**

渺船
dùchuán
ferry

舷外马达
xiánwàimǎdá
outboard motor

充气式橡皮艇
chōngqìshì xiàngpítǐng
inflatable dinghy

水翼艇
shuǐyìtǐng
hydrofoil

游艇
yóutǐng
yacht

双体船
shuāngtǐchuán
catamaran

拖船
tuōchuán
tug boat

气垫船
qìdiànchuán
hovercraft

帆缆
fānlǎn
rigging

货舱
huòcāng
hold

集装箱船
jízhuāngxiāng chuán
container ship

帆船
fānchuán
sailing boat

货船
huòchuán
freighter

油轮
yóulún
oil tanker

航空母舰
hángkōng mǔjiàn
aircraft carrier

战舰
zhànjiàn
battleship

指挥塔
zhǐhuītǎ
conning tower

潜水艇
qiánshuǐtǐng
submarine

港口 gǎngkǒu · **port**

仓库
cāngkù
warehouse

起重机
qǐzhòngjī
crane

叉车
chāchē
fork-lift truck

出入港通道
chūrùgǎng tōngdào
access road

海关
hǎiguān
customs house

船坞
chuánwù
dock

集装箱
jízhuāngxiāng
container

码头
mǎtóu
quay

货物
huòwù
cargo

渡船码头
dùchuán mǎtóu
ferry terminal

渡船
dùchuán
ferry

售票处
shòupiàochù
ticket office

乘客
chéngkè
passenger

集装箱港口 jízhuāngxiāng gǎngkǒu | **container port**

客运码头 kèyùn mǎtóu | **passenger port**

渔网
yúwǎng
net

渔船
yúchuán
fishing boat

缆绳
lǎnshéng
mooring

小船停靠区 xiǎochuántíngkàoqū | marina

渔港 yúgǎng | fishing port

港口 gǎngkǒu | harbour

栈桥 zhànqiáo | pier

防波堤
fángbōdī
jetty

船厂
chuánchǎng
shipyard

塔灯
tǎdēng
lamp

灯塔
dēngtǎ
lighthouse

浮标
fúbiāo
buoy

词汇 cíhuì • vocabulary

海岸警卫队
hǎi'àn jǐngwèiduì
coastguard

港务局长
gǎngwù júzhǎng
harbour master

抛锚
pāomáo
drop anchor (v)

干船坞
gānchuánwù
dry dock

停泊
tíngbó
moor (v)

进入船坞
jìnrùchuánwù
dock (v)

上船
shàngchuán
board (v)

离船登岸
líchuándēngàn
disembark (v)

起航
qǐháng
set sail (v)

体育运动 tǐyùyùndòng
sports

美式橄榄球 měishì gǎnlǎnqiú · American football

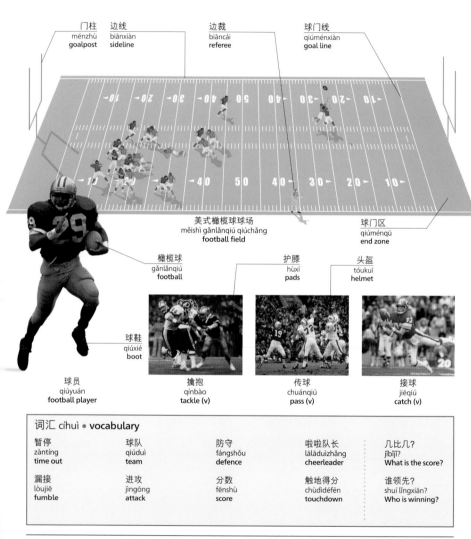

门柱
ménzhù
goalpost

边线
biānxiàn
sideline

边裁
biāncái
referee

球门线
qiúménxiàn
goal line

美式橄榄球球场
měishì gǎnlǎnqiú qiúchǎng
football field

球门区
qiúménqū
end zone

橄榄球
gǎnlǎnqiú
football

护膝
hùxī
pads

头盔
tóukuī
helmet

球鞋
qiúxié
boot

球员
qiúyuán
football player

擒抱
qínbào
tackle (v)

传球
chuánqiú
pass (v)

接球
jiēqiú
catch (v)

词汇 cíhuì · vocabulary

暂停
zàntíng
time out

球队
qiúduì
team

防守
fángshǒu
defence

啦啦队长
lālāduìzhǎng
cheerleader

几比几?
jǐbǐjǐ?
What is the score?

漏接
lòujiē
fumble

进攻
jìngōng
attack

分数
fēnshù
score

触地得分
chùdìdéfēn
touchdown

谁领先?
shuí lǐngxiān?
Who is winning?

英式橄榄球 yīngshì gǎnlǎnqiú • rugby

球门
qiúmén
goal

得分区
défēnqū
in-goal area

边线
biānxiàn
touch line

旗
qí
flag

死球线
sǐqiúxiàn
dead ball line

英式橄榄球球场 yīngshì gǎnlǎnqiú qiúchǎng | rugby pitch

球
qiú
ball

抛球
pāoqiú
throw (v)

(英式)橄榄球球衣
(yīngshì) gǎnlǎnqiú qiúyī
rugby strip

踢球
tīqiú
kick (v)

传球
chuánqiú
pass (v)

擒抱
qínbào
tackle (v)

持球触地得分
chíqiú chùdìdéfēn
try

球员
qiúyuán
player

密集争球 mìjí zhēngqiú | ruck

并列争球 bìngliè zhēngqiú | scrum

足球 zúqiú · soccer

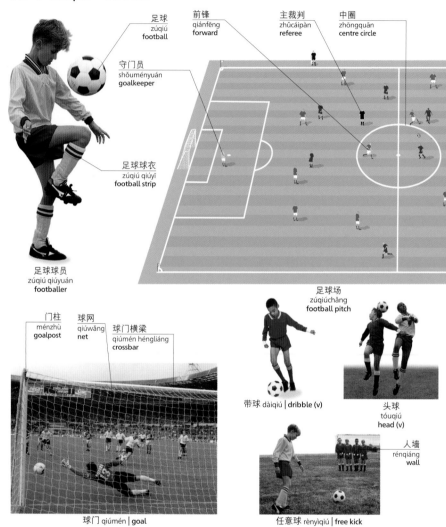

足球
zúqiú
football

前锋
qiánfēng
forward

主裁判
zhǔcáipàn
referee

中圈
zhōngquān
centre circle

守门员
shǒuményuán
goalkeeper

足球球衣
zúqiú qiúyī
football strip

足球球员
zúqiú qiúyuán
footballer

足球场
zúqiúchǎng
football pitch

门柱
ménzhù
goalpost

球网
qiúwǎng
net

球门横梁
qiúmén héngliáng
crossbar

带球 dàiqiú | dribble (v)

头球
tóuqiú
head (v)

人墙
rénqiáng
wall

球门 qiúmén | goal

任意球 rènyìqiú | free kick

罚球区
fáqiúqū
penalty area

球门线
qiúmén xiàn
goal line

球门区
qiúmén qū
goal area

球门
qiúmén
goal

防守队员
fángshǒuduìyuán
defender

边裁
biāncái
linesman

角旗
jiǎoqí
corner flag

掷界外球 zhìjièwàiqiú
throw-in

踢球 tīqiú
kick (v)

球鞋
qiúxié
boot

传球
chuánqiú
pass (v)

射门
shèmén
shoot (v)

救球
jiùqiú
save (v)

铲球
chǎnqiú
tackle (v)

词汇 cíhuì • vocabulary

体育场 tǐyùchǎng stadium	犯规 fànguī foul	黄牌 huángpái yellow card	联赛 liánsài league	加时 jiāshí extra time
进球得分 jìnqiúdéfēn score a goal (v)	角球 jiǎoqiú corner	越位 yuèwèi offside	平局 píngjú draw	替补队员 tìbǔduìyuán substitute
罚点球 fádiǎnqiú penalty	红牌 hóngpái red card	罚出场外 fáchūchǎngwài send off	半场 bànchǎng half time	换人 huànrén substitution

曲棍类运动 qūgùnlèi yùndòng • hockey

冰球 bīngqiú • ice hockey

球门线
qiúmén xiàn
goal line

进攻区
jìngōngqū
attack zone

中场
zhōngchǎng
neutral zone

防守区
fángshǒuqū
defending zone

守门员
shǒuményuán
goalkeeper

球门
qiúmén
goal

争球圈
zhēngqiúquān
face-off circle

中圈
zhōngquān
centre circle

手套
shǒutào
glove

护肩
hùjiān
pad

冰球场
bīngqiú chǎng
ice hockey rink

球杆
qiúgān
stick

冰鞋
bīngxié
ice skate

曲棍球 qūgùnqiú • field hockey

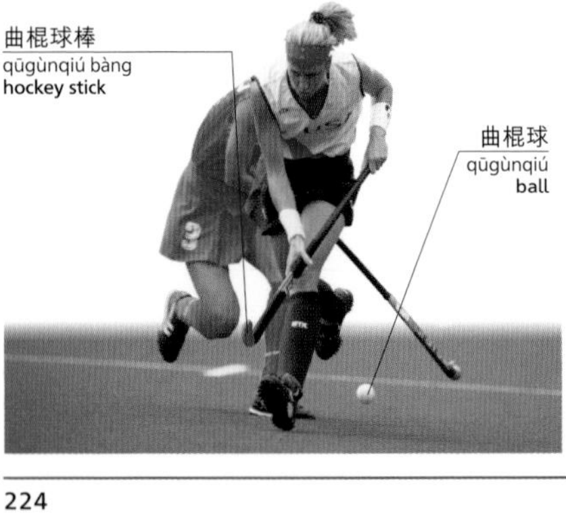

曲棍球棒
qūgùnqiú bàng
hockey stick

曲棍球
qūgùnqiú
ball

冰球
bīngqiú
puck

冰球球员 bīngqiú qiúyuán
ice hockey player

滑行
huáxíng
skate (v)

击球
jīqiú
hit (v)

板球 bǎnqiú • cricket

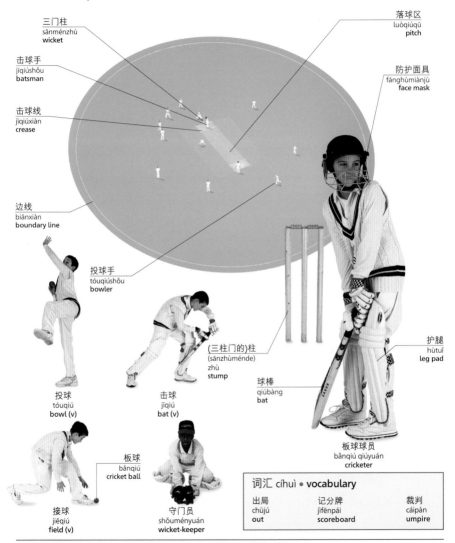

三门柱
sānménzhù
wicket

击球手
jīqiúshǒu
batsman

击球线
jīqiúxiàn
crease

边线
biānxiàn
boundary line

落球区
luòqiúqū
pitch

防护面具
fánghùmiànjù
face mask

投球手
tóuqiúshǒu
bowler

(三柱门的)柱
(sānzhùménde)
zhù
stump

护腿
hùtuǐ
leg pad

球棒
qiúbàng
bat

投球
tóuqiú
bowl (v)

击球
jīqiú
bat (v)

板球
bǎnqiú
cricket ball

接球
jiēqiú
field (v)

守门员
shǒuményuán
wicket-keeper

板球球员
bǎnqiú qiúyuán
cricketer

词汇 cíhuì • vocabulary

出局	记分牌	裁判
chūjú	jìfēnpái	cáipàn
out	**scoreboard**	**umpire**

篮球 lánqiú • basketball

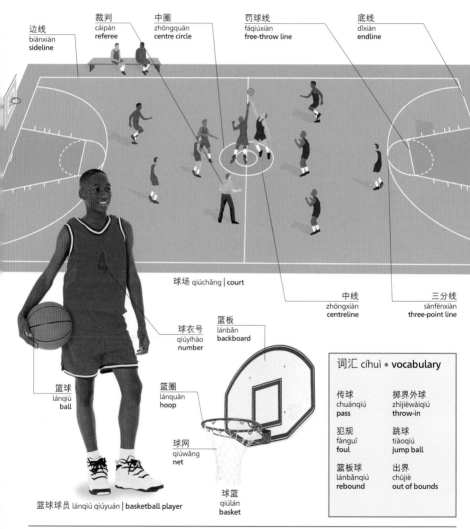

边线
biānxiàn
sideline

裁判
cáipàn
referee

中圈
zhōngquān
centre circle

罚球线
fáqiúxiàn
free-throw line

底线
dǐxiàn
endline

球场 qiúchǎng | court

中线
zhōngxiàn
centreline

三分线
sānfēnxiàn
three-point line

球衣号
qiúyīhào
number

篮板
lánbǎn
backboard

篮球
lánqiú
ball

篮圈
lánquān
hoop

球网
qiúwǎng
net

球篮
qiúlán
basket

篮球球员 lánqiú qiúyuán | basketball player

词汇 cíhuì • vocabulary

传球
chuánqiú
pass

掷界外球
zhìjièwàiqiú
throw-in

犯规
fànguī
foul

跳球
tiàoqiú
jump ball

篮板球
lánbǎnqiú
rebound

出界
chūjiè
out of bounds

动作 dòngzuò · actions

掷球
zhìqiú
throw (v)

接球
jiēqiú
catch (v)

投篮
tóulán
shoot (v)

跳投
tiàotóu
jump (v)

盯人
dīngrén
mark (v)

阻挡
zǔdǎng
block (v)

运球
yùnqiú
bounce (v)

灌篮
guànlán
dunk (v)

排球 páiqiú · volleyball

拦网
lánwǎng
block (v)

球网
qiúwǎng
net

垫球
diànqiú
dig (v)

裁判
cáipàn
referee

护膝
hùxī
knee support

球场 qiúchǎng | court

棒球 bàngqiú · baseball

球场 qiúchǎng · field

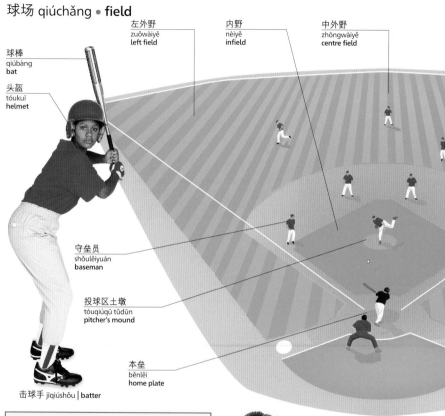

左外野
zuǒwàiyě
left field

内野
nèiyě
infield

中外野
zhōngwàiyě
centre field

球棒
qiúbàng
bat

头盔
tóukuī
helmet

守垒员
shǒulěiyuán
baseman

投球区土墩
tóuqiúqū tǔdūn
pitcher's mound

本垒
běnlěi
home plate

击球手 jīqiúshǒu | batter

词汇 cíhuì · vocabulary

击球局 jīqiújú inning	安全上垒 ānquánshànglěi safe	界外球 jièwàiqiú foul ball
得分 défēn run	出局 chūjú out	好球 hǎoqiú strike

棒球
bàngqiú
ball

棒球手套 bàngqiú shǒutào
mitt

防护面具 fánghùmiànjù
mask

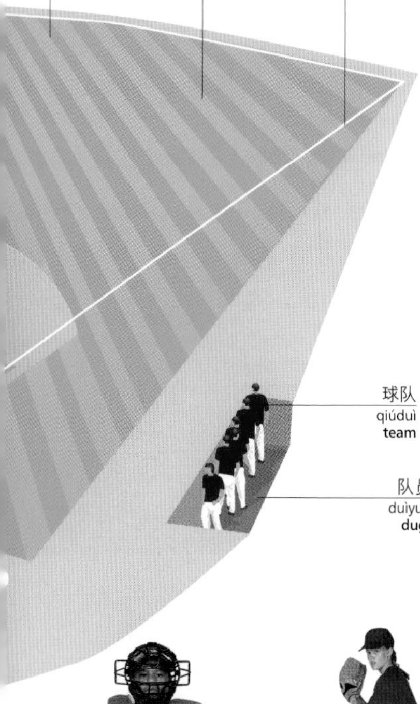
外野
wàiyě
outfield
右外野
yòuwàiyě
right field
边线
biānxiàn
foul line
球队
qiúduì
team
队员席
duìyuánxí
dugout

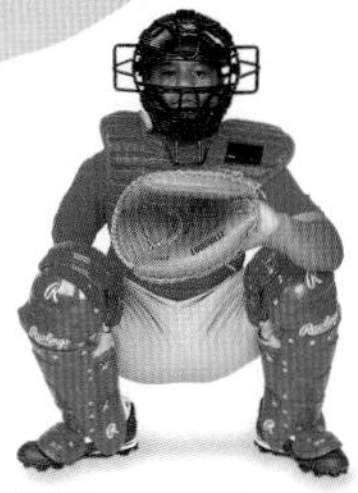

接球手 jiēqiúshǒu | catcher

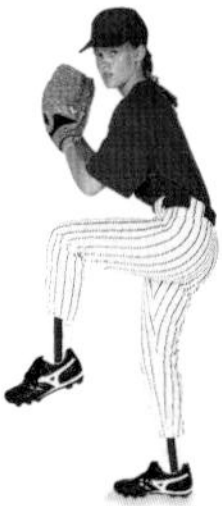

投球手 tóuqiúshǒu | pitcher

动作 dòngzuò • actions

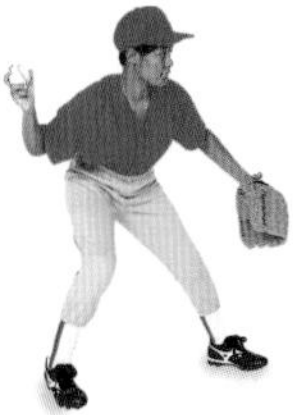

投球 tóuqiú | throw (v)

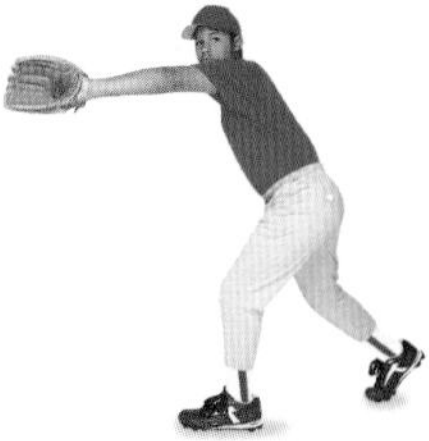

接球 jiēqiú | catch (v)

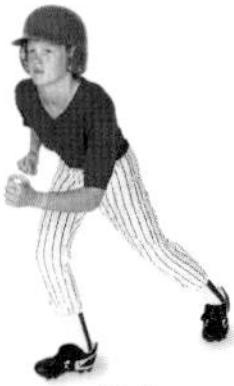

跑垒
pǎolěi
run (v)

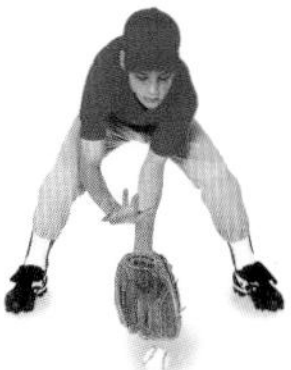

守球 shǒuqiú | field (v)

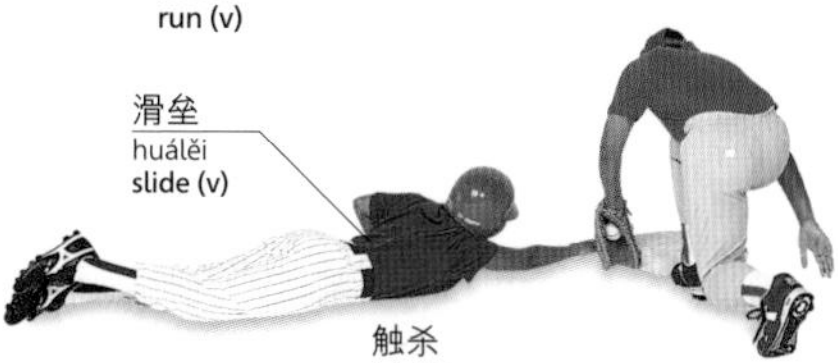
滑垒
huálěi
slide (v)
触杀
chùshā
tag (v)

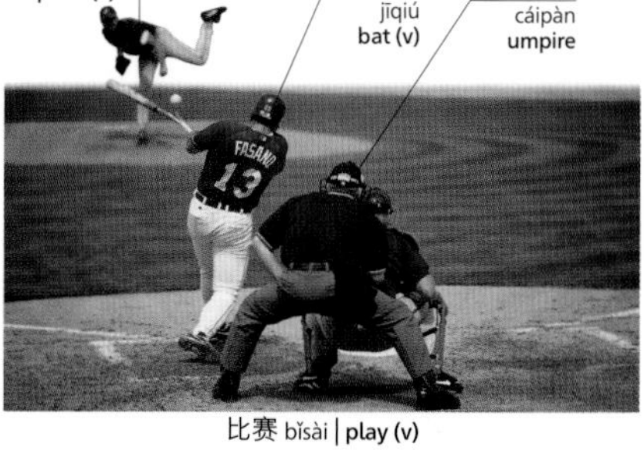
投球
tóuqiú
pitch (v)
击球
jīqiú
bat (v)
裁判
cáipàn
umpire
FASANO
13

比赛 bǐsài | play (v)

网球 wǎngqiú • tennis

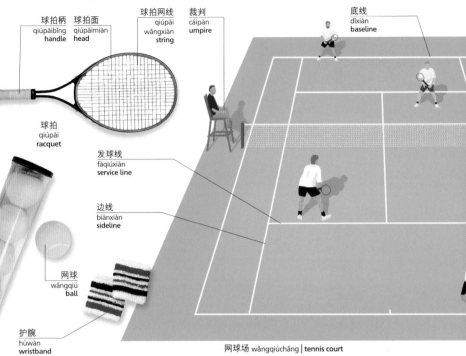

球拍柄
qiúpāibǐng
handle

球拍面
qiúpāimiàn
head

球拍网线
qiúpāi
wǎngxiàn
string

裁判
cáipàn
umpire

底线
dǐxiàn
baseline

球拍
qiúpāi
racquet

发球线
fāqiúxiàn
service line

边线
biānxiàn
sideline

网球
wǎngqiú
ball

护腕
hùwàn
wristband

网球场 wǎngqiúchǎng | tennis court

词汇 cíhuì • vocabulary

单打 dāndǎ singles	盘, 局 pán, jú set	零分 língfēn love	发球失误 fāqiúshīwù fault	削球 xiāoqiú slice	边裁 biāncái linesman
双打 shuāngdǎ doubles	比赛 bǐsài match	平分 píngfēn deuce	发球得分 fāqiúdéfēn ace	连续对打 liánxùduìdǎ rally	锦标赛 jǐnbiāosài championship
比赛 bǐsài game	抢七局 qiǎngqījú tiebreak	发球方占先 fāqiúfāng zhànxiān advantage	近网短球 jìnwǎng duǎnqiú dropshot	触网! chùwǎng! let!	(球在空中)旋转 (qiúzàikōngzhōng) xuánzhuǎn spin

击球动作 jīqiúdòngzuò · strokes

球网
qiúwǎng
net

球童
qiútóng
ball boy

发球
fāqiú
serve (v)

扣球
kòuqiú
smash

网球鞋
wǎngqiúxié
tennis shoes

网球手 wǎngqiúshǒu | player

发球
fāqiú
serve

拦击球
lánjīqiú
volley

回球
huíqiú
return

吊高球
diàogāoqiú
lob

正手
zhèngshǒu
forehand

反手
fǎnshǒu
backhand

拍类运动 pāilèi yùndòng · racquet games

羽毛球
yǔmáoqiú
shuttlecock

乒乓球拍
pīngpāngqiúpāi
bat

羽毛球(运动)
yǔmáoqiú (yùndòng)
badminton

乒乓球
pīngpāngqiú
table tennis

壁球
bìqiú
squash

短拍壁球
duǎnpāibìqiú
racquetball

高尔夫球 gāo'ěrfūqiú · golf

球洞
qiúdòng
hole

发球区
fāqiúqū
teeing ground

果岭
guǒlǐng
green

沙坑
shākēng
bunker

旗
qí
flag

挥杆
huīgān
swing (v)

球道
qiúdào
fairway

长草区
chángcǎoqū
rough

水障碍
shuǐzhàng'ài
water hazard

高尔夫球场
gāo'ěrfū qiúchǎng
golf course

短途小车
duǎntú xiǎochē
buggy

站位
zhànwèi
stance

高尔夫球员 gāo'ěrfū qiúyuán | golfer

会所 huìsuǒ | clubhouse

球具 qiújù • equipment

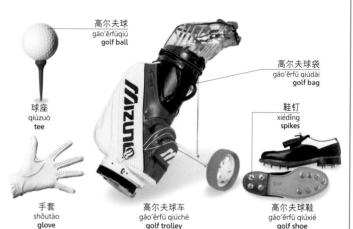

高尔夫球
gāo'ěrfūqiú
golf ball

高尔夫球袋
gāo'ěrfū qiúdài
golf bag

鞋钉
xiédīng
spikes

球座
qiúzuò
tee

手套
shǒutào
glove

高尔夫球车
gāo'ěrfū qiúchē
golf trolley

高尔夫球鞋
gāo'ěrfū qiúxié
golf shoe

高尔夫球杆 gāo'ěrfū qiúgān • golf clubs

木杆
mùgān
wood

推杆
tuīgān
putter

铁杆
tiěgān
iron

挖起杆
wāqǐgān
wedge

动作 dòngzuò • actions

开球
kāiqiú
tee-off (v)

远打
yuǎndǎ
drive (v)

轻击
qīngjī
putt (v)

切击
qiējī
chip (v)

词汇 cíhuì • vocabulary

一杆入洞 yīgān rùdòng hole in one	标准杆数 biāozhǔn gǎnshù par	差点 chàdiǎn handicap	球童 qiútóng caddy	向后挥杆 xiàng hòu huīgān backswing	击球 jīqiú stroke
低于标准杆数 dīyú biāozhǔn gǎnshù under par	高于标准杆数 gāoyú biāozhǔn gǎnshù over par	巡回赛 xúnhuísài tournament	观众 guānzhòng spectators	练习挥杆 liànxí huīgān practice swing	打球线 dǎqiúxiàn line of play

---

田径运动 tiánjìng yùndòng • athletics

分道
fēndào
lane

跑道
pǎodào
track

终点线
zhōngdiǎn xiàn
finishing line

起跑线
qǐpǎo xiàn
starting line

运动场
yùndòngchǎng
field

田径选手
tiánjìng
xuǎnshǒu
athlete

起跑器
qǐpǎoqì
starting
blocks

短跑选手
duǎnpǎo xuǎnshǒu
sprinter

铁饼
tiěbǐng
discus

铅球
qiānqiú
shotput

标枪
biāoqiāng
javelin

词汇 cíhuì • vocabulary

赛跑 sàipǎo race	纪录 jìlù record	终点摄影记录 zhōngdiǎn shèyǐng jìlù photo finish	撑杆跳 chēnggāntiào pole vault
时间 shíjiān time	打破纪录 dǎpò jìlù break a record (v)	马拉松 mǎlāsōng marathon	个人最好成绩 gèrén zuìhǎo chéngjì personal best

秒表
miǎobiǎo
stopwatch

接力棒
jiēlìbàng
baton

横杆
hénggān
crossbar

接力
jiēlì
relay race

跳高
tiàogāo
high jump

跳远
tiàoyuǎn
long jump

跨栏
kuàlán
hurdles

体操 tǐcāo • gymnastics

跳板
tiàobǎn
springboard

跳马
tiàomǎ
horse

空翻
kōngfān
somersault

体操选手
tǐcāo xuǎnshǒu
gymnast

平衡木 pínghéngmù | beam

丝带
sīdài
ribbon

垫子
diànzi
mat

跳马(项目)
tiàomǎ (xiàngmù)
vault

自由体操
zìyóutǐcāo
floor exercises

侧手翻
cèshǒufān
cartwheel

艺术体操
yìshù tǐcāo
rhythmic gymnastics

词汇 cíhuì • vocabulary

单杠 dāngàng **horizontal bar**	鞍马 ānmǎ **pommel horse**	吊环 diàohuán **rings**	奖牌 jiǎngpái **medals**	银牌 yínpái **silver**
双杠 shuānggàng **parallel bars**	高低杠 gāodīgàng **asymmetric bars**	领奖台 lǐngjiǎngtái **podium**	金牌 jīnpái **gold**	铜牌 tóngpái **bronze**

格斗运动 gédòu yùndòng • combat sports

对手 duìshǒu **opponent**

护盔 hùkuī **guard**

手套 shǒutào **glove**

腰带 yāodài **belt**

跆拳道 táiquándào | **tae-kwon-do**

空手道 kōngshǒudào | **karate**

柔道 róudào | **judo**

防护面具 fánghùmiànjù **mask**

竹剑 zhújiàn **sword**

合气道 héqìdào | **aikido**

剑道 jiàndào | **kendo**

中国武术 zhōngguówǔshù **kung fu**

泰拳 tàiquán | **kickboxing**

摔跤 shuāijiāo | **wrestling**

拳击 quánjī | **boxing**

动作 dòngzuò • actions

摔倒 shuāidǎo | fall

抓握 zhuāwò | hold

摔 shuāi | throw

压倒 yādǎo | pin

侧踢 cètī | kick

出拳 chūquán | punch

击打 jīdǎ | strike

跳踢 tiàotī | jump

挡 dǎng | block

劈 pī | chop

词汇 cíhuì • vocabulary

拳击台 quánjī tái **boxing ring**	回合 huíhé **round**	拳头 quántóu **fist**	黑带 hēidài **black belt**	卡波卫勒舞 kǎbōwèilèwǔ **capoeira**
拳击手套 quánjī shǒutào **boxing gloves**	拳击比赛 quánjī bǐsài **bout**	击倒 (对手) jīdǎo (duìshǒu) **knock out**	自卫 zìwèi **self-defence**	相扑 xiāngpū **sumo wrestling**
护齿 hùchǐ **mouth guard**	拳击练习 quánjī liànxí **sparring**	沙袋 shādài **punchbag**	武术 wǔshù **martial arts**	太极拳 tàijíquán **Tai Chi**

游泳 yóuyǒng • swimming
泳具 yǒngjù • equipment

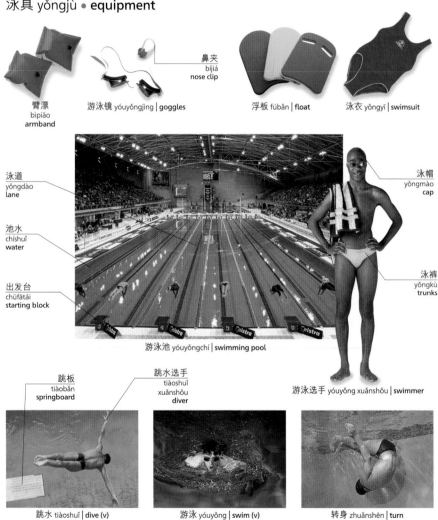

臂漂
bìpiāo
armband

游泳镜 yóuyǒngjìng | goggles

鼻夹
bíjiá
nose clip

浮板 fúbǎn | float

泳衣 yǒngyī | swimsuit

泳道
yǒngdào
lane

池水
chíshuǐ
water

出发台
chūfātái
starting block

泳帽
yǒngmào
cap

泳裤
yǒngkù
trunks

游泳池 yóuyǒngchí | swimming pool

游泳选手 yóuyǒng xuǎnshǒu | swimmer

跳板
tiàobǎn
springboard

跳水选手
tiàoshuǐ
xuǎnshǒu
diver

跳水 tiàoshuǐ | dive (v)

游泳 yóuyǒng | swim (v)

转身 zhuǎnshēn | turn

泳姿 yǒngzī · styles

自由泳 zìyóuyǒng | front crawl

蛙泳 wāyǒng | breaststroke

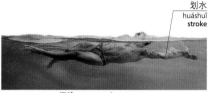

划水
huáshuǐ
stroke

仰泳 yǎngyǒng | backstroke

打水
dǎshuǐ
kick

蝶泳 diéyǒng | butterfly

水肺潜水 shuǐfèi qiánshuǐ · scuba diving

氧气瓶
yǎngqìpíng
air cylinder

潜水服
qiánshuǐfú
wetsuit

潜水面罩
qiánshuǐ miànzhào
mask

脚蹼
jiǎopǔ
flipper

呼吸调节器
hūxītiáojié qì
regulator

负重腰带
fùzhòng yāodài
weight belt

水下呼吸管
shuǐxià hūxīguǎn
snorkel

词汇 cíhuì · vocabulary

跳水 tiàoshuǐ dive	踩水 cǎishuǐ tread water (v)	锁柜 suǒguì lockers	水球 shuǐqiú water polo	浅水区 qiǎnshuǐqū shallow end	抽筋 chōujīn cramp
高台跳水 gāotái tiàoshuǐ high dive	出发跳水 chūfā tiàoshuǐ racing dive	救生员 jiùshēngyuán lifeguard	深水区 shēnshuǐqū deep end	花样游泳 huāyàng yóuyǒng synchronized swimming	溺水 nìshuǐ drown (v)

帆船运动 fānchuán yùndòng • **sailing**

指南针
zhǐnánzhēn
compass

锚
máo
anchor

前桅帆
qiánwéifān
headsail

系索耳
xìsuǒ'ěr
cleat

侧舷
cèxián
sidedeck

船头
chuántóu
bow

舵柄
duòbǐng
tiller

船体
chuántǐ
hull

桅杆
wéigān
mast

帆缆
fānlǎn
rigging

主帆
zhǔfān
mainsail

帆杆
fāngān
boom

船尾
chuánwěi
stern

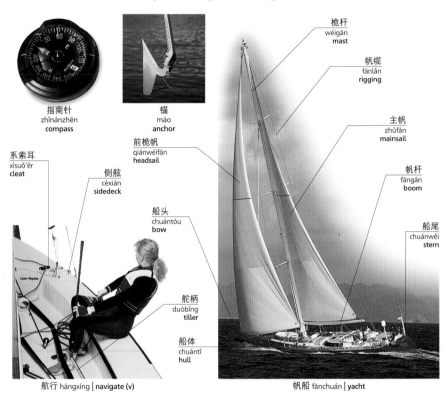

航行 hángxíng | navigate (v)

帆船 fānchuán | yacht

救生器具 jiùshēngqìjù • **safety**

照明弹
zhàomíngdàn
flare

救生圈
jiùshēngquān
lifebuoy

救生衣
jiùshēngyī
life jacket

救生筏
jiùshēngfá
life raft

水上运动 shuǐshàng yùndòng · watersports

桨手
jiǎngshǒu
rower

桨
jiǎng
oar

皮筏
pífá
kayak

双叶桨
shuāngyèjiǎng
paddle

划船 huáchuán | row (v)

划独木舟
huádúmùzhōu
kayaking

帆
fān
sail

冲浪板
chōnglàngbǎn
surfboard

滑水橇
huáshuǐqiāo
ski

帆板运动员
fānbǎn
yùndòngyuán
windsurfer

冲浪
chōnglàng
surfing

滑水
huáshuǐ
waterskiing

快艇
kuàitǐng
speed boating

帆板
fānbǎn
board

套脚带
tàojiǎodài
footstrap

皮划艇
píhuátǐng
rafting

水上摩托
shuǐshàng mótuō
jet skiing

帆板运动 fānbǎn yùndòng | windsurfing

词汇 cíhuì · vocabulary

滑水者 huáshuǐzhě waterskier	艇员 tǐngyuán crew	风 fēng wind	浪花 lànghuā surf	帆脚索 fānjiǎosuǒ sheet	稳向板 wěnxiàngbǎn centreboard
冲浪运动员 chōnglàng yùndòngyuán surfer	抢风航行 qiǎngfēng hángxíng tack (v)	波浪 bōlàng wave	激流 jīliú rapids	舵 duò rudder	(船)倾覆 (chuán) qīngfù capsize (v)

马上运动 mǎshàng yùndòng • horse riding

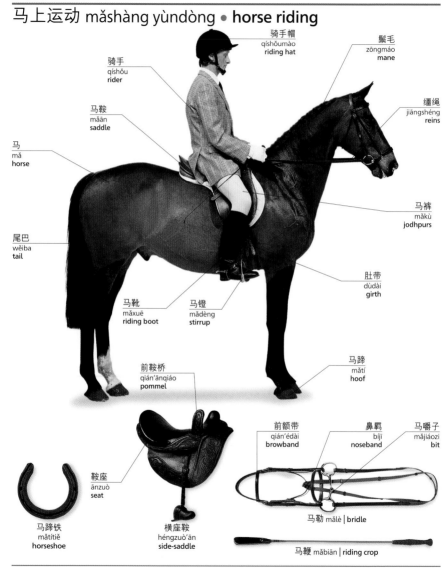

骑手帽
qíshǒumào
riding hat

鬃毛
zōngmáo
mane

骑手
qíshǒu
rider

缰绳
jiāngshéng
reins

马鞍
mǎān
saddle

马
mǎ
horse

马裤
mǎkù
jodhpurs

尾巴
wěiba
tail

肚带
dùdài
girth

马靴
mǎxuē
riding boot

马镫
mǎdèng
stirrup

马蹄
mǎtí
hoof

前鞍桥
qián'ānqiáo
pommel

前额带
qián'édài
browband

鼻羁
bíjī
noseband

马嚼子
mǎjiáozi
bit

鞍座
ānzuò
seat

马蹄铁
mǎtítiě
horseshoe

横座鞍
héngzuò'ān
side-saddle

马勒 mǎlè | **bridle**

马鞭 mǎbiān | **riding crop**

赛事 sàishì • events

赛马
sàimǎ
racehorse

障碍
zhàng'ài
fence

赛马(比赛)
sàimǎ (bǐsài)
horse race

障碍赛
zhàng'àisài
steeplechase

轻驾车赛
qīngjiàchēsài
harness race

牛仔竞技表演
niúzǎijìngjì biǎoyǎn
rodeo

越障碍赛
yuèzhàng'àisài
showjumping

双套马车赛
shuāngtào mǎchēsài
carriage race

长途旅行 chángtú lǚxíng | **trekking**　　花式骑术 huāshìqíshù | **dressage**　　马球 mǎqiú | **polo**

词汇 cíhuì • vocabulary

慢步 mànbù walk	慢跑 mànpǎo canter	跳跃 tiàoyuè jump	笼头 lóngtou halter	围场 wéichǎng paddock	无障碍赛马 wúzhàng'àisàimǎ flat race
小跑 xiǎopǎo trot	疾驰 jíchí gallop	马夫 mǎfū groom	马厩 mǎjiù stable	竞技场 jìngjìchǎng arena	赛马场 sàimǎchǎng racecourse

钓鱼 diàoyú ● **fishing**

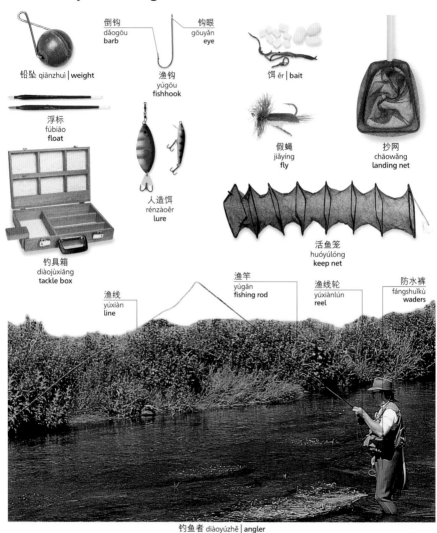

铅坠 qiānzhuì | **weight**

倒钩
dǎogōu
barb

钩眼
gōuyǎn
eye

渔钩
yúgōu
fishhook

饵 ěr | **bait**

假蝇
jiǎyíng
fly

抄网
chāowǎng
landing net

浮标
fúbiāo
float

人造饵
rénzàoěr
lure

活鱼笼
huóyúlóng
keep net

钓具箱
diàojùxiāng
tackle box

渔线
yúxiàn
line

渔竿
yúgān
fishing rod

渔线轮
yúxiànlún
reel

防水裤
fángshuǐkù
waders

钓鱼者 diàoyúzhě | **angler**

垂钓种类 chuídiào zhǒnglèi · types of fishing

淡水垂钓
dànshuǐ chuídiào
freshwater fishing

假蝇垂钓
jiǎyíng chuídiào
fly fishing

休闲垂钓
xiūxián chuídiào
sport fishing

深海垂钓
shēnhǎi chuídiào
deep sea fishing

激浪投钓
jīlàng tóudiào
surfcasting

活动 huódòng · activities

撒网
sāwǎng
cast (v)

捕捉
bǔzhuō
catch (v)

收线
shōuxiàn
reel in (v)

网捕
wǎngbǔ
net (v)

放生
fàngshēng
release (v)

词汇 cíhuì · vocabulary

装饵 zhuāng'ěr **bait (v)**	钓具 diàojù **tackle**	雨衣 yǔyī **waterproofs**	钓鱼许可证 diàoyú xǔkězhèng **fishing permit**	渔篓 yúlǒu **creel**
咬钩 yǎogōu **bite (v)**	线轴 xiànzhóu **spool**	杆 gān **pole**	海洋捕捞 hǎiyáng bǔlāo **marine fishing**	渔叉捕鱼 yúchābǔyú **spearfishing**

滑雪 huáxuě · **skiing**

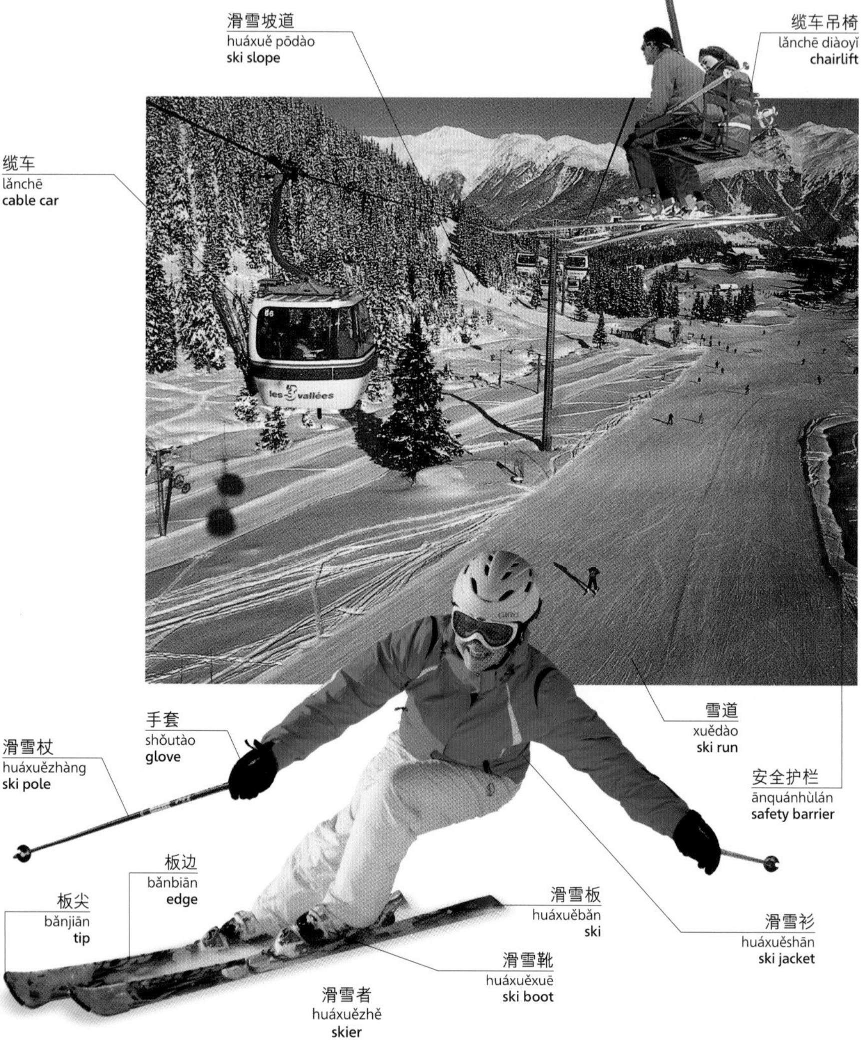

滑雪坡道
huáxuě pōdào
ski slope

缆车吊椅
lǎnchē diàoyǐ
chairlift

缆车
lǎnchē
cable car

滑雪杖
huáxuězhàng
ski pole

手套
shǒutào
glove

雪道
xuědào
ski run

安全护栏
ānquánhùlán
safety barrier

板边
bǎnbiān
edge

滑雪板
huáxuěbǎn
ski

滑雪衫
huáxuěshān
ski jacket

板尖
bǎnjiān
tip

滑雪靴
huáxuěxuē
ski boot

滑雪者
huáxuězhě
skier

项目 xiàngmù • events

高山速降
gāoshān sùjiàng
downhill skiing

旗门杆
qíméngān
gate

小回转
xiǎohuízhuǎn
slalom

跳台滑雪
tiàotái huáxuě
ski jump

越野滑雪
yuèyě huáxuě
cross-country skiing

冬季运动 dōngjì yùndòng • winter sports

攀冰
pānbīng
ice climbing

溜冰
liūbīng
ice-skating

花样滑冰
huāyàng huábīng
figure skating

滑雪镜
huáxuějìng
goggles

冰鞋
bīngxié
skate

单板滑雪
dānbǎn huáxuě
snowboarding

长橇滑雪
chángqiāo huáxuě
bobsleigh

小型橇
xiǎoxíngqiāo
luge

机动雪橇
jīdòng xuěqiāo
snowmobile

乘橇滑行
chéngqiāo huáxíng
sledding

词汇 cíhuì • vocabulary

高山滑雪
gāoshān huáxuě
alpine skiing

大回转
dàhuízhuǎn
giant slalom

雪道外
xuědàowài
off-piste

冰上溜石
bīngshàng liūshí
curling

狗拉雪橇
gǒulā xuěqiāo
dog sledding

速滑
sùhuá
speed skating

冬季两项
dōngjì liǎngxiàng
biathlon

雪崩
xuěbēng
avalanche

其他运动 qítāyùndòng · **other sports**

滑翔机
huáxiángjī
glider

悬挂式滑翔机
xuánguàshì
huáxiángjī
hang-glider

滑翔
huáxiáng
gliding

降落伞
jiàngluòsǎn
parachute

悬挂滑翔
xuánguà huáxiáng
hang-gliding

绳索
shéngsuǒ
rope

攀岩
pānyán
rock climbing

跳伞
tiàosǎn
parachuting

滑翔伞
huáxiángsǎn
paragliding

特技跳伞
tèjìtiàosǎn
skydiving

悬绳下降
xuánshéng xiàjiàng
abseiling

蹦极
bèngjí
bungee jumping

汽车拉力赛
qìchē lālìsài
rally driving

赛车手
sàichēshǒu
racing driver

赛车
sàichē
motor racing

摩托车越野赛
mótuōchē yuèyěsài
motorcross

摩托车赛
mótuōchēsài
motorbike racing

滑板
huábǎn
skateboard

滑板运动
huábǎn yùndòng
skateboarding

轮滑
lúnhuá
inline skating

球棒
qiúbàng
stick

长曲棍球
cháng qūgùnqiú
lacrosse

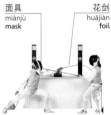
面具
miànjù
mask

花剑
huājiàn
foil

击剑
jījiàn
fencing

保龄球瓶
bǎolíngqiú píng
pin

弓
gōng
bow

箭
jiàn
arrow

箭袋
jiàndài
quiver

靶
bǎ
target

射箭
shèjiàn
archery

射击
shèjī
target shooting

保龄球
bǎolíngqiú
bowling ball

保龄球运动
bǎolíngqiú yùndòng
bowling

美式台球
měishìtáiqiú
pool

斯诺克台球
sīnuòkètáiqiú
snooker

健身 jiànshēn • fitness

健身车
jiànshēnchē
exercise bike

力量训练器
lìliàng xùnliànqì
free weights

横杠
hénggàng
bar

健身器械
jiànshēn qìxiè
gym machine

长椅
chángyǐ
bench

划船机
huáchuánjī
rowing machine

健身房
jiànshēnfáng
gym

跑步机
pǎobùjī
treadmill

交叉训练器
jiāochā xùnliànqì
cross trainer

私人教练
sīrén jiàoliàn
personal trainer

踏步机
tàbùjī
step machine

游泳池
yóuyǒngchí
swimming pool

桑拿浴
sāngnáyù
sauna

锻炼 duànliàn • exercises

伸展腿
shēnzhǎntuǐ
stretch

弓箭步压腿
gōngjiànbù yātuǐ
lunge

紧身衣
jǐnshēnyī
tights

俯卧撑
fǔwòchēng
press-up

哑铃
yǎlíng
dumbbell

蹲起
dūnqǐ
squat

仰卧起坐
yǎngwòqǐzuò
sit-up

二头肌训练
èrtóujī xùnliàn
bicep curl

蹬腿
dēngtuǐ
leg press

杠铃横杆
gànglíng
hénggān
weight bar

运动鞋
yùndòngxié
trainers

扩胸
kuòxiōng
chest press

重量训练
zhòngliàng xùnliàn
weight training

慢跑
mànpǎo
jogging

普拉提
pǔlātí
Pilates

词汇 cíhuì • vocabulary

训练 xùnliàn **train (v)**	原地跑 yuándìpǎo **jog on the spot (v)**	伸展 shēnzhǎn **extend (v)**	跳绳 tiàoshéng **skipping**	循环训练法 xúnhuán xùnliànfǎ **circuit training**
热身 rèshēn **warm up (v)**	弯曲(四肢) wānqū (sìzhī) **flex (v)**	引体向上 yǐntǐ xiàngshàng **pull up (v)**	搏击操 bójīcāo **boxercise**	

中文 zhōngwén • english

休闲 xiūxián
leisure

剧院 jùyuàn • theatre

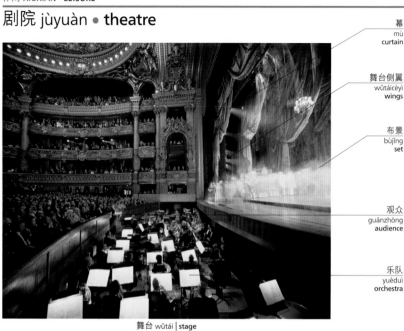

幕
mù
curtain

舞台侧翼
wǔtáicèyì
wings

布景
bùjǐng
set

观众
guānzhòng
audience

乐队
yuèduì
orchestra

舞台 wǔtái | stage

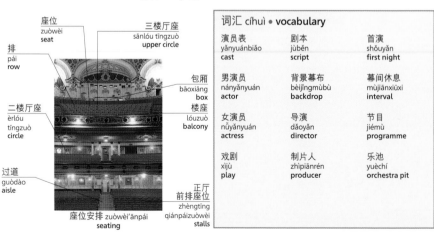

座位
zuòwèi
seat

三楼厅座
sānlóu tīngzuò
upper circle

排
pái
row

包厢
bāoxiāng
box

楼座
lóuzuò
balcony

二楼厅座
èrlóu
tīngzuò
circle

过道
guòdào
aisle

正厅
前排座位
zhèngtīng
qiánpáizuòwèi
stalls

座位安排 zuòwèi'ānpái
seating

词汇 cíhuì • vocabulary

演员表	剧本	首演
yǎnyuánbiǎo	jùběn	shǒuyǎn
cast	**script**	**first night**
男演员	背景幕布	幕间休息
nányǎnyuán	bèijǐngmùbù	mùjiānxiūxi
actor	**backdrop**	**interval**
女演员	导演	节目
nǚyǎnyuán	dǎoyǎn	jiémù
actress	**director**	**programme**
戏剧	制片人	乐池
xìjù	zhìpiānrén	yuèchí
play	**producer**	**orchestra pit**

音乐会 yīnyuèhuì | concert

音乐剧 yīnyuèjù | **musical**

戏装
xìzhuāng
costume

芭蕾舞 bālěiwǔ | ballet

词汇 cíhuì • vocabulary

引座员 yǐnzuòyuán usher	声带 shēngdài soundtrack	演出什么时候开始? yǎnchū shénme shíhou kāishǐ? **What time does it start?**
古典音乐 gǔdiǎn yīnyuè classical music	鼓掌喝彩 gǔzhǎnghècǎi applaud (v)	我想要两张今晚演出的票。 wǒ xiǎng yào liǎngzhāng jīnwǎn yǎnchūde piào. **I'd like two tickets for tonight's performance.**
乐谱 yuèpǔ musical score	再来一次 zàiláiyícì encore	

歌剧 gējù | opera

电影院 diànyǐngyuàn • cinema

爆米花
bàomǐhuā
popcorn

大厅
dàtīng
lobby

售票处
shòupiàochù
box office

海报
hǎibào
poster

电影放映厅
diànyǐng fàngyìngtīng
cinema hall

银幕
yínmù
screen

词汇 cíhuì • vocabulary

喜剧片 xǐjùpiàn comedy	爱情片 àiqíngpiàn romance
惊险片 jīngxiǎnpiàn thriller	科幻片 kēhuànpiàn science fiction film
恐怖片 kǒngbùpiàn horror film	冒险片 màoxiǎnpiàn adventure film
西部片 xībùpiàn western	动画片 dònghuàpiàn animated film

乐队 yuèduì • orchestra

弦乐器 xiányuèqì • strings

竖琴
shùqín
harp

指挥
zhǐhuī
conductor

低音提琴
dīyīntíqín
double bass

小提琴
xiǎotíqín
violin

指挥台
zhǐhuītái
podium

中提琴
zhōngtíqín
viola

大提琴
dàtíqín
cello

乐谱
yuèpǔ
score

高音谱号
gāoyīn pǔhào
treble clef

音符
yīnfú
note

五线谱
wǔxiànpǔ
staff

低音谱号
dīyīn pǔhào
bass clef

钢琴 gāngqín | piano

记谱法 jìpǔfǎ | notation

词汇 cíhuì • vocabulary

序曲 xùqǔ **overture**	奏鸣曲 zòumíngqǔ **sonata**	休止符 xiūzhǐfú **rest**	升号 shēnghào **sharp**	本位号 běnwèihào **natural**	音阶 yīnjiē **scale**
交响乐 jiāoxiǎngyuè **symphony**	乐器 yuèqì **instruments**	音高 yīngāo **pitch**	降号 jiànghào **flat**	小节线 xiǎojiéxiàn **bar**	指挥棒 zhǐhuībàng **baton**

木管乐器 mùguǎnyuèqì · **woodwind**

短笛
duǎndí
piccolo

长笛
chángdí
flute

双簧管
shuānghuángguǎn
oboe

英国管
yīngguóguǎn
cor anglais

单簧管
dānhuángguǎn
clarinet

低音单簧管
dīyīn dānhuángguǎn
bass clarinet

巴松管
bāsōngguǎn
bassoon

倍低音管
bèidīyīnguǎn
double bassoon

萨克斯管
sàkèsīguǎn
saxophone

打击乐器 dǎjīyuèqì · **percussion**

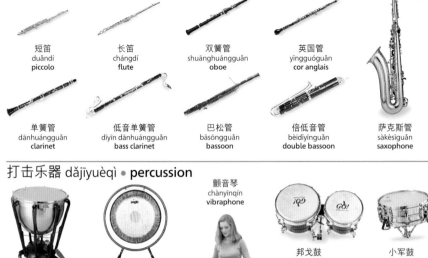

颤音琴
chànyīnqín
vibraphone

定音鼓
dìngyīngǔ
kettledrum

锣
luó
gong

邦戈鼓
bānggēgǔ
bongos

小军鼓
xiǎojūngǔ
snare drum

钹
bó
cymbals

铃鼓
línggǔ
tambourine

脚踏板
jiǎotàbǎn
foot pedal

三角铁
sānjiǎotiě
triangle

沙锤
shāchuí
maracas

铜管乐器 tóngguǎn yuèqì · **brass**

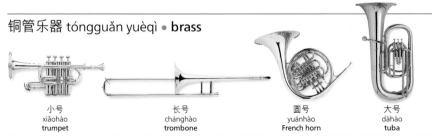

小号
xiǎohào
trumpet

长号
chánghào
trombone

圆号
yuánhào
French horn

大号
dàhào
tuba

音乐会 yīnyuèhuì • concert

吉他手
jítāshǒu
guitarist

鼓手
gǔshǒu
drummer

主唱
zhǔchàng
lead singer

麦克风
màikèfēng
microphone

扩音器
kuòyīnqì
speaker

歌迷
gēmí
fans

摇滚音乐会 yáogǔn yīnyuèhuì | rock concert

乐器 yuèqì • instruments

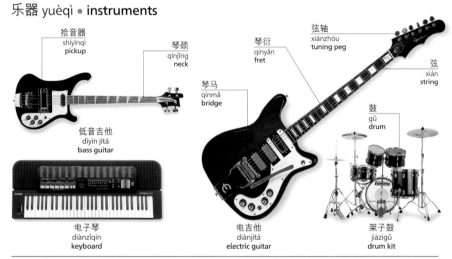

拾音器
shíyīnqì
pickup

琴颈
qínjǐng
neck

琴衍
qínyǎn
fret

弦轴
xiánzhóu
tuning peg

弦
xián
string

琴马
qínmǎ
bridge

鼓
gǔ
drum

低音吉他
dīyīn jítā
bass guitar

电子琴
diànzǐqín
keyboard

电吉他
diànjítā
electric guitar

架子鼓
jiàzigǔ
drum kit

音乐风格 yīnyuè fēnggé · **musical styles**

爵士乐 juéshìyuè | jazz

蓝调音乐 lándiào yīnyuè | blues

朋克音乐 péngkè yīnyuè | punk

民间音乐 mínjiān yīnyuè | folk music

流行音乐 liúxíng yīnyuè | pop

舞曲 wǔqǔ | dance

说唱音乐 shuōchàng yīnyuè
rap

重金属摇滚 zhòngjīnshǔyáogǔn
heavy metal

古典音乐 gǔdiǎn yīnyuè
classical music

词汇 cíhuì · **vocabulary**

歌曲	歌词	旋律	节拍	雷盖音乐	乡村音乐	聚光灯
gēqǔ	gēcí	xuánlǜ	jiépāi	léigài yīnyuè	xiāngcūn yīnyuè	jùguāngdēng
song	**lyrics**	**melody**	**beat**	**reggae**	**country**	**spotlight**

观光 guānguāng • sightseeing

游客
yóukè
tourist

游览胜地 yóulǎn shèngdì | tourist attraction

旅行路线
lǚxíng lùxiàn
itinerary

敞篷
chǎngpéng
open-top

This is an official London Sightseeing Bus.

LONDON PRIDE

观光巴士 guānguāngbāshì | tour bus

导游
dǎoyóu
tour guide

团体旅游
tuántǐlǚyóu
guided tour

小雕像
xiǎodiāoxiàng
statuette

纪念品
jìniànpǐn
souvenirs

词汇 cíhuì • vocabulary

开门 kāimén open	旅行指南 lǚxíngzhǐnán guidebook	便携式摄像机 biànxiéshì shèxiàngjī camcorder	左 zuǒ left	…在哪里? …zàinǎli? Where is …?
关门 guānmén closed	胶片 jiāopiàn film	照相机 zhàoxiàngjī camera	右 yòu right	我迷路了。 wǒ mílùle. I'm lost.
入场费 rùchǎngfèi entrance fee	电池 diànchí batteries	(行路的)指引 (xínglùde) zhǐyǐn directions	直行 zhíxíng straight on	你能告诉我到…的路吗? nǐ néng gàosù wǒ dào…delù ma? Can you tell me the way to …?

名胜 míngshèng · **attractions**

绘画
huìhuà
painting

展品
zhǎnpǐn
exhibit

展览
zhǎnlǎn
exhibition

古迹
gǔjì
famous ruin

艺术馆
yìshùguǎn
art gallery

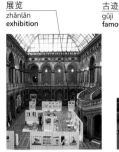

纪念碑
jìniànbēi
monument

博物馆
bówùguǎn
museum

历史建筑
lìshǐ jiànzhù
historic building

赌场
dǔchǎng
casino

庭园
tíngyuán
gardens

国家公园
guójiā gōngyuán
national park

游览信息 yóulǎnxìnxī · **information**

日程
rìchéng
times

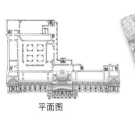

平面图
píngmiàntú
floor plan

地图
dìtú
map

时刻表
shíkèbiǎo
timetable

旅游问询处
lǚyóu wènxúnchù
tourist information

户外活动 hùwàihuódòng • **outdoor activities**

小道
xiǎodào
footpath

日晷
rìguǐ
sundial

咖啡馆
kāfēiguǎn
café

公园 gōngyuán | **park**

草坪
cǎopíng
grass

长椅
chángyǐ
bench

法式花园
fǎshì huāyuán
formal gardens

过山车
guòshānchē
roller coaster

游乐园
yóulèyuán
fairground

主题公园
zhǔtí gōngyuán
theme park

野生动物园
yěshēng dòngwùyuán
safari park

动物园
dòngwùyuán
zoo

活动 huódòng • activities

骑自行车
qízíxíngchē
cycling

慢跑
mànpǎo
jogging

滑板
huábǎn
skateboarding

滚轴溜冰
gǔnzhóu liūbīng
rollerblading

骑马专用道
qímǎ zhuānyòngdào
bridle path

食物篮
shíwùlán
hamper

观鸟
guānniǎo
bird-watching

骑马
qímǎ
horse riding

远足
yuǎnzú
hiking

野餐
yěcān
picnic

游乐场 yóulèchǎng • playground

沙箱
shāxiāng
sandpit

儿童戏水池
értóng xìshuǐchí
paddling pool

秋千
qiūqiān
swing

跷跷板 qiāoqiāobǎn | seesaw

滑梯 huátī | slide

攀登架 pāndēngjià | climbing frame

海滩 hǎitān • beach

旅馆
lǚguǎn
hotel

遮阳伞
zhēyángsǎn
beach umbrella

海滩小屋
hǎitān xiǎowū
beach hut

沙
shā
sand

海浪
hǎilàng
wave

海
hǎi
sea

海滨游泳袋
hǎibīn yóuyǒngdài
beach bag

比基尼泳装
bǐjīníyǒngzhuāng
bikini

晒日光浴 shài rìguāngyù | sunbathe (v)

救生员
jiùshēngyuán
lifeguard

救生瞭望塔
jiùshēng liàowàngtǎ
lifeguard tower

防风屏
fángfēngpíng
windbreak

海滨步道
hǎibīn bùdào
promenade

轻便折叠躺椅
qīngbiàn zhédiétǎngyǐ
deck chair

太阳镜
tàiyángjìng
sunglasses

遮阳帽
zhēyángmào
sunhat

防晒油
fángshàiyóu
suntan lotion

防晒液
fángshàiyè
sunblock

浮水气球
fúshuǐqìqiú
beach ball

游泳圈
yóuyǒngquān
rubber ring

游泳衣
yóuyǒngyī
swimsuit

铲子
chǎnzi
spade

桶
tǒng
bucket

海滩浴巾
hǎitān yùjīn
beach towel

沙堡
shābǎo
sandcastle

贝壳
bèiké
shell

露营 lùyíng • camping

卫生间
wèishēngjiān
toilets

垃圾箱
lājīxiāng
waste disposal

浴室
yùshì
shower block

接电装置
jiēdiàn zhuāngzhì
electric hook-up

防雨罩
fángyǔzhào
flysheet

地钉
dìdìng
tent peg

防风绳
fángfēng shéng
guy rope

旅行拖车
lǚxíng tuōchē
caravan

露营地 lùyíngdì | campsite

词汇 cíhuì • vocabulary

露营
lùyíng
camp (v)

宿营地
sùyíngdì
pitch

野餐长椅
yěcān chángyǐ
picnic bench

木炭
mùtàn
charcoal

营地管理处
yíngdì guǎnlǐchù
site manager's office

支帐篷
zhīzhàngpeng
pitch a tent (v)

吊床
diàochuáng
hammock

引火物
yǐnhuǒwù
firelighter

自由宿营地
zìyóu sùyíngdì
pitches available

帐篷杆
zhàngpenggǎn
tent pole

野营车
yěyíngchē
camper van

点火
diǎnhuǒ
light a fire (v)

满
mǎn
full

行军床
xíngjūn chuáng
camp bed

拖车
tuōchē
trailer

营火
yínghuǒ
campfire

支架
zhījià
frame

铺地防潮布
pūdì fángcháobù
ground sheet

背包
bèibāo
backpack

保温瓶
bǎowēnpíng
vacuum flask

水瓶
shuǐpíng
water bottle

帐篷
zhàngpeng
tent

驱虫剂
qūchóngjì
insect repellent

营地灯
yíngdìdēng
torch

蚊帐
wénzhàng
mosquito net

保暖内衣
bǎonuǎn nèiyī
thermals

徒步靴
túbùxuē
walking boots

雨衣
yǔyī
waterproofs

睡袋
shuìdài
sleeping bag

睡垫
shuìdiàn
sleeping mat

野营炉
yěyínglú
camping stove

烧烤架
shāokǎojià
barbecue

充气床垫 chōngqì chuángdiàn | air mattress

家庭娱乐 jiātíngyúlè · home entertainment

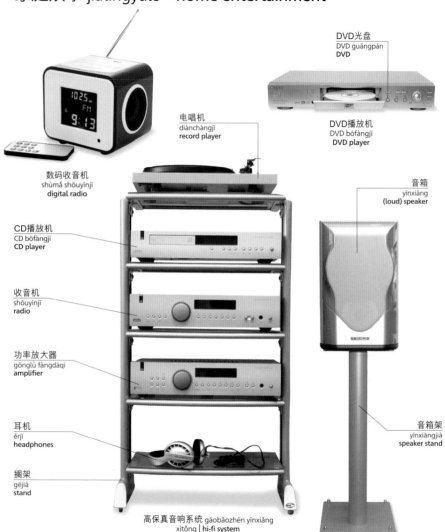

DVD光盘
DVD guāngpán
DVD

电唱机
diànchàngjī
record player

DVD播放机
DVD bōfàngjī
DVD player

数码收音机
shùmǎ shōuyīnjī
digital radio

音箱
yīnxiāng
(loud) speaker

CD播放机
CD bōfàngjī
CD player

收音机
shōuyīnjī
radio

功率放大器
gōnglǜ fàngdàqì
amplifier

耳机
ěrjī
headphones

搁架
gējià
stand

音箱架
yīnxiāngjià
speaker stand

高保真音响系统 gāobǎozhēn yīnxiǎng
xìtǒng | hi-fi system

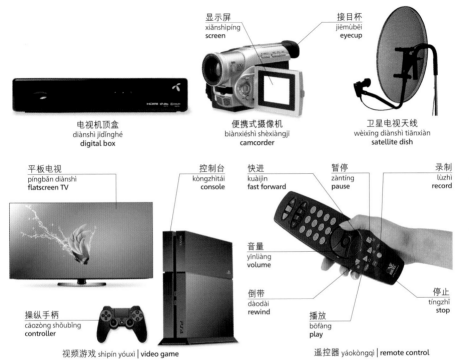

显示屏
xiǎnshìpíng
screen

接目杯
jiēmùbēi
eyecup

电视机顶盒
diànshì jǐdǐnghé
digital box

便携式摄像机
biànxiéshì shèxiàngjī
camcorder

卫星电视天线
wèixīng diànshì tiānxiàn
satellite dish

平板电视
píngbǎn diànshì
flatscreen TV

控制台
kòngzhìtái
console

快进
kuàijìn
fast forward

暂停
zàntíng
pause

录制
lùzhì
record

音量
yīnliàng
volume

停止
tíngzhǐ
stop

操纵手柄
cāozòng shǒubǐng
controller

倒带
dàodài
rewind

播放
bōfàng
play

视频游戏 shìpín yóuxì | video game

遥控器 yáokòngqì | remote control

词汇 cíhuì · vocabulary

激光唱盘 jīguāng chàngpán compact disc	故事片 gùshìpiàn feature film	节目 jiémù programme	收费频道 shōufèi píndào pay per view channel	看电视 kàndiànshì watch television (v)
盒式录音带 héshì lùyīndài cassette tape	广告 guǎnggào advertisement	立体声 lìtǐshēng stereo	换频道 huàn píndào change channel (v)	关电视 guāndiànshì turn the television off (v)
盒式磁带录音机 héshì cídàilùyīnjī cassette player	数字式 shùzìshì digital	有线电视 yǒuxiàn diànshì cable television	调收音机 tiáoshōuyīnjī tune the radio (v)	开电视 kāidiànshì turn the television on (v)
流媒体 liúméitǐ streaming	高清晰度 gāo qīngxī dù high-definition	无线网络 wúxiàn wǎngluò Wi-Fi		

摄影 shèyǐng · photography

快门键
kuàimén jiàn
shutter release

光圈调节环
guāngquān tiáojiéhuán
aperture dial

镜头
jìngtóu
lens

滤镜
lǜjìng
filter

镜头盖
jìngtóugài
lens cap

单镜头反光照相机 dānjìngtóu fǎnguāngzhàoxiàngjī | SLR camera

闪光灯
shǎnguāngdēng
flash gun

曝光表
bàoguāngbiǎo
lightmeter

变焦镜头
biànjiāo jìngtóu
zoom lens

三脚架
sānjiǎojià
tripod

相机种类 xiàngjī zhǒnglèi · types of camera

宝丽来相机
bǎolìlái xiàngjī
Polaroid camera

数码相机
shùmǎ xiàngjī
digital camera

闪光灯
shǎnguāngdēng
flash

照相手机
zhàoxiàng shǒujī
cameraphone

一次性相机
yícìxìng xiàngjī
disposable camera

照相 zhàoxiàng • photograph (v)

胶卷
jiāojuǎn
film spool

胶片
jiāopiàn
film

调焦
tiáojiāo
focus (v)

冲洗
chōngxǐ
develop (v)

底片
dǐpiàn
negative

全景照
quánjǐngzhào
landscape

人像照
rénxiàngzhào
portrait

相片 xiàngpiàn | photograph

相册
xiàngcè
photo album

相框
xiàngkuàng
photo frame

问题 wèntí • problems

曝光不足
pùguāng bùzú
underexposed

曝光过度
pùguāng guòdù
overexposed

调焦不准
tiáojiāo bùzhǔn
out of focus

红眼
hóngyǎn
red eye

词汇 cíhuì • vocabulary

取景器
qǔjǐngqì
viewfinder

相机盒
xiàngjīhé
camera case

曝光
pùguāng
exposure

暗室
ànshì
darkroom

样片
yàngpiàn
print

无光泽
wúguāngzé
matte

有光泽
yǒuguāngzé
gloss

放大
fàngdà
enlargement

请冲洗这个胶卷。
qǐng chōngxǐ zhège jiāojuǎn.
I'd like this film processed.

游戏 yóuxì • **games**

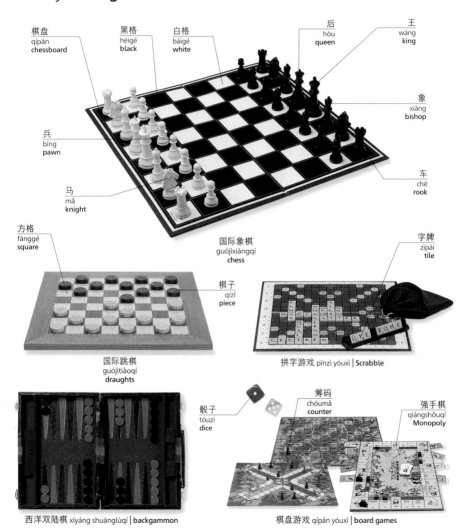

棋盘
qípán
chessboard

黑格
hēigé
black

白格
báigé
white

后
hòu
queen

王
wáng
king

象
xiàng
bishop

兵
bīng
pawn

车
chē
rook

马
mǎ
knight

国际象棋
guójìxiàngqí
chess

方格
fānggé
square

棋子
qízǐ
piece

国际跳棋
guójìtiàoqí
draughts

字牌
zìpái
tile

拼字游戏 pīnzì yóuxì | Scrabble

骰子
tóuzi
dice

筹码
chóumǎ
counter

强手棋
qiángshǒuqí
Monopoly

西洋双陆棋 xīyáng shuānglùqí | backgammon

棋盘游戏 qípán yóuxì | board games

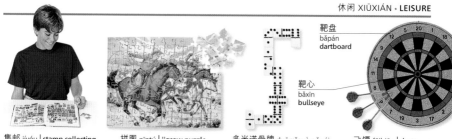

靶盘 bǎpán dartboard

靶心 bǎxīn bullseye

集邮 jíyóu | stamp collecting

拼图 pīntú | jigsaw puzzle

多米诺骨牌 duōmǐnuò gǔpái dominoes

飞镖 fēibiāo | darts

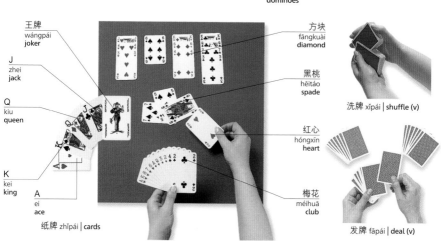

王牌 wángpái joker

J zhei jack

Q kiu queen

K kei king

A ei ace

纸牌 zhǐpái | cards

方块 fāngkuài diamond

黑桃 hēitáo spade

红心 hóngxīn heart

梅花 méihuā club

洗牌 xǐpái | shuffle (v)

发牌 fāpái | deal (v)

词汇 cíhuì • vocabulary

走棋 zǒuqí move	赢 yíng win (v)	输家 shūjiā loser	点 diǎn point	桥牌 qiáopái bridge	掷骰子。 zhìtóuzi. Roll the dice.
玩 wán play (v)	赢家 yíngjiā winner	游戏 yóuxì game	得分 défēn score	一副牌 yīfùpái pack of cards	该谁了？ gāishuíle? Whose turn is it?
玩家 wánjiā player	输 shū lose (v)	赌注 dǔzhù bet	扑克牌 pūkèpái poker	同花 tónghuā suit	该你了。 gāinǐle. It's your move.

工艺美术 1 gōngyìměishù yī · arts and crafts 1

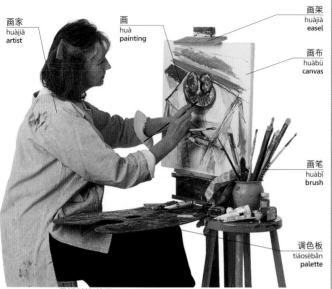

画家
huàjiā
artist

画
huà
painting

画架
huàjià
easel

画布
huàbù
canvas

画笔
huàbǐ
brush

调色板
tiáosèbǎn
palette

(用颜料等)绘画 (yòng yánliào děng) huìhuà | painting

颜料 yánliào · paints

油画颜料
yóuhuà yánliào
oil paints

水彩画颜料
shuǐcǎi huàyánliào
watercolour paint

彩色蜡笔
cǎisèlàbǐ
pastels

丙烯颜料
bǐngxī yánliào
acrylic paint

广告颜料 guǎnggào yánliào
poster paint

颜色 yánsè · colours

红色 hóngsè | red

蓝色 lánsè | blue

黄色 huángsè
yellow

绿色 lǜsè | green

橘色 júsè | orange

紫色 zǐsè | purple

白色 báisè | white

黑色 hēisè | black

灰色 huīsè | grey

粉红色 fěnhóngsè
pink

褐色 hèsè | brown

靛青色 diànqīngsè
indigo

其他工艺 qítā gōngyì • other crafts

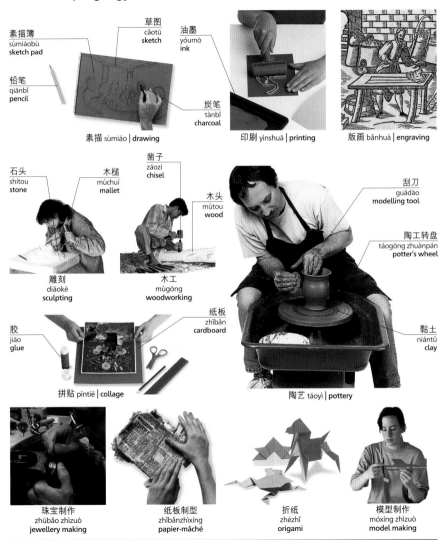

素描簿
sùmiáobù
sketch pad

铅笔
qiānbǐ
pencil

草图
cǎotú
sketch

油墨
yóumò
ink

炭笔
tànbǐ
charcoal

素描 sùmiáo | drawing

印刷 yìnshuā | printing

版画 bǎnhuà | engraving

石头
shítou
stone

木槌
mùchuí
mallet

凿子
záozi
chisel

木头
mùtou
wood

刮刀
guādāo
modelling tool

陶工转盘
táogōng zhuànpán
potter's wheel

雕刻
diāokè
sculpting

木工
mùgōng
woodworking

黏土
niántǔ
clay

胶
jiāo
glue

纸板
zhǐbǎn
cardboard

拼贴 pīntiē | collage

陶艺 táoyì | pottery

珠宝制作
zhūbǎo zhìzuò
jewellery making

纸板制型
zhǐbǎnzhìxíng
papier-mâché

折纸
zhézhǐ
origami

模型制作
móxíng zhìzuò
model making

工艺美术 2 gōngyìměishù èr • **arts and crafts 2**

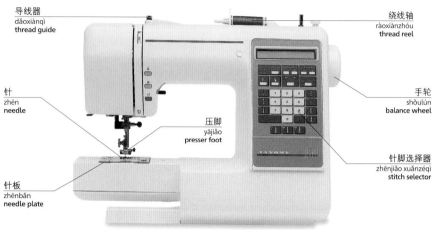

导线器
dǎoxiànqì
thread guide

绕线轴
ràoxiànzhóu
thread reel

针
zhēn
needle

手轮
shǒulún
balance wheel

压脚
yājiǎo
presser foot

针脚选择器
zhēnjiǎo xuǎnzéqì
stitch selector

针板
zhēnbǎn
needle plate

缝纫机 féngrènjī | **sewing machine**

剪刀
jiǎndāo
scissors

纸样
zhǐyàng
pattern

针垫
zhēndiàn
pincushion

卷尺
juǎnchǐ
tape measure

布料
bùliào
material

大头针
dàtóuzhēn
pin

针线筐 zhēnxiànkuāng
sewing basket

线
xiàn
thread

领钩环
lǐnggōuhuán
eye

线轴
xiànzhóu
bobbin

领钩
lǐnggōu
hook

顶针
dǐngzhēn
thimble

划粉
huáfěn
tailor's chalk

人体模型
réntǐ móxíng
tailor's dummy

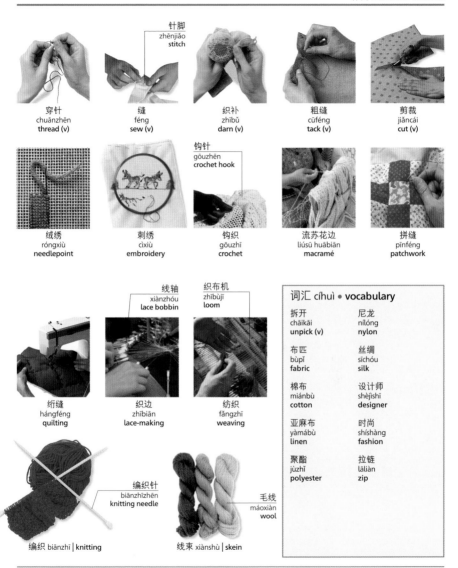

针脚
zhēnjiǎo
stitch

穿针
chuānzhēn
thread (v)

缝
féng
sew (v)

织补
zhībǔ
darn (v)

粗缝
cūféng
tack (v)

剪裁
jiǎncái
cut (v)

钩针
gōuzhēn
crochet hook

绒绣
róngxiù
needlepoint

刺绣
cìxiù
embroidery

钩织
gōuzhī
crochet

流苏花边
liúsū huābiān
macramé

拼缝
pīnféng
patchwork

线轴
xiànzhóu
lace bobbin

织布机
zhībùjī
loom

绗缝
hángféng
quilting

织边
zhībiān
lace-making

纺织
fǎngzhī
weaving

词汇 cíhuì • vocabulary

拆开
chāikāi
unpick (v)

尼龙
nílóng
nylon

布匹
bùpǐ
fabric

丝绸
sīchóu
silk

棉布
miánbù
cotton

设计师
shèjìshī
designer

亚麻布
yàmábù
linen

时尚
shíshàng
fashion

聚酯
jùzhǐ
polyester

拉链
lāliàn
zip

编织针
biānzhīzhēn
knitting needle

毛线
máoxiàn
wool

编织 biānzhī | knitting

线束 xiànshù | skein

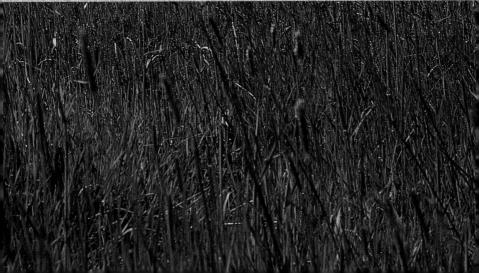

环境 huánjìng
environment

宇宙空间 yǔzhòukōngjiān · space

水星
shuǐxīng
Mercury

地球
dìqiú
Earth

火星
huǒxīng
Mars

木星
mùxīng
Jupiter

天王星
tiānwángxīng
Uranus

海王星
hǎiwángxīng
Neptune

冥王星
míngwángxīng
Pluto

金星
jīnxīng
Venus

太阳
tàiyáng
Sun

月球
yuèqiú
Moon

土星
tǔxīng
Saturn

太阳系 tàiyángxì | solar system

彗尾
huìwěi
tail

星
xīng
star

星系
xīngxì
galaxy

星云
xīngyún
nebula

小行星
xiǎoxíngxīng
asteroid

彗星
huìxīng
comet

词汇 cíhuì · vocabulary

宇宙
yǔzhòu
universe

黑洞
hēidòng
black hole

满月
mǎnyuè
full moon

轨道
guǐdào
orbit

行星
xíngxīng
planet

新月
xīnyuè
new moon

重力
zhònglì
gravity

流星
liúxīng
meteor

弦月
xiányuè
crescent moon

(日、月)食 (rì, yuè) shí | eclipse

中文 zhōngwén · **english**

太空探索 tàikōngfú • **space exploration**

雷达
léidá
radar

助推器
zhùtuīqì
thruster

航天飞机
hángtiān fēijī
space shuttle

太空服
tàikōngfú
space suit

推进器
tuījìnqì
booster

舱门
cāngmén
crew hatch

宇航员 yǔhángyuán
astronaut

登月舱 dēngyuècāng | **lunar module**

发射架
fāshèjià
launch pad

发射
fāshè
launch

人造卫星
rénzàowèixīng
satellite

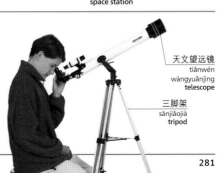

空间站
kōngjiān zhàn
space station

天文学 tiānwénxué • **astronomy**

星座
xīngzuò
constellation

双筒望远镜
shuāngtǒng wàngyuǎnjìng
binoculars

天文望远镜
tiānwén
wàngyuǎnjìng
telescope

三脚架
sānjiǎojià
tripod

地球 dìqiú • Earth

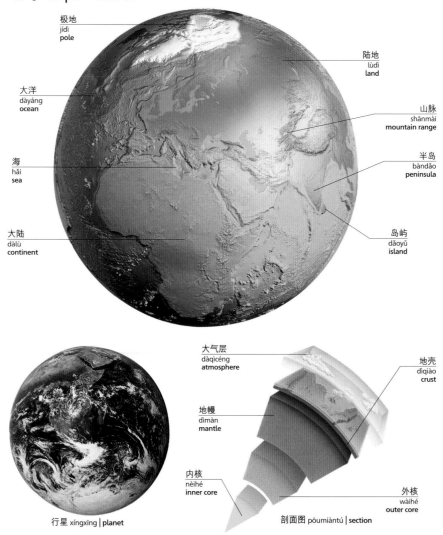

极地
jídì
pole

陆地
lùdì
land

大洋
dàyáng
ocean

山脉
shānmài
mountain range

海
hǎi
sea

半岛
bàndǎo
peninsula

大陆
dàlù
continent

岛屿
dǎoyǔ
island

大气层
dàqìcéng
atmosphere

地壳
dìqiào
crust

地幔
dìmàn
mantle

内核
nèihé
inner core

外核
wàihé
outer core

行星 xíngxīng | **planet**

剖面图 pōumiàntú | **section**

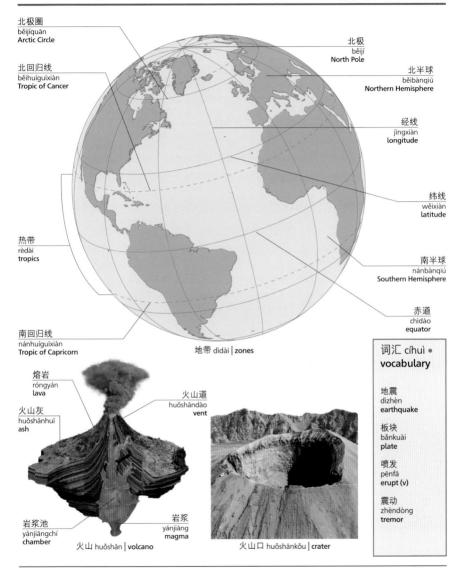

北极圈
běijíquān
Arctic Circle

北极
běijí
North Pole

北回归线
běihuíguīxiàn
Tropic of Cancer

北半球
běibànqiú
Northern Hemisphere

经线
jīngxiàn
longitude

纬线
wěixiàn
latitude

热带
rèdài
tropics

南半球
nánbànqiú
Southern Hemisphere

南回归线
nánhuíguīxiàn
Tropic of Capricorn

赤道
chìdào
equator

地带 dìdài | zones

熔岩
róngyán
lava

火山道
huǒshāndào
vent

火山灰
huǒshānhuī
ash

岩浆池
yánjiāngchí
chamber

岩浆
yánjiāng
magma

火山 huǒshān | volcano

火山口 huǒshānkǒu | crater

词汇 cíhuì ·
vocabulary

地震
dìzhèn
earthquake

板块
bǎnkuài
plate

喷发
pēnfā
erupt (v)

震动
zhèndòng
tremor

地貌 dìmào · landscape

山
shān
mountain

山坡
shānpō
slope

河岸
hé'àn
bank

河流
héliú
river

急流
jíliú
rapids

岩石
yánshí
rocks

冰河 bīnghé | glacier

山谷 shāngǔ | valley

丘陵
qiūlíng
hill

高原
gāoyuán
plateau

峡谷
xiágǔ
gorge

岩洞
yándòng
cave

平原 píngyuán | plain

沙漠 shāmò | desert

森林 sēnlín | forest

树林 shùlín | wood

雨林
yǔlín
rainforest

沼泽
zhǎozé
swamp

草场
cǎochǎng
meadow

草原
cǎoyuán
grassland

瀑布
pùbù
waterfall

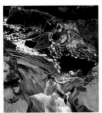
溪流
xīliú
stream

湖
hú
lake

间歇喷泉
jiànxiē pēnquán
geyser

海岸
hǎi'àn
coast

悬崖
xuányá
cliff

珊瑚礁
shānhújiāo
coral reef

河口
hékǒu
estuary

天气 tiānqì • weather

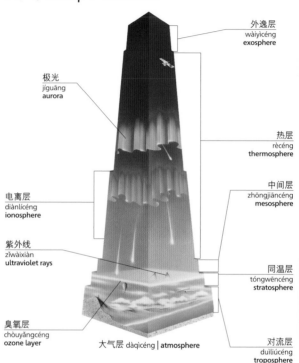

外逸层
wàiyìcéng
exosphere

极光
jíguāng
aurora

热层
rècéng
thermosphere

电离层
diànlícéng
ionosphere

中间层
zhōngjiāncéng
mesosphere

紫外线
zǐwàixiàn
ultraviolet rays

同温层
tóngwēncéng
stratosphere

臭氧层
chòuyǎngcéng
ozone layer

大气层 dàqìcéng | atmosphere

对流层
duìliúcéng
troposphere

阳光 yángguāng | sunshine

风 fēng | wind

词汇 cíhuì • vocabulary

雨夹雪 yǔjiáxuě sleet	阵雨 zhènyǔ shower	热 rè hot	干燥 gānzào dry	多风 duōfēng windy	我热/冷。 wǒ rè/lěng. I'm hot/cold.
冰雹 bīngbáo hail	阳光明媚 yángguāng míngmèi sunny	冷 lěng cold	潮 cháo wet	狂风 kuángfēng gale	正在下雨。 zhèngzài xiàyǔ. It's raining.
雷 léi thunder	多云 duōyún cloudy	温暖 wēnnuǎn warm	湿润 shīrùn humid	温度 wēndù temperature	…度 …dù It's … degrees.

闪电 shǎndiàn lightning

云 yún | cloud

雨 yǔ | rain

暴风雨 bàofēngyǔ | storm

霭 ǎi | mist

雾 wù | fog

彩虹 cǎihóng | rainbow

冰柱 bīngzhù icicle

雪 xuě | snow

霜 shuāng | frost

冰 bīng | ice

结冰 jiébīng | freeze

飓风 jùfēng | hurricane

龙卷风 lóngjuǎnfēng tornado

季风 jìfēng | monsoon

洪水 hóngshuǐ | flood

岩石 yánshí · rocks

火成岩 huǒchéngyán · igneous

花岗岩
huāgāngyán
granite

黑曜岩
hēiyàoyán
obsidian

玄武岩
xuánwǔyán
basalt

浮石
fúshí
pumice

沉积岩 chénjīyán · sedimentary

砂岩
shāyán
sandstone

石灰岩
shíhuīyán
limestone

白垩
bái'è
chalk

燧石
suìshí
flint

砾岩
lìyán
conglomerate

煤
méi
coal

变质岩 biànzhìyán · metamorphic

板岩
bǎnyán
slate

页岩
yèyán
schist

片麻岩
piànmáyán
gneiss

大理石
dàlǐshí
marble

宝石 bǎoshí · gems

红宝石
hóngbǎoshí
ruby

海蓝宝石
hǎilánbǎoshí
aquamarine

紫水晶
zǐshuǐjīng
amethyst

钻石
zuànshí
diamond

玉石
yùshí
jade

黑玉
hēiyù
jet

绿宝石
lǜbǎoshí
emerald

蛋白石
dànbáishí
opal

蓝宝石
lánbǎoshí
sapphire

月长石
yuèchángshí
moonstone

石榴石
shíliúshí
garnet

黄玉
huángyù
topaz

电气石
diànqìshí
tourmaline

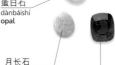

矿物 kuàngwù • minerals

石英
shíyīng
quartz

云母
yúnmǔ
mica

硫磺
liúhuáng
sulphur

赤铁矿
chìtiěkuàng
hematite

方解石
fāngjiěshí
calcite

孔雀石
kǒngquèshí
malachite

绿松石
lǜsōngshí
turquoise

缟玛瑙
gǎomǎnǎo
onyx

玛瑙
mǎnǎo
agate

石墨
shímò
graphite

金属 jīnshǔ • metals

金
jīn
gold

银
yín
silver

铂
bó
platinum

镍
niè
nickel

铁
tiě
iron

铜
tóng
copper

锡
xī
tin

铝
lǚ
aluminium

汞
gǒng
mercury

锌
xīn
zinc

动物1 dòngwùyī • animals 1
哺乳动物 bǔrǔ dòngwù • mammals

腮须
sāixū
whiskers

尾
wěi
tail

兔子
tùzi
rabbit

仓鼠
cāngshǔ
hamster

小家鼠
xiǎojiāshǔ
mouse

老鼠
lǎoshǔ
rat

刺猬
cìwei
hedgehog

松鼠
sōngshǔ
squirrel

蝙蝠
biānfú
bat

浣熊
huànxióng
raccoon

狐狸
húli
fox

狼
láng
wolf

小狗
xiǎogǒu
puppy

小猫
xiǎomāo
kitten

小海豹
xiǎohǎibào
pup

狗
gǒu
dog

猫
māo
cat

水獭
shuǐtǎ
otter

海豹
hǎibào
seal

鳍状肢
qízhuàngzhī
flipper

喷水孔
pēnshuǐkǒng
blowhole

海豚
hǎitún
dolphin

海狮
hǎishī
sea lion

海象
hǎixiàng
walrus

鲸
jīng
whale

鹿角
lùjiǎo
antler

鬃毛
zōngmáo
mane

蹄
tí
hoof

驼峰
tuófēng
hump

鹿
lù
deer

斑马
bānmǎ
zebra

长颈鹿
chángjǐnglù
giraffe

骆驼
luòtuo
camel

象鼻
xiàngbí
trunk

长牙
chángyá
tusk

角
jiǎo
horn

河马
hémǎ
hippopotamus

象
xiàng
elephant

犀牛
xīniú
rhinoceros

虎
hǔ
tiger

鬃毛
zōngmáo
mane

狮子
shīzi
lion

猴子
hóuzi
monkey

大猩猩
dàxīngxing
gorilla

树袋熊
shùdài xióng
koala

育儿袋
yù'érdài
pouch

熊猫
xióngmāo
panda

爪
zhǎo
claw

袋鼠
dàishǔ
kangaroo

熊
xióng
bear

北极熊
běijí xióng
polar bear

动物 2 dòngwùèr · animals 2

鸟 niǎo · birds

尾
wěi
tail

金丝雀
jīnsīquè
canary

麻雀
máquè
sparrow

蜂鸟
fēngniǎo
hummingbird

燕子
yànzi
swallow

乌鸦
wūyā
crow

鸽子
gēzi
pigeon

啄木鸟
zhuómùniǎo
woodpecker

隼
sǔn
falcon

猫头鹰
māotóuyíng
owl

海鸥
hǎi'ōu
gull

鹰
yīng
eagle

鹈鹕
tíhú
pelican

火烈鸟
huǒlièniǎo
flamingo

鹳
guàn
stork

鹤
hè
crane

企鹅
qǐ'é
penguin

鸵鸟
tuóniǎo
ostrich

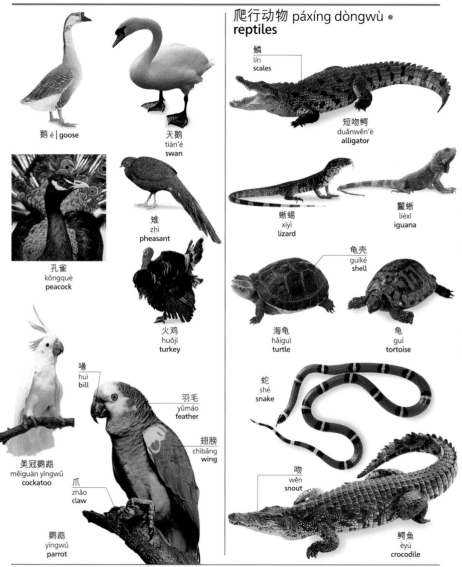

鹅 é | goose

天鹅
tiān'é
swan

孔雀
kǒngquè
peacock

雉
zhì
pheasant

火鸡
huǒjī
turkey

喙
huì
bill

羽毛
yǔmáo
feather

翅膀
chìbǎng
wing

美冠鹦鹉
měiguàn yīngwǔ
cockatoo

爪
zhǎo
claw

鹦鹉
yīngwǔ
parrot

爬行动物 páxíng dòngwù • reptiles

鳞
lín
scales

短吻鳄
duǎnwěn'è
alligator

蜥蜴
xīyì
lizard

鬣蜥
lièxī
iguana

龟壳
guīké
shell

海龟
hǎiguī
turtle

龟
guī
tortoise

蛇
shé
snake

吻
wěn
snout

鳄鱼
èyú
crocodile

动物 3 dòngwùsān • animals 3
两栖动物 liǎngqī dòngwù • amphibians

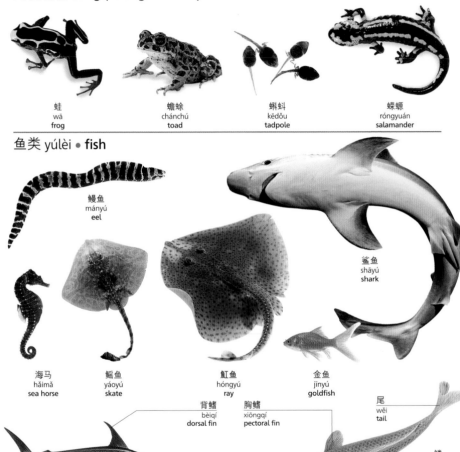

蛙
wā
frog

蟾蜍
chánchú
toad

蝌蚪
kēdǒu
tadpole

蝾螈
róngyuán
salamander

鱼类 yúlèi • fish

鳗鱼
mányú
eel

鲨鱼
shāyú
shark

海马
hǎimǎ
sea horse

鳐鱼
yáoyú
skate

魟鱼
hóngyú
ray

金鱼
jīnyú
goldfish

背鳍
bèiqí
dorsal fin

胸鳍
xiōngqí
pectoral fin

尾
wěi
tail

鳃
sāi
gill

鳞
lín
scale

剑鱼 jiànyú | swordfish

鲤鱼 lǐyú | koi carp

无脊椎动物 wújǐzhuī dòngwù · invertebrates

蚂蚁
mǎyǐ
ant

白蚁
báiyǐ
termite

蜜蜂
mìfēng
bee

黄蜂
huángfēng
wasp

甲壳虫
jiǎqiàochóng
beetle

蟑螂
zhāngláng
cockroach

蛾
é
moth

触角
chùjiǎo
antenna

蝴蝶
húdié
butterfly

茧
jiǎn
cocoon

毛虫
máochóng
caterpillar

蟋蟀 xīshuài | cricket

蚱蜢
zhàměng
grasshopper

螳螂
tángláng
praying mantis

螫针
zhēzhēn
sting

蝎子
xiēzi
scorpion

蜈蚣
wúgōng
centipede

蜻蜓
qīngtíng
dragonfly

苍蝇
cāngyíng
fly

蚊子
wénzi
mosquito

瓢虫
piáochóng
ladybird

蜘蛛
zhīzhū
spider

蛞蝓
kuòyú
slug

蜗牛
wōniú
snail

蚯蚓 qiūyǐn | worm

海星
hǎixīng
starfish

贻贝
yíbèi
mussel

螃蟹 pángxiè | crab

龙虾 lóngxiā | lobster

章鱼 zhāngyú | octopus

鱿鱼 yóuyú | squid

水母 shuǐmǔ | jellyfish

植物 zhíwù • plants

树 shù • tree

叶
yè
leaf

树枝
shùzhī
branch

细枝
xìzhī
twig

树皮
shùpí
bark

柳树
liǔshù
willow

根
gēn
root

树干
shùgàn
trunk

橡树 xiàngshù | oak

白杨
báiyáng
poplar

桉树
ānshù
eucalyptus

落叶松
luòyèsōng
larch

山毛榉
shānmáojǔ
beech

桦树
huàshù
birch

松树
sōngshù
pine

雪松
xuěsōng
cedar

枫树
fēngshù
maple

榆树
yúshù
elm

椴树
duànshù
lime

浆果
jiāngguǒ
berry

冬青树
dōngqīngshù
holly

棕榈树
zōnglǘshù
palm

显花植物 xiǎnhuā zhíwù • flowering plant

花
huā
flower

雄蕊
xióngruǐ
stamen

花瓣
huābàn
petal

花萼
huā'è
calyx

叶梗
yègěng
stalk

主茎
zhǔjīng
stem

花蕾
huālěi
bud

毛茛
máogèn
buttercup

雏菊
chújú
daisy

蓟
jì
thistle

蒲公英
púgōngyīng
dandelion

石南花
shínánhuā
heather

罂粟
yīngsù
poppy

毛地黄
máodihuáng
foxglove

忍冬
rěndōng
honeysuckle

向日葵
xiàngrikuí
sunflower

苜蓿
mùxu
clover

野风信子
yěfēngxìnzǐ
bluebells

樱草
yīngcǎo
primrose

羽扇豆
yǔshàndòu
lupins

荨麻
qiánmá
nettle

市区 shìqū · city

街道
jiēdào
street

路沿
lùyán
kerb

街角
jiējiǎo
street corner

商店
shāngdiàn
shop

十字路口
shízìlùkǒu
intersection

单行道
dānxíngdào
one-way system

人行道
rénxíngdào
pavement

办公楼
bàngōnglóu
office block

公寓楼
gōngyùlóu
apartment block

小巷
xiǎoxiàng
alley

停车场
tíngchēchǎng
car park

路标
lùbiāo
street sign

安全岛护栏
ānquán
dǎohùlán
bollard

路灯
lùdēng
streetlight

建筑物 jiànzhùwù • buildings

市政厅
shìzhèngtīng
town hall

图书馆
túshūguǎn
library

电影院
diànyǐngyuàn
cinema

剧院
jùyuàn
theatre

大学
dàxué
university

学校
xuéxiào
school

摩天大楼
mótiān dàlóu
skyscraper

区域 qūyù • areas

工业区
gōngyèqū
industrial estate

市区
shìqū
city

郊区
jiāoqū
suburb

村庄
cūnzhuāng
village

词汇 cíhuì • vocabulary

步行区 bùxíngqū pedestrian zone	小街 xiǎojiē side street	检修井 jiǎnxiūjǐng manhole	排水沟 páishuǐgōu gutter	教堂 jiàotáng church
林阴道 línyīndào avenue	广场 guǎngchǎng square	公共汽车站 gōnggòngqìchē zhàn bus stop	工厂 gōngchǎng factory	下水道 xiàshuǐdào drain

建筑 jiànzhù · architecture

建筑与结构 jiànzhù yǔ jiégòu · buildings and structures

尖顶饰
jiāndǐngshì
finial

角楼
jiǎolóu
turret

尖顶
jiāndǐng
spire

壕沟
háogōu
moat

摩天大楼
mótiān dàlóu
skyscraper

城堡
chéngbǎo
castle

三角墙
sānjiǎoqiáng
gable

圆顶
yuándǐng
dome

塔
tǎ
tower

教堂
jiàotáng
church

清真寺
qīngzhēnsì
mosque

拱型圆顶
gǒngxíng yuándǐng
vault

檐口
yánkǒu
cornice

寺庙
sìmiào
temple

犹太教会堂
yóutàijiào huìtáng
synagogue

柱
zhù
pillar

水坝
shuǐbà
dam

桥梁
qiáoliáng
bridge

大教堂 dàjiàotáng | cathedral

建筑风格 jiànzhù fēnggé • styles

哥特式 gētèshì | Gothic

柱顶楣梁
zhùdǐng méiliáng
architrave

文艺复兴时期风格
wényìfùxīng shíqī fēnggé
Renaissance

巴洛克式
bāluòkèshì
Baroque

拱
gǒng
arch

檐壁
yánbì
frieze

圣坛
shèngtán
choir

洛可可式
luòkěkěshì
Rococo

三角楣
sānjiǎoméi
pediment

扶墙
fúqiáng
buttress

新古典主义风格
xīn gǔdiǎnzhǔyì fēnggé
Neoclassical

新艺术风格
xīn yìshù fēnggé
Art Nouveau

装饰艺术风格
zhuāngshìyìshù fēnggé
Art Deco

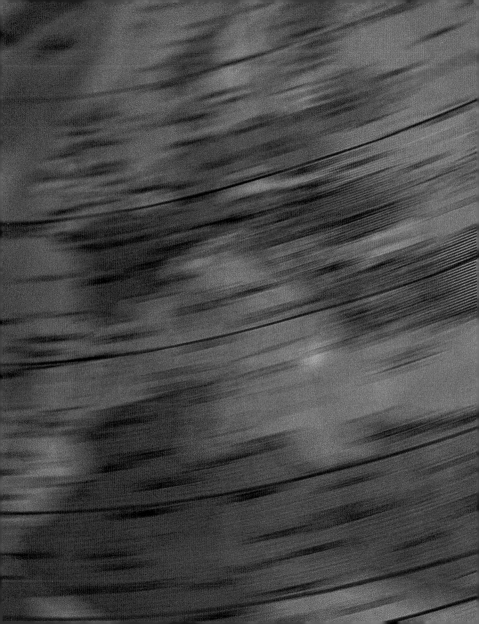

日常便览 rìcháng biànlǎn
reference

时间 shíjiān · **time**

分针
fēnzhēn
minute hand

时针
shízhēn
hour hand

钟表
zhōngbiǎo
clock

词汇 cíhuì · **vocabulary**

秒
miǎo
second

分钟
fēnzhōng
minute

小时
xiǎoshí
hour

现在
xiànzài
now

以后
yǐhòu
later

半小时
bàn xiǎoshí
half an hour

一刻钟
yí kèzhōng
a quarter of an hour

二十分钟
èrshí fēnzhōng
twenty minutes

四十分钟
sìshí fēnzhōng
forty minutes

几点了?
jǐ diǎn le?
What time is it?

三点了。
sāndiǎn le.
It's three o'clock.

一点五分
yìdiǎn wǔ fēn
five past one

一点十分
yìdiǎn shí fēn
ten past one

一点十五分
yìdiǎn shíwǔ fēn
quarter past one

一点二十分
yìdiǎn èrshí fēn
twenty past one

秒针
miǎozhēn
second hand

一点二十五分
yìdiǎn èrshíwǔ fēn
twenty five past one

一点半
yìdiǎnbàn
one thirty

一点三十五分
yìdiǎn sānshíwǔ fēn
twenty five to two

一点四十分
yìdiǎn sìshí fēn
twenty to two

一点四十五分
yìdiǎn sìshíwǔ fēn
quarter to two

一点五十分
yìdiǎn wǔshí fēn
ten to two

一点五十五分
yìdiǎn wǔshíwǔ fēn
five to two

两点钟
liǎngdiǎn zhōng
two o'clock

昼夜 zhòuyè · night and day

午夜 wǔyè | midnight

日出 rìchū | sunrise

拂晓 fúxiǎo | dawn

早晨 zǎochén | morning

日落
rìluò
sunset

正午
zhèngwǔ
midday

黄昏 huánghūn | dusk

傍晚 bàngwǎn | evening

下午 xiàwǔ | afternoon

词汇 cíhuì · vocabulary

早 zǎo early	你来早了。 nǐ lái zǎo le. You're early.	请准时些。 qǐng zhǔnshí xiē. Please be on time.	几点结束? jǐdiǎn jiéshù? What time does it finish?
准时 zhǔnshí on time	你迟到了。 nǐ chídào le. You're late.	待会儿见。 dàihuìer jiàn. I'll see you later.	天晚了。 tiān wǎnle. It's getting late.
迟 chí late	我马上就到。 wǒ mǎshàng jiùdào. I'll be there soon.	几点开始? jǐdiǎn kāishǐ? What time does it start?	会持续多久? huì chíxù duōjiǔ? How long will it last?

日历 rìlì • calendar

月
yuè
month

年
nián
year

一月
yīyuè
January

2010

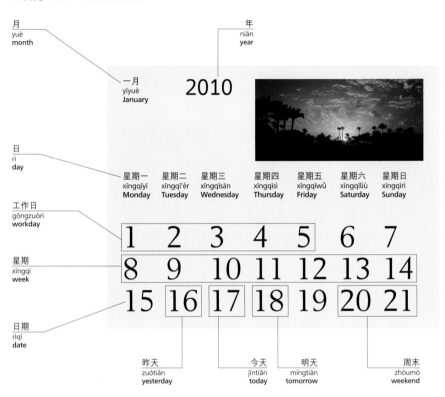

日
rì
day

| 星期一
xīngqīyī
Monday | 星期二
xīngqī'èr
Tuesday | 星期三
xīngqīsān
Wednesday | 星期四
xīngqīsì
Thursday | 星期五
xīngqīwǔ
Friday | 星期六
xīngqīliù
Saturday | 星期日
xīngqīrì
Sunday |

工作日
gōngzuòrì
workday

星期
xīngqī
week

1	2	3	4	5	6	7
8	9	10	11	12	13	14
15	16	17	18	19	20	21

日期
rìqī
date

昨天
zuótiān
yesterday

今天
jīntiān
today

明天
míngtiān
tomorrow

周末
zhōumò
weekend

词汇 cíhuì • vocabulary

| 一月
yīyuè
January | 三月
sānyuè
March | 五月
wǔyuè
May | 七月
qīyuè
July | 九月
jiǔyuè
September | 十一月
shíyīyuè
November |
| 二月
èryuè
February | 四月
sìyuè
April | 六月
liùyuè
June | 八月
bāyuè
August | 十月
shíyuè
October | 十二月
shíèryuè
December |

年 nián • **years**

1900 一九〇〇年 yījiǔlínglíng nián • nineteen hundred

1901 一九〇一年 yījiǔlíngyī nián • nineteen hundred and one

1910 一九一〇年 yījiǔyīlíng nián • nineteen ten

2000 二〇〇〇年 èrlínglíng nián • two thousand

2001 二〇〇一年 èrlínglíngyī nián • two thousand and one

季节 jìjié • **seasons**

春天
chūntiān
spring

夏天
xiàtiān
summer

秋天
qiūtiān
autumn

冬天
dōngtiān
winter

词汇 cíhuì • **vocabulary**

世纪 shìjì **century**	本周 běnzhōu **this week**	后天 hòutiān **the day after tomorrow**	今天几号? jīntiān jǐhào? **What's the date today?**
十年 shínián **decade**	上周 shàngzhōu **last week**	每周 měizhōu **weekly**	今天是二〇一七年二月七日。 jīntiān shì èrlíngyīqī nián èryuè qīrì. **It's February seventh, two thousand and seventeen.**
千年 qiānnián **millennium**	下周 xiàzhōu **next week**	每月 měiyuè **monthly**	
两周 liǎngzhōu **fortnight**	前天 qiántiān **the day before yesterday**	每年 měinián **annual**	

数字 shùzì • numbers

0	零 líng • zero		20	二十 èrshí • twenty
1	一 yī • one		21	二十一 èrshíyī • twenty-one
2	二 èr • two		22	二十二 èrshí'èr • twenty-two
3	三 sān • three		30	三十 sānshí • thirty
4	四 sì • four		40	四十 sìshí • forty
5	五 wǔ • five		50	五十 wǔshí • fifty
6	六 liù • six		60	六十 liùshí • sixty
7	七 qī • seven		70	七十 qīshí • seventy
8	八 bā • eight		80	八十 bāshí • eighty
9	九 jiǔ • nine		90	九十 jiǔshí • ninety
10	十 shí • ten		100	一百 yībǎi • one hundred
11	十一 shíyī • eleven		110	一百一十 yībǎiyīshí • one hundred and ten
12	十二 shí'èr • twelve		200	二百 èrbǎi • two hundred
13	十三 shísān • thirteen		300	三百 sānbǎi • three hundred
14	十四 shísì • fourteen		400	四百 sìbǎi • four hundred
15	十五 shíwǔ • fifteen		500	五百 wǔbǎi • five hundred
16	十六 shíliù • sixteen		600	六百 liùbǎi • six hundred
17	十七 shíqī • seventeen		700	七百 qībǎi • seven hundred
18	十八 shíbā • eighteen		800	八百 bābǎi • eight hundred
19	十九 shíjiǔ • nineteen		900	九百 jiǔbǎi • nine hundred

中文 zhōngwén • english

1,000　一千 yīqiān • one thousand

10,000　一万 yīwàn • ten thousand

20,000　两万 liǎngwàn • twenty thousand

50,000　五万 wǔwàn • fifty thousand

55,500　五万五千五百 wǔwàn wǔqiān wǔbǎi • fifty-five thousand five hundred

100,000　十万 shíwàn • one hundred thousand

1,000,000　一百万 yībǎiwàn • one million

1,000,000,000　十亿 shíyì • one billion

第一 dìyī first

第二 dì'èr second

第三 dìsān third

第四 dìsì • fourth

第五 dìwǔ • fifth

第六 dìliù • sixth

第七 dìqī • seventh

第八 dìbā • eighth

第九 dìjiǔ • ninth

第十 dìshí • tenth

第十一 dìshíyī • eleventh

第十二 dìshíèr • twelfth

第十三 dìshísān • thirteenth

第十四 dìshísì • fourteenth

第十五 dìshíwǔ • fifteenth

第十六 dìshíliù • sixteenth

第十七 dìshíqī • seventeenth

第十八 dìshíbā • eighteenth

第十九 dìshíjiǔ • nineteenth

第二十 dì'èrshí • twentieth

第二十一 dì'èrshíyī • twenty-first

第二十二 dì'èrshíèr • twenty-second

第二十三 dì'èrshísān • twenty-third

第三十 dìsānshí • thirtieth

第四十 dìsìshí • fortieth

第五十 dìwǔshí • fiftieth

第六十 dìliùshí • sixtieth

第七十 dìqīshí • seventieth

第八十 dìbāshí • eightieth

第九十 dìjiǔshí • ninetieth

第一百 dìyībǎi • (one) hundredth

度量衡 dùliánghéng • **weights and measures**

面积 miànjī • **area**

平方英尺
píngfāng
yīngchǐ
square foot

平方米
píngfāng mǐ
square metre

距离 jùlí •
distance

公里
gōnglǐ
kilometre

英里
yīnglǐ
mile

秤盘
chèngpán
pan

千克
qiānkè
kilogram

克
kè
gram

磅
bàng
pound

盎司
àngsī
ounce

磅秤 bàngchèng | **scales**

词汇 cíhuì • **vocabulary**

码 mǎ **yard**	吨 dūn **tonne**	测量 cèliáng **measure (v)**
米 mǐ **metre**	毫克 háokè **milligram**	称重量 chēng zhòngliàng **weigh (v)**

长度 chángdù • **length**

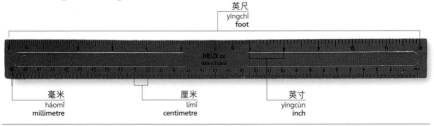

英尺
yīngchǐ
foot

毫米
háomǐ
millimetre

厘米
límǐ
centimetre

英寸
yīngcùn
inch

容量 róngliàng • capacity

半升
bànshēng
half-litre

品脱
pǐntuō
pint

容积
róngjī
volume

量壶 liànghú | measuring jug

毫升
háoshēng
millilitre

液体量器 yètǐ liángqì | liquid measure

词汇 cíhuì •
vocabulary

加仑
jiālún
gallon

夸脱
kuātuō
quart

升
shēng
litre

容器 róngqì • container

硬纸盒
yìngzhǐhé
carton

包
bāo
packet

瓶
píng
bottle

袋
dài
bag

塑料盒 sùliàohé | tub

广口瓶 guǎngkǒupíng | jar

罐
guàn
can

罐头盒 guàntóuhé | tin

喷水器 pēnshuǐqì | liquid dispenser

块
kuài
bar

软管
ruǎnguǎn
tube

卷
juǎn
roll

纸盒
zhǐhé
pack

喷雾罐
pēnwùguàn
spray can

世界地图 shìjiè dìtú • **world map**

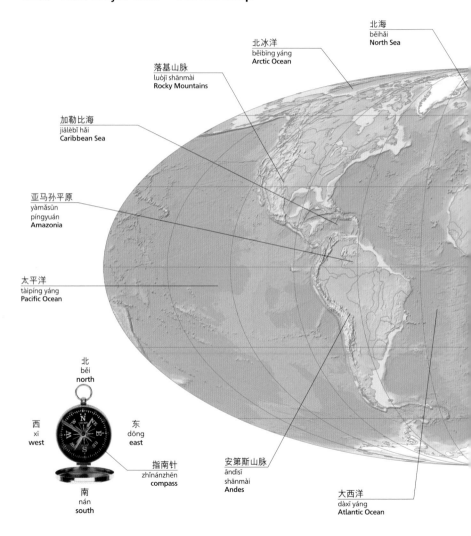

北海
běihǎi
North Sea

北冰洋
běibīng yáng
Arctic Ocean

落基山脉
luòjī shānmài
Rocky Mountains

加勒比海
jiālèbǐ hǎi
Caribbean Sea

亚马孙平原
yàmǎsūn
píngyuán
Amazonia

太平洋
tàipíng yáng
Pacific Ocean

北
běi
north

西
xī
west

东
dōng
east

指南针
zhǐnánzhēn
compass

南
nán
south

安第斯山脉
āndìsī
shānmài
Andes

大西洋
dàxī yáng
Atlantic Ocean

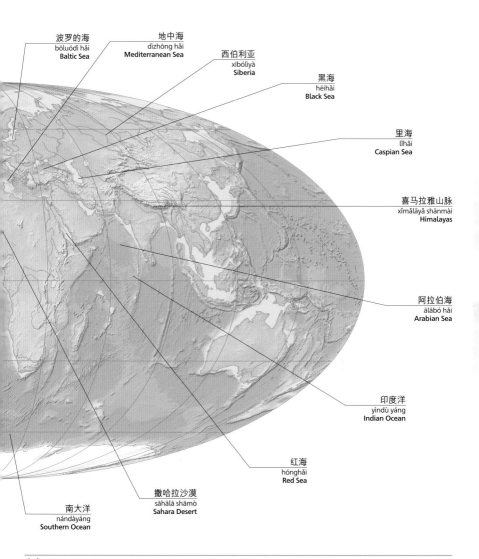

波罗的海
bōluódì hǎi
Baltic Sea

地中海
dìzhōng hǎi
Mediterranean Sea

西伯利亚
xībólìyà
Siberia

黑海
hēihǎi
Black Sea

里海
lǐhǎi
Caspian Sea

喜马拉雅山脉
xǐmǎlāyǎ shānmài
Himalayas

阿拉伯海
ālābó hǎi
Arabian Sea

印度洋
yìndù yáng
Indian Ocean

红海
hónghǎi
Red Sea

撒哈拉沙漠
sāhālā shāmò
Sahara Desert

南大洋
nándàyáng
Southern Ocean

北美洲 běiměizhōu · North and Central America

巴巴多斯 bābāduōsī ·
Barbados

加拿大 jiānádà · **Canada**

哥斯达黎加 gēsīdálíjiā ·
Costa Rica

古巴 gǔbā · **Cuba**

牙买加 yámǎijiā · **Jamaica**

墨西哥 mòxīgē · **Mexico**

巴拿马 bānámǎ · **Panama**

特立尼达和多巴哥 tèlìnídá hé
duōbāgē · **Trinidad and Tobago**

美利坚合众国
měilìjiānhézhòngguó ·
United States of America

阿拉斯加 ālāsījiā · **Alaska**

安提瓜和巴布达 āntíguā hé
bābùdá · **Antigua and Barbuda**

巴哈马 bāhāmǎ · **Bahamas**

巴巴多斯 bābāduōsī · **Barbados**

伯利兹 bólìzī · **Belize**

加拿大 jiānádà · **Canada**

哥斯达黎加 gēsīdálíjiā · **Costa Rica**

古巴 gǔbā · **Cuba**

多米尼克 duōmǐníkè · **Dominica**

多米尼加 duōmǐníjiā ·
Dominican Republic

萨尔瓦多 sà'ěrwǎduō · **El Salvador**

格陵兰 gélínglán · **Greenland**

格林纳达 gélínnàdá · **Grenada**

危地马拉 wēidìmǎlā · **Guatemala**

海地 hǎidì · **Haiti**

夏威夷 xiàwēiyí · **Hawaii**

洪都拉斯 hóngdūlāsī · **Honduras**

牙买加 yámǎijiā · **Jamaica**

墨西哥 mòxīgē · **Mexico**

尼加拉瓜 níjiālāguā · **Nicaragua**

巴拿马 bānámǎ · **Panama**

波多黎各 bōduōlígè · **Puerto Rico**

圣基茨和尼维斯 shèngjīcí hé

níwéisī · **St Kitts and Nevis**

圣卢西亚 shènglúxīyà · **St Lucia**

圣文森特和格林纳丁斯
shèngwénsēntè hé gélínnàdīngsī ·
St Vincent and The Grenadines

特立尼达和多巴哥 tèlìnídá hé
duōbāgē · **Trinidad and Tobago**

美利坚合众国
měilìjiānhézhòngguó ·
United States of America

南美洲 nánměizhōu · **South America**

阿根廷 āgēntíng · **Argentina**

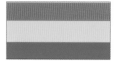

玻利维亚 bōlìwéiyà · **Bolivia**

巴西 bāxī · **Brazil**

智利 zhìlì · **Chile**

哥伦比亚 gēlúnbǐyà · **Colombia**

厄瓜多尔 èguāduōěr · **Ecuador**

秘鲁 bìlǔ · **Peru**

乌拉圭 wūlāguī · **Uruguay**

委内瑞拉 wěinèiruìlā · **Venezuela**

阿根廷 āgēntíng · **Argentina**
玻利维亚 bōlìwéiyà · **Bolivia**
巴西 bāxī · **Brazil**
智利 zhìlì · **Chile**
哥伦比亚 gēlúnbǐyà · **Colombia**
厄瓜多尔 èguāduōěr · **Ecuador**
福克兰群岛（马尔维纳斯群岛）
fúkèlán qúndǎo (mǎ'ěrwéinàsī qúndǎo) · **Falkland Islands**
法属圭亚那 fǎshǔ guīyànà · **French Guiana**
加拉帕戈斯群岛 jiālāpàgēsī qúndǎo · **Galápagos Islands**
圭亚那 guīyànà · **Guyana**

巴拉圭 bālāguī · **Paraguay**
秘鲁 bìlǔ · **Peru**
苏里南 sūlǐnán · **Suriname**
乌拉圭 wūlāguī · **Uruguay**
委内瑞拉 wěinèiruìlā · **Venezuela**

词汇 cíhuì · **vocabulary**

国家 guójiā country	省 shěng province	地域 dìyù zone
民族 mínzú nation	领土 lǐngtǔ territory	行政区 xíngzhèngqū district
大陆 dàlù continent	殖民地 zhímíndì colony	地区 dìqū region
主权国家 zhǔquán guójiā state	公国 gōngguó principality	首都 shǒudū capital

欧洲 ōuzhōu • Europe

法国 fǎguó • France

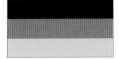

德国 déguó • Germany

意大利 yìdàlì • Italy

波兰 bōlán • Poland

葡萄牙 pútáoyá • Portugal

俄罗斯联邦 éluósīliánbāng •
Russian Federation

西班牙 xībānyá • Spain

阿尔巴尼亚 ā'ěrbāníyà • Albania

安道尔 āndào'ěr • Andorra

奥地利 àodìlì • Austria

巴利阿里群岛 bālìālǐ qúndǎo •
Balearic Islands

白俄罗斯 bái'éluósī • Belarus

比利时 bǐlìshí • Belgium

波斯尼亚和黑塞哥维那(波黑)
bōsīníyà hé hēisàigēwéinà(bōhēi) •
Bosnia and Herzogovina

保加利亚 bǎojiālìyà • Bulgaria

科西嘉岛 kēxījiādǎo • Corsica

克罗地亚 kèluódìyà • Croatia

捷克 jiékè • Czech Republic

丹麦 dānmài • Denmark

爱沙尼亚 àishā'níyà • Estonia

芬兰 fēnlán • Finland

法国 fǎguó • France

德国 déguó • Germany

希腊 xīlà • Greece

匈牙利 xiōngyálì • Hungary

冰岛 bīngdǎo • Iceland

爱尔兰 ài'ěrlán • Ireland

意大利 yìdàlì • Italy

加里宁格勒 jiālǐnínggélè •
Kaliningrad

科索沃 kēsuǒwò • Kosovo

拉脱维亚 lātuōwéiyà • Latvia

列支敦士登 lièzhīdūnshìdēng •
Liechtenstein

立陶宛 lìtáowǎn • Lithuania

卢森堡 lúsēnbǎo • Luxembourg

马其顿 mǎqídùn • Macedonia

马耳他 mǎ'ěrtā • Malta

摩尔多瓦 mó'ěrduōwǎ • Moldova

摩纳哥 mónàgē • Monaco

黑山 hēishān • Montenegro

荷兰 hélán • Netherlands

挪威 nuówēi • Norway

波兰 bōlán • Poland

葡萄牙 pútáoyá • Portugal

罗马尼亚 luómǎníyà • Romania

俄罗斯联邦 éluósīliánbāng •
Russian Federation

圣马力诺 shèngmǎlìnuò •
San Marino

撒丁岛 sādīngdǎo • Sardinia

塞尔维亚 sài'ěrwéiyà • Serbia

西西里岛 xīxīlǐdǎo • Sicily

斯洛伐克 sīluòfákè • Slovakia

斯洛文尼亚 sīluòwénníyà •
Slovenia

西班牙 xībānyá • Spain

瑞典 ruìdiǎn • Sweden

瑞士 ruìshì • Switzerland

乌克兰 wūkèlán • Ukraine

英国 yīngguó • United Kingdom

梵蒂冈 fàndìgāng • Vatican City

非洲 fēizhōu • Africa

埃及 āijí • Egypt

埃塞俄比亚 āisài'ébǐyà • Ethiopia

肯尼亚 kěnníyà • Kenya

尼日利亚 nírìlìyà • Nigeria

南非 nánfēi • South Africa

乌干达 wūgāndá • Uganda

阿尔及利亚 ā'ěrjílìyà • Algeria

安哥拉 āngēlā • Angola

贝宁 bèiníng • Benin

博茨瓦纳 bócíwǎnà • Botswana

布基纳法索 bùjīnà fǎsuǒ •
Burkina Faso

布隆迪 bùlóngdí • Burundi

卡奔达(安哥拉) kǎbēndá (āngēlā) •
Cabinda

喀麦隆 kāmàilóng • Cameroon

中非共和国 zhōngfēi gònghéguó •
Central African Republic

乍得 zhàdé • Chad

科摩罗群岛 kēmóluóqúndǎo •
Comoros

刚果 gāngguǒ • Congo

刚果民主共和国 gāngguǒ mínzhǔ
gònghéguó • Democratic
Republic of the Congo

吉布提 jíbùtí • Djibouti

埃及 āijí • Egypt

赤道几内亚 chìdàojǐnèiyà •
Equatorial Guinea

厄立特里亚 èlìtèlǐyà • Eritrea

埃塞俄比亚 āisài'ébǐyà • Ethiopia

加蓬 jiāpéng • Gabon

冈比亚 gāngbǐyà • Gambia

加纳 jiānà • Ghana

几内亚 jǐ'nèiyà • Guinea

几内亚比绍 jǐ'nèiyà bǐshào •
Guinea-Bissau

科特迪瓦 kētèdíwǎ • Ivory Coast

肯尼亚 kěnníyà • Kenya

莱索托 láisuǒtuō • Lesotho

利比里亚 lìbǐlǐyà • Liberia

利比亚 lìbǐyà • Libya

马达加斯加 mǎdájiāsījiā •
Madagascar

马拉维 mǎlāwéi • Malawi

马里 mǎlǐ • Mali

毛里塔尼亚 máolǐtǎníyà •
Mauritania

毛里求斯 máolǐqiúsī • Mauritius

摩洛哥 móluògē • Morocco

莫桑比克 mòsāngbǐkè •
Mozambique

纳米比亚 nàmǐbǐyà • Namibia

尼日尔 nírìěr • Niger

尼日利亚 nírìlìyà • Nigeria

卢旺达 lúwàngdá • Rwanda

圣多美和普林西比 shèngduōměi
hé pǔlínxībǐ • São Tomé and
Principe

塞内加尔 sàinèijiā'ěr • Senegal

塞拉利昂 sàilālì'áng • Sierra Leone

索马里 suǒmǎlǐ • Somalia

南非 nánfēi • South Africa

南苏丹 nán sūdān • South Sudan

苏丹 sūdān • Sudan

斯威士兰 sīwēishìlán • Swaziland

坦桑尼亚 tǎnsāngníyà • Tanzania

多哥 duōgē • Togo

突尼斯 tūnísī • Tunisia

乌干达 wūgāndá • Uganda

西撒哈拉 xīsāhālā • Western
Sahara

赞比亚 zànbǐyà • Zambia

津巴布韦 jīnbābùwéi • Zimbabwe

亚洲 yàzhōu • Asia

孟加拉国 mèngjiālāguó •
Bangladesh

中国 zhōngguó • China

印度 yìndù • India

日本 rìběn • Japan

约旦 yuēdàn • Jordan

菲律宾 fēilǜbīn • Philippines

韩国 hánguó • South Korea

泰国 tàiguó • Thailand

土耳其 tǔ'ěrqí • Turkey

阿富汗 āfùhàn • Afghanistan

亚美尼亚 yàměiníyà • Armenia

阿塞拜疆 ā'sàibàijiāng •
Azerbaijan

巴林 bālín • Bahrain

孟加拉国 mèngjiālāguó •
Bangladesh

不丹 bùdān • Bhutan

文莱 wénlái • Brunei

柬埔寨 jiǎnpǔzhài • Cambodia

中国 zhōngguó • China

塞浦路斯 sàipǔlùsī • Cyprus

东帝汶 dōngdìwèn • East Timor

斐济 fěijì • Fiji

格鲁吉亚 gélǔjíyà • Georgia

印度 yìndù • India

印度尼西亚 yìndùníxīyà •
Indonesia

伊朗 yīlǎng • Iran

伊拉克 yīlākè • Iraq

以色列 yǐsèliè • Israel

日本 rìběn • Japan

约旦 yuēdàn • Jordan

哈萨克斯坦 hāsàkèsītǎn •
Kazakhstan

科威特 kēwēitè • Kuwait

吉尔吉斯坦 jí'ěrjísītǎn • Kyrgyzstan

老挝 lǎowō • Laos

黎巴嫩 líbānèn • Lebanon

马来西亚 mǎláixīyà • Malaysia

马尔代夫 mǎ'ěrdàifū • Maldives

蒙古 měnggǔ • Mongolia

缅甸 miǎndiàn • Myanmar
(Burma)

尼泊尔 níbó'ěr • Nepal

朝鲜 cháoxiǎn • North Korea

阿曼 āmàn • Oman

巴基斯坦 bājīsītǎn • Pakistan

巴布亚新几内亚 bābùyà xīnjǐnèiyà
• Papua New Guinea

菲律宾 fēilǜbīn • Philippines

卡塔尔 kǎtǎ'ěr • Qatar

沙特阿拉伯 shātè'ālābó •
Saudi Arabia

新加坡 xīnjiāpō • Singapore

所罗门群岛 suǒluómén qúndǎo •
Solomon Islands

韩国 hánguó • South Korea

大洋洲 dàyángzhōu ·
Australasia

印度尼西亚 yìndùníxīyà ·
Indonesia

沙特阿拉伯 shātè'ālābó · **Saudi Arabia**

越南 yuènán · **Vietnam**

澳大利亚 àodàlìyà · **Australia**

新西兰 xīnxīlán · **New Zealand**

澳大利亚 àodàlìyà · **Australia**
新西兰 xīnxīlán · **New Zealand**
塔斯马尼亚(岛) tǎsīmǎníyà(dǎo) ·
Tasmania

斯里兰卡 sīlǐlánkǎ · **Sri Lanka**

叙利亚 xùlìyà · **Syria**

塔吉克斯坦 tǎjíkèsītǎn · **Tajikistan**

泰国 tàiguó · **Thailand**

土耳其 tǔ'ěrqí · **Turkey**

土库曼斯坦 tǔkùmànsītǎn ·
Turkmenistan

阿拉伯联合酋长国 ālābó liánhé
qiúzhǎngguó · **United Arab
Emirates**

乌兹别克斯坦 wūzībiékèsītǎn ·
Uzbekistan

瓦努阿图 wǎnǔ'ātú · **Vanuatu**

越南 yuènán · **Vietnam**

也门 yěmén · **Yemen**

小品词与反义词 xiǎopǐncí yǔ fǎnyìcí ·
particles and antonyms

到..v.去
dào...qù
to

从...来
cóng...lái
from

为
wèi
for

向...方向
xiàng...fāngxiàng
towards

在...上方
zài...shàngfāng
over

在...下方
zài...xiàfāng
under

沿着...
yánzhe...
along

越过
yuèguò
across

在...前面
zài...qiánmian
in front of

在...后面
zài...hòumian
behind

连同
liántóng
with

没有...
méiyǒu...
without

在...上
zài...shàng
onto

到...里
dào...lǐ
into

在...之前
zài...zhīqián
before

在...之后
zài...zhīhòu
after

在...里
zài...lǐ
in

在...外
zài...wài
out

不迟于...
bùchíyú...
by

直到...
zhídào...
until

在...上面
zài...shàngmian
above

在...下面
zài...xiàmian
below

早
zǎo
early

迟
chí
late

在...里面
zài...lǐmiàn
inside

在...外面
zài...wàimiàn
outside

现在
xiànzài
now

以后
yǐhòu
later

向上
xiàngshàng
up

向下
xiàngxià
down

一直
yìzhí
always

从不
cóngbù
never

在
zài
at

超出
chāochū
beyond

经常
jīngcháng
often

很少
hěnshǎo
rarely

穿越
chuānyuè
through

在...周围
zài...zhōuwéi
around

昨天
zuótiān
yesterday

明天
míngtiān
tomorrow

在...之上
zài...zhīshàng
on top of

在...旁边
zài...pángbiān
beside

第一
dìyī
first

最后
zuìhòu
last

在...之间
zài...zhījiān
between

在...对面
zài...duìmiàn
opposite

每...
měi...
every

一些
yìxiē
some

在...附近
zài...fùjìn
near

离...远
lí...yuǎn
far

关于
guānyú
about

准确地
zhǔnquède
exactly

这里
zhèlǐ
here

那里
nàlǐ
there

一点儿
yìdiǎn'er
a little

很多
hěnduō
a lot

大 dà **large**	小 xiǎo **small**	热 rè **hot**	冷 lěng **cold**
宽 kuān **wide**	窄 zhǎi **narrow**	开 kāi **open**	关 guān **closed**
高大 gāodà **tall**	矮小 ǎixiǎo **short**	满 mǎn **full**	空 kōng **empty**
高 gāo **high**	低 dī **low**	新 xīn **new**	旧 jiù **old**
厚 hòu **thick**	薄 báo **thin**	明亮 míngliàng **light**	黑暗 hēiàn **dark**
轻 qīng **light**	重 zhòng **heavy**	容易 róngyì **easy**	困难 kùnnán **difficult**
硬 yìng **hard**	软 ruǎn **soft**	空闲 kòngxián **free**	忙碌 mánglù **occupied**
潮湿 cháoshī **wet**	干燥 gānzào **dry**	强壮 qiángzhuàng **strong**	虚弱 xūruò **weak**
好 hǎo **good**	坏 huài **bad**	胖 pàng **fat**	瘦 shòu **thin**
快 kuài **fast**	慢 màn **slow**	年轻 niánqīng **young**	年老 niánlǎo **old**
正确 zhèngquè **correct**	错误 cuòwù **wrong**	更好 gènghǎo **better**	更差 gèngchà **worse**
干净 gānjìng **clean**	脏 zāng **dirty**	黑色 hēisè **black**	白色 báisè **white**
好看 hǎokàn **beautiful**	丑 chǒu **ugly**	有趣 yǒuqù **interesting**	无聊 wúliáo **boring**
贵 guì **expensive**	便宜 piányi **cheap**	生病的 shēngbìngde **sick**	健康的 jiànkāngde **well**
安静 ānjìng **quiet**	吵闹 chǎonào **noisy**	开始 kāishǐ **beginning**	结束 jiéshù **end**

中文 zhōngwén · **english**

常用语 cháng yòngyǔ ● useful phrases

**基本用语 jīběn yòngyǔ ●
essential phrases**

是
shì
Yes

不
bù
No

也许
yěxǔ
Maybe

请
qǐng
Please

谢谢
xièxie
Thank you

不用谢
búyòngxiè
You're welcome

抱歉；打扰一下
bàoqiàn, dǎrǎoyíxià
Excuse me

对不起
duìbuqǐ
I'm sorry

不要
búyào
Don't

好
hǎo
OK

很好
hěnhǎo
That's fine

正确
zhèngquè
That's correct

不对
búduì
That's wrong

**问候 wènhòu ●
greetings**

你好
nǐ hǎo
Hello

再见
zàijiàn
Goodbye

早上好
zǎoshang hǎo
Good morning

下午好
xiàwǔ hǎo
Good afternoon

晚上好
wǎnshang hǎo
Good evening

晚安
wǎn'ān
Good night

你好吗?
nǐ hǎo ma?
How are you?

我叫…
wǒ jiào…
My name is …

您怎么称呼?
nín zěnme chēnghu?
What is your name?

他/她叫什么名字?
tā/tā jiào shénme míngzì?
What is his/her name?

我介绍一下…
wǒ jièshào yíxià…
May I introduce …

这是…
zhèshì…
This is …

很高兴见到你
hěngāoxìng jiàndào nǐ
Pleased to meet you

待会儿见
dài huì'er jiàn
See you later

**标志 biāozhì ●
signs**

游客问询处
yóukè wènxúnchù
Tourist information

入口
rùkǒu
Entrance

出口
chūkǒu
Exit

紧急出口
jǐnjí chūkǒu
Emergency exit

推
tuī
Push

危险
wēixiǎn
Danger

禁止吸烟
jìnzhǐxīyān
No smoking

故障
gùzhàng
Out of order

开放时间
kāifàng shíjiān
Opening times

免费入场
miǎnfèi rùchǎng
Free admission

减价
jiǎnjià
Reduced

打折
dǎzhé
Sale

进前敲门
jìnqiánqiāomén
Knock before
entering

禁止践踏草坪
jìnzhǐ jiàntàcǎopíng
Keep off the grass

**求助 qiúzhù ●
help**

你能帮帮我吗?
nǐ néng bāngbāng wǒ ma?
Can you help me?

我不懂
wǒ bù dǒng
I don't understand

我不知道
wǒ bù zhīdào
I don't know

你说英语吗?
nǐ shuō yīngyǔ ma?
Do you speak
English?

我会说英语
wǒ huì shuō yīngyǔ
I speak English

请说得再慢些
qǐng shuōdé zài màn xiē
Please speak more
slowly

请帮我写下来
qǐng bāng wǒ xiě xiàlái
Please write it down
for me

我丢了…
wǒ diūle…
I have lost …

方向 fāngxiàng · directions

我迷路了
wǒ mílùle
I am lost

...在哪里?
zàinǎli
Where is the ...?

最近的...在哪里?
zuìjìnde...zàinǎli
Where is the nearest ...?

洗手间在哪儿?
xǐshǒujiān zàinǎer?
Where are the toilets?

我怎么去...?
wǒ zěnme qù...?
How do I get to ...?

右转
yòuzhuǎn
To the right

左转
zuǒzhuǎn
To the left

向前直行
xiàngqián zhíxíng
Straight ahead

到...有多远?
dào ...yǒu duōyuǎn?
How far is ...?

交通标志 jiāotōng biāozhì · road signs

各方通行
gèfāng tōngxíng
All directions

谨慎驾驶
jǐnshèn jiàshǐ
Caution

禁入
jìnrù
No entry

减速
jiǎnsù
Slow down

绕行
ràoxíng
Diversion

靠右侧行驶
kào yòucè xíngshǐ
Keep to the right

高速公路
gāosùgōnglù
Motorway

禁止停车
jìnzhǐ tíngchē
No parking

禁止通行
jìnzhǐ tōngxíng
No through road

单行道
dānxíngdào
One-way street

让路
rànglù
Give way

只限本区居民(停车)
zhǐxiànběnqūjūmín (tíngchē)
Residents only

道路管制
dàolùguǎnzhì
Roadworks

危险弯道
wēixiǎnwāndào
Dangerous bend

住宿 zhùsù · accommodation

我订了房间
wǒ dìng le fángjiān
I have a reservation

餐厅在哪儿?
cāntīng zàinǎ'er
Where is the dining room?

几点吃早餐?
jǐdiǎn chī zǎocān?
What time is breakfast?

我将在...点回来
wǒ jiāng zài...diǎn huílái
I'll be back at ... o'clock

我明天离开
wǒ míngtiān líkāi
I'm leaving tomorrow

饮食 yǐnshí · eating and drinking

干杯!
gānbēi
Cheers!

很好吃/很难吃
hěn hǎochī/hěn nánchī
It's delicious/awful

我不喝酒/抽烟
wǒ bù hējiǔ / chōuyān
I don't drink/smoke

我不吃肉
wǒ bù chīròu
I don't eat meat

够了，谢谢
gòule, xièxie
No more for me, thank you

请再来点儿
qǐng zàilái diǎn'ér
May I have some more?

我们要结账
wǒmen yào jiézhàng
May we have the bill?

请开张收据
qǐng kāi zhāng shōujù
Can I have a receipt?

吸烟区
xīyānqū
Smoking area

健康 jiànkāng · health

我不舒服
wǒ bù shūfu
I don't feel well

我难受
wǒ nánshòu
I feel sick

我这儿疼
wǒ zhè'er téng
It hurts here

我发烧了
wǒ fāshāole
I have a temperature

我怀孕...个月了
wǒ huáiyùn...gè yuèle
I'm ... months pregnant

我需要...处方
wǒ xūyào...chǔfāng
I need a prescription for

我通常服用...
wǒ tōngcháng fúyòng...
I normally take ...

我对...过敏
wǒ duì...guòmǐn
I'm allergic to ...

他/她没事吧?
tā/tā méishì ba?
Will he/she be all right?

中文索引 zhōngwén suŏyĭn · Chinese index

中文 zhōngwén • english

zhōngwén

zhōngwén

中文 zhōngwén · english

zhōngwén

英文索引 yīngwén suǒyǐn · English index

A

à la carte 152
abdomen 12
abdominals 16
above 320
abseiling 248
acacia 110
accelerator 200
access road 216
accessories 36, 38
accident 46
account number 96
accountant 97, 190
accounts department 175
accused 180
ace 230, 273
Achilles tendon 16
acorn squash 125
acquaintance 24
acquitted 181
across 320
acrylic paints 274
actions 237, 229, 227, 233, 183
activities 263, 245, 162, 77
actor 254, 191
actors 179
actress 254
acupressure 55
acupuncture 55
Adam's apple 19
add v 165
address 98
adhesive tape 47
adjustable spanner 80
admissions 168
admitted 48
adult 23
advantage 230
adventure film 255
advertisement 269
adzuki beans 131
aerate v 91
Afghanistan 318
Africa 317
after 320
afternoon 305
aftershave 73
aftersun 108
agate 289
agenda 174
aikido 236
aileron 210
air bag 201
air conditioning 200
air cylinder 239
air filter 202, 204

air letter 98
air mattress 267
air stewardess 190
air vent 210
aircraft 210
aircraft carrier 215
airliner 210, 212
airport 212
aisle 106, 168, 210, 254
alarm clock 70
Alaska 314
Albania 316
alcoholic drinks 145
alfalfa 184
Algeria 317
Allen key 80
allergy 44
alley 298
alligator 293
allspice 132
almond 129
almond oil 134
almonds 151
along 320
alpine 87
alpine skiing 247
alternating current 60
alternative therapy 54
alternator 203
altitude 211
aluminium 289
Amazonia 312
ambulance 94
American football 220
amethyst 288
amniocentesis 52
amniotic fluid 52
amount 96
amp 60
amphibians 294
amplifier 268
anaesthetist 48
analogue 179
anchor 214, 240
Andes 312
Andorra 316
angle 164
angler 244
Angola 317
angry 25
animals 292, 294
animated film 255
ankle 13, 15
ankle length 34
anniversary 26
annual 86, 307
anorak 31, 33
answer 163
answer v 99, 163

answering machine 99
ant 295
antenatal 52
antenna 295
antifreeze 199, 203
anti-inflammatory 109
antique shop 114
antiseptic 47
antiseptic wipe 47
antiwrinkle 41
antler 291
apartment block 298
apéritif 153
aperture dial 270
apex 165
app 99
appeal 181
appearance 30
appendix 18
applaud v 255
apple 126
apple corer 68
apple juice 149
appliances 66
application 176
appointment 45, 175
apricot 126
April 306
apron 30, 50, 69, 212
aquamarine 288
Arabian Sea 313
arable farm 183
arc 164
arch 15, 85, 301
archery 249
architect 190
architecture 300
architrave 301
Arctic Circle 283
Arctic Ocean 312
area 165, 310
areas 299
arena 243
Argentina 315
arithmetic 165
arm 13
armband 238
armchair 63
Armenia 318
armpit 13
armrest 200, 210
aromatherapy 55
around 320
arrangements 111
arrest 94
arrivals 213
arrow 249

art 162
art college 169
Art Deco 301
art gallery 261
Art Nouveau 301
art shop 115
artery 19
artichoke 124
artist 274
arts and crafts 274, 276
ash 283
ashtray 150
Asia 318
asparagus 124
assault 94
assistant 24
assisted delivery 53
asteroid 280
asthma 44
astigmatism 51
astronaut 281
astronomy 281
asymmetric bars 235
at 320
athlete 234
athletics 234
Atlantic Ocean 312
ATM 97
atmosphere 282, 286
atrium 104
attachment 177
attack 220
attack zone 224
attend v 174
attic 58
attractions 261
aubergine 125
auburn 39
audience 254
August 306
aunt 22
aurora 286
Australasia 319
Australia 319
Austria 316
autocue 179
automatic 200
automatic door 196
autumn 31, 307
avalanche 247
avenue 299
avocado 128
awning 148
axe 95
axle 205
ayurveda 55
Azerbaijan 318

B

baby 23, 30
baby bath 74
baby care 74
baby changing facilities 104
baby monitor 75
baby products 107
baby sling 75
babygro 30
back 13
back brush 73
back seat 200
backboard 226
backdrop 254
backgammon 272
backhand 231
backpack 31, 37, 267
backstroke 239
backswing 233
bacon 118, 157
bad 321
badge 94
badminton 231
bag 311
bagel 139
baggage reclaim 213
baggage trailer 212
bags 37
baguette 138
Bahamas 314
bail 181
bait 244
bait v 245
bake v 67, 138
baked 159
baker 114, 139
bakery 107, 138
baking 69
baking tray 69
balance wheel 276
balcony 59, 254
bald 39
bale 184
Balearic Islands 316
ball 15, 75, 221, 224, 226, 228, 230
ball boy 231
ballet 255
balsamic vinegar 135
Baltic Sea 313
bamboo 86,122
banana 128
bandage 47
Bangladesh 318
banister 59
bank 96, 284
bank charge 96
bank manager 96

english

english

emotions 25
employee 24
employer 24
empty 321
emulsion 83
enamel 50
encore 255
encyclopedia 163
end 321
end zone 220
endive 123
endline 226
endocrine 19
endocrinology 49
energy-saving bulb 60
engaged/busy 99
engaged couple 24
engine 202, 204, 208, 210
engine room 214
engineering 169
English breakfast 157
English mustard 135
engraving 275
enlarge v 172
enlargement 271
enquiries 168
ENT 49
entrance 59
entrance fee 260
envelope 98, 173
environment 280
epidural 52
epiglottis 19
epilepsy 44
episiotomy 52
equals 165
equation 165
equator 283
equipment 165, 233, 238
Equitorial Guinea 317
equity 97
Eritrea 317
erupt v 283
escalator 104
espresso 148
essay 163
essential oils 55
estate 199
estate agent 115, 189
Estonia 316
estuary 285
Ethiopia 317
eucalyptus 296
Europe 316
evening 305
evening dress 34
evening menu 152
events 243, 247
evergreen 86
evidence 181
examination 163
excess baggage 212
exchange rate 97

excited 25
excuse me 322
executive 174
exercise bike 250
exercises 251
exfoliate v 41
exhaust pipe 203, 204
exhibit v 261
exhibition 261
exit 210
exit ramp 194
exosphere 286
expectant 52
experiment 166
expiry date 109
exposure 271
extend v 251
extension 58
extension lead 78
exterior 198
external hard drive 176
extra time 223
extraction 50
extractor 66
eye 14, 51, 244, 276
eye shadow 40
eye test 51
eyebrow 14, 51
eyebrow brush 40
eyebrow pencil 40
eyecup 269
eyelash 14, 51
eyelet 37
eyelid 51
eyeliner 40
eyepiece 167

F

fabric 277
fabric conditioner 76
face 14
face cream 73
face mask 225
face-off circle 224
face pack 41
face powder 40
facial 41
factory 299
faint v 25, 44
fair 41
fairground 262
fairway 232
falcon 292
Falkland Islands 315
fall 237
fall in love v 26
Fallopian tube 20
family 22
famous ruin 261
fan 60, 202
fan belt 203
fans 258
far 320
fare 197, 209

farm 182, 183, 184
farmhouse 182
farmland 182
farmyard 182
farmer 182, 189
fashion 277
fast 321
fast food 154
fast forward 269
fastening 37
fat 119, 321
fat free 137
father 22
father-in-law 23
fault 230
feather 293
feature film 269
February 306
feed v 183
feijoa 128
female 12, 20
feminine hygiene 108
femur 17
fence 85, 182, 243
fencing 249
feng shui 55
fennel 122, 133
fennel seeds 133
fenugreek 132
fern 86
ferry 215, 216
ferry terminal 216
fertilization 20
fertilize v 91
fertilizer 91
festivals 27
fever 44
fiancé 24
fiancée 24
fibre 127
fibula 17
field 182, 222, 228, 234
field v 225, 229
field hockey 224
fifteen 308
fifteenth 309
fifth 309
fiftieth 309
fifty 308
fifty five thousand, five hundred 309
fifty thousand 309
fig 129
fighter plane 211
figure skating 247
Fiji 319
file 81, 177
filing cabinet 172
fill v 82
filler 83
fillet 119, 121
filleted 121
filling 50, 140, 155
film 260, 271

film set 179
film spool 271
filo pastry 140
filter 270
filter coffee 148
filter paper 167
fin 210, 239
finance 97
financial advisor 97
fingerprint 94
finial 300
finishing line 234
Finland 316
fire 95
fire alarm 95
fire brigade 95
fire engine 95
fire escape 95
fire extinguisher 95
fire station 95
firefighters 95
firelighter 266
fireman 189
fireplace 63
firm 124
first 309
first aid 47
first-aid box 47
first floor 104
first night 254
fish 107, 120, 294
fish and chips 155
fish farm 183
fish slice 68
fisherman 189
fishhook 244
fishing 244, 245
fishing boat 217
fishing permit 245
fishing port 217
fishing rod 244
fishmonger 188
fishmonger's 114, 120
fist 15, 237
fitness 250
five 308
five hundred 308
flag 221, 232
flageolet beans 131
flakes 132
flamingo 292
flan 142
flan dish 69
flare 240
flash 270
flash gun 270
flask 166
flat 59, 256
flat race 243
flat wood bit 80
flatbread 139
flatscreen TV 269
flavoured oil 134
flax 184
fleece 74

flesh 124, 127, 129
flex v 251
flight attendant 210
flight number 213
flint 288
flip chart 174
flip-flop 37
flipper 290
float 238, 244
float ball 61
flock 183
flood 287
floor 58, 62, 71
floor exercises 235
floor plan 261
Florentine 141
floret 122
florist 110, 188
floss v 50
flours 138
flower 297
flowerbed 85, 90
flowering plant 297
flowering shrub 87
flowers 110
flu 44
flute 139, 257
fly 244, 295
fly v 211
fly fishing 245
flyover 194
flysheet 266
foal 185
focus v 271
focusing knob 167
foetus 52
fog 287
foil 249
folder 177
foliage 110
folk music 259
follicle 20
font 177
food 118, 130, 149
food hall 105
food processor 66
foot 12, 15, 310
foot pedal 257
football 220, 222
football field 220
football player 220
football strip 31, 222
footballer 222
footboard 71
footpath 262
footstrap 241
for 320
forceps 53, 167
forearm 12
forecourt 199
forehand 231
forehead 14
foreign currency 97
foreskin 21
forest 285

english

english

english

english

english

puff pastry 140
pull up v 251
pulp 127
pulse 47
pulses 130
pumice 288
pumice stone 73
pump 37, 207
pumpkin 125
pumpkin seed 131
punch 237
punchbag 237
puncture 203, 207
pup 290
pupil 51, 162
puppy 290
purple 274
purse 37
pushchair 75
putt v 233
putter 233
pyjamas 33
pyramid 164

Q

Qatar 318
quadriceps 16
quail 119
quail egg 137
quart 311
quarter of an hour
    304
quarterdeck 214
quartz 289
quay 216
queen 272, 273
question 163
question v 163
quilt 71
quilting 277
quince 128
quinoa 130
quiver 249

R

rabbit 118, 290
raccoon 290
race 234
racecourse 243
racehorse 243
racing bike 205, 206
racing dive 239
racing driver 249
rack 166
racquet 230
racquet games 231
racquetball 231
radar 214, 281
radiator 60, 202
radicchio 123
radio 179, 268
radio antenna 214
radio station 179
radiology 49

radish 124
radius 17, 164
rafter 186
rafting 241
rail 208
rail network 209
rain 287
rainbow 287
rainbow trout 120
raincoat 31, 32
rainforest 285
raisin 129
rake 88
rake v 90
rally 230
rally driving 249
RAM 176
Ramadan 26
ramekin 69
rap 259
rapeseed 184
rapeseed oil 135
rapids 240, 284
rash 44
rasher 119
raspberry 127
raspberry jam 134
rat 290
rattle 74
raw 124, 129
ray 294
razor blade 73
razor-shell 121
read v 162
reading light 210
reading list 168
reading room 168
reamer 80
rear light 207
rear-view mirror 198
rear wheel 197
receipt 152
receive v 177
receiver 99
reception 100
receptionist 100, 190
record 234, 269
record player 268
record shop 115
recording studio 179
rectangle 164
rectum 21
recycling bin 61
red 145, 274
red card 223
red eye 271
red kidney beans 131
red lentils 131
red meat 118
red mullet 120
Red Sea 313
reduce v 172
reel 244
reel in v 245
refectory 168

referee 220, 222, 226
referral 49
reflector 50, 204,
    207
reflector strap 205
reflexology 54
refrigerator 67
reggae 259
region 315
register 100
registered post 98
regulator 239
reheat v 154
reiki 55
reins 242
relationships 24
relatives 23
relaxation 55
relay race 235
release v 245
remote control 269
Renaissance 301
renew v 168
rent 58
rent v 58
repair kit 207
report 174
reporter 179
reproduction 20
reproductive 19
reproductive
    organs 20
reptiles 293
research 169
reserve v 168
respiratory 19
rest 256
restaurant 101, 152
result 49
resurfacing 187
resuscitation 47
retina 51
retire v 26
return 231
return address 98
return date 168
rev counter 201
reverse v 195
reverse charge call 99
rewind 269
rhinoceros 291
rhombus 164
rhubarb 127
rhythmic gymnastics
    235
rib 17, 119
rib cage 17
ribbon 27, 39, 111,
    141, 235
ribs 155
rice 130, 158, 184
rice pudding 140
rider 242
riding boot 242
riding crop 242

riding hat 242
rigging 215, 240
right 260
right field 229
right-hand drive
    201
rim 206
rind 119, 127, 136,
    142
ring 36
ring finger 15
ring ties 89
rings 235
rinse v 38, 76
ripe 129
rise v 139
river 284
road bike 206
road markings 194
road signs 195
roadroller 187
roads 194
roadworks 187, 195
roast 158
roast v 67
roasted 129
robe 38, 169
rock climbing 248
rock concert 258
rock garden 84
rocket 123
rocks 284, 288
Rocky Mountains 312
Rococo 301
rodeo 243
roll 139, 311
roll v 67
roller 83
roller blind 63
roller coaster 262
rollerblading 263
rolling pin 69
romance 255
Romania 316
romper suit 30
roof 58, 203
roof garden 84
roof tile 187
roof rack 198
rook 272
room 58
room key 100
room number 100
room service 101
rooms 100
root 39, 50, 124,
    296
rope 248
rose 89, 110, 145
rosé 145
rosemary 133
rotor blade 211
rotten 127
rough 232
round 237

round neck 33
roundabout 195
route number 196
router 78
row 210, 254
row v 241
rower 241
rowing boat 214
rowing machine 250
rubber 163
rubber band 173
rubber boots 89
rubber ring 265
rubber stamp 173
rubbish bin 61, 67
ruby 288
ruck 221
rudder 210, 241
rug 63
rugby 221
rugby pitch 221
rugby strip 221
ruler 163, 165
rum 145
rum and cola
    151
rump steak 119
run 228
run v 228
runner bean 122
runway 212
rush 86
Russian Federation
    318
Rwanda 317
rye bread 138

S

sad 25
saddle 206, 242
safari park 262
safe 228
safety 75, 240
safety barrier 246
safety goggles 81,
    167
safety pin 47
saffron 132
sage 133
Sahara Desert 313
sail 241
sailing 240
sailing boat 215
sailor 189
salad 149
salamander 294
salami 142
salary 175
sales assistant 104
sales department
    175
salmon 120
saloon 199
salt 64, 152

english

english

english

english

鸣谢 míngxiè • acknowledgments

DORLING KINDERSLEY would like to thank Christine Lacey for design assistance, Georgina Garner for editorial and administrative help, Kopal Agarwal, Polly Boyd, Sonia Gavira, Cathy Meeus, Antara Raghavan, and Priyanka Sharma for editorial help, Claire Bowers for compiling the DK picture credits, Nishwan Rasool for picture research, and Suruchi Bhatia, Miguel Cunha, Mohit Sharma, and Alex Valizadeh for app development and creation.

The publisher would like to thank the following for their kind permission to reproduce their photographs:

Abbreviations key: (a-above; b-below/bottom; c-centre; f-far; l-left; r-right; t-top)

123RF.com: Andrey Popov / andreypopov 23bc; Andriy Popov 34tl; Brad Wynnyk 172bc; Daniel Ernst 179tc; Hongqi Zhang 24cla, 175cr; Ingvar Bjork 60c; Kobby Dagan 259c; leonardo255 269c; Liubov Vadimovna (Luba) Nel 39cla; Ljupco Smokovski 75crb; Oleksandr Marynchenko 60bl; Olga Popova 33c; oneblink 49bc; Robert Churchill 94c; Roman Gorielov 33bc; Ruslan Kudrin 35bc, 35br; Subbotina 39cra; Sutichak Yachaingkham 39tc; Tarzhanova 37tc; Vitaly Valua 39tl; Wavebreak Media Ltd 188bl; Wilawan Khasawong 75cb; **Action Plus: Alamy Images:** 154t; A.T. Willett 287bcl; Alex Segre 105ca, 195cl; Ambrophoto 24cra; Blend Images 168cr; Cultura RM 33r; Doug Houghton 107br; Hugh Threlfall 35tl; 176tr; Ian Allenden 48br; Ian Dagnall 270t; Levgen Chepil 250bc; Imagebroker 199tl, 249c; Keith Morris 178c; Martyn Evans 210b; MBI 175tl; Michael Burrell 213cra; Michael Foyle 184bl; Oleksiy Maksymenko 105tc; Paul Weston 168br; Prisma Bildagentur AG 246b; Radharc Images 197cr; RBtravel 112tl; Ruslan Kudrin 176tl; Sasa Huzjak 258t; Sergey Kravchenko 37ca; Sergio Azenha 270bc; Stanca Sanda (iPad is a trademark of Apple Inc., registered in the U.S. and other countries) 176bc; Stock Connection 287bcr; tarczas 35cr; Vitaly Suprun 176cl; Wavebreak Media ltd 39cl, 174b, 175tr; **Allsport/Getty Images:** 238cl; **Alvey and Towers:** 209 acr, 215bcl, 215bcr, 241cr; **Peter Anderson:** 188cbr, 271br. **Anthony Blake Photo Library:** Charlie Stebbings 114cl; John Sims 114cl; **Andyalte:** 98tl; **Arcaid:** John Edward Linden 301bl; Martine Hamilton Knight, Architects: Chapman Taylor Partners, 213cl; Richard Bryant 301br; **Argos:** 41tcl, 66cbl, 66cl, 66br, 66bcl, 69cl, 70bcl, 71t, 77tl, 269tc, 270tl; **Axiom:** Eitan Simanor 105bcr; Ian Cumming 104; Vicki Couchman 148cr; **Beken Of Cowes Ltd:** 215bc; **Bosch:** 76tcr, 76tc, 76tcl; **Camera Press:** 38tr, 256t, 257cr; Barry J. Holmes 148tr; Jane Hanger 159cr; Mary Germanou 259bc; **Corbis:** 78b; Anna Clopet 247cr; Ariel Skelley / Blend Images 52l; Bettmann 181tl, 181br; Blue Jean Images 48bl; Bo Zauders 156t; Bob Rowan 152bl; Bob Winsett 247cbl; Brian Bailey 247br; Chris Rainer 247ctl; Craig Aurness 215bl; David H.Wells 249cbr; Dennis Marsico 274bl; Dimitri Lundt 236bc; Duomo 211tl; Gail Mooney 277ctcr; George Lepp 248c; Gerald Nowak 239b; Gunter Marx 248cr; Jack Hollingsworth 231bl; Jacqui Hurst 277cbr; James L. Amos 247bl, 191ctr, 220bcr; Jan Butchofsky 277cbc; Johnathan Blair 243cr; Jose F. Poblete 191br; Jose Luis Pelaez.Inc 153tc; Karl Weatherly 220bl, 247tcr; Kelly Mooney Photography 259tl; Kevin Fleming 249bc; Kevin R. Morris 105tr, 243tl, 243tc; Kim Sayer 249tcr; Lynn Goldsmith 258t; Macduff Everton 231bcl; Mark Gibson 249bl; Mark L. Stephenson 249ctl; Michael Pole 115tr; Michael S. Yamashita 247ctcl; Mike King 247cbl; Neil Rabinowitz 214br; Pablo Corral 115bc; Paul A. Sounders 169br, 249ctcl; Paul J. Sutton 224c, 224br; Phil Schermeister 227b, 248tr; R. W Jones 309; Richard Morrell 189bc; Rick Doyle 241ctr; Robert Holmes 97br, 277ctc; Roger Ressmeyer 169tr; Russ Schleipman 229; The Purcell Team 211ctr; Vince Streano 194t; Wally McNamee 220br, 220bcl, 224bl; Wavebreak Media LTD 191bc; Yann Arhus-Bertrand 249tl; **Demetrio Carrasco / Dorling Kindersley (c) Herge / Les Editions Casterman:** 112ccl; **Dorling Kindersley:** Banbury Museum 35c; Five Napkin Burger 152t; **Dixons:** 270cl, 270cr, 270bl, 270bcl, 270bcr, 270ccr; **Dreamstime.com:** Alexander Podshivalov 179tr, 191cr; Alexxl66 268tl; Andersatplest 176ctc; Andrey Popov 191bl; Arne9001 190tl; Chaoss 26c; Designsstock 269cl; Monkey Business Images 26clb; Paul Michael Hughes 162tr; Serghei Starus 190bc; **Education Photos:** John Walmsley 26tl; **Empics Ltd:** Adam Day 236br; Andy Heading 243c; Steve White 249cbc; **Getty Images:** 48bcl, 94tr, 100t, 114bcr, 154bl, 287tr; George Doyle & Ciaran Griffin 22cr; David Leahy 162tl; Don Farrall / Digital Vision 176c; Ethan Miller 270bl; Inti St Clair 179bl; Liam Norris 188br; Sean Justice / Digital Vision 24br; **Dennis Gilbert:** 106tc; **Hulsta:** 70t; **Ideal Standard Ltd:** 72r; **The Image Bank/ Getty Images:** 58; **Impact Photos:** Eliza Armstrong 115cr; Philip Achache 246t; **The Interior Archive:** Henry Wilson, Alfie's Market 114bl; Luke White, Architect: David Mikhail, 59tl; Simon Upton, Architect: Phillippe Starck, St Martins Lane Hotel 100bcr, 100br; **iStockphoto.com:** asterix0597 163tl; EdStock 190br; RichLegg 26bc; SorinVidis 27cr; **Jason Hawkes Aerial Photography:** 216t; **Dan Johnson:** 35r; **Kos Pictures Source:** 215cbl, 240tc, 240tr; David Williams 216b; **Lebrecht Collection:** Kate Mount 169bc; **MP Visual.com:** Mark Swallow 202t; **NASA:** 280cr, 280ccl, 281tl; **P&O Princess Cruises:** 214bl; **P A Photos:** 181br; **The Photographers' Library:** 186bl, 186bc, 186t; **Plain and Simple Kitchens:** 66t; **Powerstock Photolibrary:** 169tl, 256t, 287tc; **PunchStock:** Image Source 195tr; **Rail Images:** 208c, 208 cbl, 209br;

Red Consultancy: Odeon cinemas 257br; **Redferns:** 259br; Nigel Crane 259c; **Rex Features:** 106br, 259tc, 259tr, 259bl, 280b; Charles Ommaney 114tcr; J.F.F Whitehead 243cl; Patrick Barth 101tl; Patrick Frilet 189cbl; Scott Wiseman 287bl; **Royalty Free Images:** Getty Images/Eyewire 154bl; **Science & Society Picture Library:** Science Museum 202b; **Science Photo Library:** IBM Research 190cla; NASA 281cr; **SuperStock:** Ingram Publishing 62; Juanma Aparicio / age fotostock 172t; Nordic Photos 269tl; **Skyscan:** 168t, 182c, 298; Quick UK Ltd 212; **Sony:** 268bc; **Robert Streeter:** 154br; **Neil Sutherland:** 82tr, 83tl, 90t, 118c, 188tr, 196tl, 196tr, 299cl, 299bl; **The Travel Library:** Stuart Black 264t; **Travelex:** 97cl; **Vauxhall:** Technik 198t, 199tl, 199tr, 199ctcl, 199cctcr, 199tctl, 199cttcr, 200; **View Pictures:** Dennis Gilbert, Architects: ACDP Consulting, 106t; Dennis Gilbert, Chris Wilkinson Architects, 209tr; Peter Cook, Architects: Nicholas Crimshaw and partners, 208t; **Betty Walton:** 185br; **Colin Walton:** 2, 4, 7, 9, 10, 28, 40l, 42, 56, 92, 95c, 99tl, 99tcl, 102, 116, 120t, 138t, 146, 150t, 160, 170, 191ccl, 192, 218, 252, 260br, 260l, 261tr, 261c, 261cr, 271cbl, 271cbr, 271cbl, 278, 287br, 302.

DK PICTURE LIBRARY:
Akhil Bahkshi; Patrick Baldwin; Geoff Brightling; British Museum; John Bulmer; Andrew Butler; Joe Cornish; Brian Cosgrove; Andy Crawford and Kit Hougton; Philip Dowell; Alistair Duncan; Gables; Bob Gathany; Norman Hollands; Kew Gardens; Peter James Kindersley; Vladimir Kozlik; Sam Lloyd; London Northern Bus Company Ltd; Tracy Morgan; David Murray and Jules Selmes; Musée Vivant du Cheval, France; Museum of Broadcast Communications; Museum of Natural History; NASA; National History Museum; Norfolk Rural Life museum; Stephen Oliver; RNLI; Royal Ballet School; Guy Ryecart; Science Museum; Neil Setchfield; Ross Simms and the Winchcombe Folk Police Museum; Singapore Symphony Orchestra; Smart Museum of Art; Tony Souter; Erik Svensson and Jeppe Wikstrom; Sam Tree of Keygrove Marketing Ltd; Barrie Watts; Alan Williams; Jerry Young.

Additional photography by Colin Walton.

Colin Walton would like to thank:
A&A News, Uckfield; Abbey Music, Tunbridge Wells; Arena Mens Clothing, Tunbridge Wells; Burrells of Tunbridge Wells; Gary at Di Marco's; Jeremy's Home Store, Tunbridge Wells; Noakes of Tunbridge Wells; Ottakar's, Tunbridge Wells; Selby's of Uckfield; Sevenoaks Sound and Vision; Westfield, Royal Victoria Place, Tunbridge Wells.

All other images © Dorling Kindersley
For further information see: www.dkimages.com